THE DASH DIET COOKBOOK

by
Susan Castelli

Copyright © 2020 by Susan Castelli

All right reserved. No part of this publication may be reproduced in any form without permission in writing form the publisher, except for brief quotations used for publishable articles or reviews.

Legal Disclaimer

The information contained in this book and its contents is not designed to replace any form of medical or professional advice; and is not meant to replace the need for independent medical, financial, legal, or other professional advice or service that may require. The content and information in this book have been provided for educational and entertainment purposes only.

The content and information contained in this book have been compiled from sources deemed reliable, and they are accurate to the best of the Author's knowledge, information and belief.

However, the Author cannot guarantee its accuracy and validity and therefore cannot be held liable for any errors and/or omissions.

Further, changes are periodically made to this book as needed. Where appropriate and/or necessary, you must consult a professional (including but not limited to your doctor, attorney, financial advisor, or other such professional) before using any of the suggested remedies, techniques, and/or information in this book.

Upon using this book's contents and information, you agree to hold harmless the Author from any damaged, costs and expenses, including any legal fees potentially resulting from the application of any of the information in this book. This disclaimer applies to any loss, damages, or injury caused by the use and application of this book's content, whether directly and indirectly, whether for breach of contract, tort, negligence, personal injury, criminal intent, or under any other circumstances.

You agree to accept all risks of using the information presented in this book. You agree that by continuing to read this book, where appropriate and/or necessary, you shall consult a professional (including but not limited to your doctor, attorney, financial advisor, or other such professional) before remedies, techniques, and/or information in this book.

Table of Contents

Introduction..1
Chapter 1: What is the Dash Diet......................2
Chapter 2: Blood pressure and general health.6
Chapter 3: Benefits of Dash Diet......................12
Chapter 4: Food requirements..........................14
Chapter 5: Breakfast & Smoothie......................18
- Swiss Chard Omelet.................................18
- Hearty Pineapple Oatmeal........................18
- Sweet Potatoes with Coconut Flakes........18
- Banana Smoothie......................................18
- Strawberry Smoothie................................18
- Summer Smoothie......................................2
- Tropical Smoothie.....................................2
- Paradise Smoothie....................................2
- Fruity Smoothie..2
- Grape Shake...2
- Melon Shake..2
- Mango and Pear Smoothie........................2
- Mixed Berries Smoothie............................3
- Healthy Bagels...3
- Watermelon Shake...................................3
- Morning Punch...3
- Cherries Oatmeal......................................3
- Veggie Omelette.......................................4
- Avocado cup...4
- Eggs with Cheese......................................4
- Quinoa Quiche..5
- Fruits Breakfast Salad................................5
- Mediterranean Toast.................................5
- Italian Bruschetta.....................................5
- Quinoa Breakfast Bars...............................5
- Cherries Oatmeal......................................6
- Cheese & Kale Omelette............................6
- Chicken Breakfast Burritos........................6
- Chia Seeds Breakfast Mix..........................6

- Apple Cinnamon Crisp...............................6
- Strawberry Chia Breakfast Pudding............7
- Zingy Onion and Thyme Crackers...............7
- Coffee Frappe...7
- Sweet Corn Muffins...................................7
- Banana Chocolate.....................................7
- Mexican Omelet..8
- Spinach & Ham Muffins.............................8
- Crunchy Flax and Almond Crackers............8
- Basil and Tomato Baked Eggs....................8
- Mushroom Snacks.....................................9
- Delicious Pancakes...................................9
- French Toast..9
- Scrambled Eggs..9
- Green Smoothie......................................10
- Greens and Giger Smoothie.....................10
- Banana Bread...10
- Fruits Bowls..10
- Banana and Buckwheat Porridge.............11
- Delightful Berry Quinoa Bowl..................11
- Fantastic Bowl..11
- Quinoa and Cinnamon Bowl....................11
- Breakfast Parfait.....................................12
- Healthy Granola Bowl.............................12
- Cinnamon and Pumpkin Porridge............12
- Quinoa and Date Bowl............................12
- Crispy Tofu...13
- Pumpkin Pie Oatmeal..............................13
- Powerful Oatmeal...................................13
- Chia Porridge...13
- Simple Blueberry Oatmeal......................13
- Apple "Porridge"....................................14
- The Unique Smoothie Bowl....................14
- Cinnamon and Coconut Porridge............14
- Morning Porridge...................................14

Sweet Potato Porridge 15
German Oatmeal.. 15
Banana Oatmeal 15

Chapter 6: Soups and Salads 16
Tofu Soup 16
Tomato Soup 16
Vichyssoise 16
Pumpkin and Rosemary Soup 16
Mangetout Soup 17
Nicoise Salad 17
Zucchini Soup 17
Black Bean Soup 17
Chicken and Dill Soup 18
Cheese Soup with crispy bacon 18
Cherry Stew 18
Raspberry and cranberry soup 18
Sirloin Carrot Soup 18
Classical Wonton Soup 18
Pumpkin and Coconut Soup 19
Kale And Spinach Soup 19
Onion Soup 19
Vegetarian Soup in a Crock Pot 19
Rhubarb Stew 20
Gazpacho 20
Mixed Beans Soup 20
Beef Stew 20
Homemade Turkey Soup 21
Meatball Soup 21
Sorrel Soup 21
Mexican Pozole 22
Carrot and Ginger Soup 22
Cauliflower Soup 22
Minestrone Soup 22
Brussels Soup 23
Crab and Watermelon Soup 23
Garlic Tomato Soup 23
Lobster Bisque 23
Eggplant Soup 24

Sweet Potato Soup 24
Organic Chicken Thigh Soup 24
Butternut Squash Soup 24
Soup a la Kiev 25
Summer Strawberry Stew 25
Blueberry Stew 25
Chipotle Chicken Chowder 25
Peach Stew 25
Summer Tomato Soup 26
Summer Tomato Sorbet 26
Carrot and Coriander Soup 26
Pappa al pomodoro 26
Zucchini Cream Soup 26
Salmon and Vegetable Soup 27
Mango Salad 27
Tomato and Cucumber Salad 27
Fresh Fruit Salad 27
Green Papaya Salad 27
Quinoa And Fruit Salad 28
Shrimp and Veggie Salad 28
Salmon and Spinach Salad 28
Peach Stew 28
Corn Salad 29
Fattoush Salad 29
Broccoli Salad 29
Baby Spinach Salad 29
Classic Tuna Salad 29
Greek Salad 30
Delicious Tuna Salad 30
Yogurt And Cucumber Salad 30
Tasty Eggplant Salad 30
Potato & Octopus Salad 30
Balsamic Beet Salad 31
Squash Garden Salad 31
Beet and Walnut Salad 31
Steamed Saucy Garlic Greens 32
Daikon Radish Salad 32
Calamari Salad 32

Chicken Raisin Salad 32
Pickled Onion Salad 32
Pickled Grape Salad with Pear, and Cheese 33
Tuna and Potato Salad 33
Spinach Parmesan Dip 33

Chapter 7: Poultry 35
Crispy Chicken Egg Rolls 35
Chicken Brats 35
Italian Meatballs 35
Garlic Parmesan Wings 35
White Chicken Chili 36
Chicken and Broccoli Stir-Fry 36
Zucchini Tagine with Minced Meatballs 36
Quick Chicken Fajitas 37
Roasted Turkey 37
Honey Garlic Chicken Drumsticks 37
Southwestern Chicken and Pasta 38
Chicken Sliders 38
Buffalo Chicken Salad Wrap 38
White Chicken Chili 38
Turkey Club Burger 39
Mango Chicken Stir-Fry 39
Chicken Couscous 39
Esotic Jerk Chicken 40
Chicken Vegetable Creole 40
Crispy Oven-Fried Chicken 41
Turkey Stir-Fry 41
Chicken and Broccoli Stir-Fry 41
Quick Chicken Fajitas 42
Roasted Turkey 42
Honey Garlic Chicken Drumsticks 42
Southwestern Chicken and Pasta 42
Chicken Sliders 43
Buffalo Chicken Salad Wrap 43
Honey-Mustard Chicken 43
Grilled Chicken, Avocado, and Apple Salad 43
Turkey Cutlets with Herbs 44
Chili Chicken Curry 44

Honey-Mustard Chicken 44
Grilled Chicken, Avocado, and Apple Salad 45
Chicken and Spanish Rice 45
Turkey Cutlets with Herbs 45
Chili Chicken Curry 46
Saucy Chicken 46
Chicken Fried Rice 46
Mexican Chicken 46
Chicken Breast Stew 47
Vegetable Chicken Enchiladas 47
Turkey Meatloaf 47
Shepherd's Pie 48
Turkey Breast and Sweet Potato Mix 48
Italian Chicken 48
Chicken Breast and Cinnamon Veggie Mix 49

Chapter 8: Beef, Pork and Lamb 50
Buffalo & Ranch Chicken Meatloaf 50
Mexican Beef Mix 50
Maple Beef Tenderloin 50
Beef and Cabbage Stew 50
Greek Beef 51
Roast and Veggies 51
Pork Medallions 51
Pork Salad with Walnuts and Peaches 51
Pork, White Bean, and Spinach Soup 52
Orange-Beef Stir-Fry 52
Steak Tacos 52
Beef-and-Bean Chili 53
Asian Pork Tenderloin 53
Curried Pork Tenderloin in Apple Cider 53
New York Strip Steak 54
Mediterranean Pork Pasta 54
Pork Medallions with Herbs de Provence 54
Pork and Mint Corn 55
Pork Chops and Snow Peas 55
Pork Meatballs 55
Pork with Sprouts 55
Beef Stew with Fennel and Shallots 55

Grilled Portobello Mushroom Burger	56
Pork and Green Onions	56
Chili Verde	57
Pork and Carrots Soup	57
Chili Pork	57
Asian Pork Tenderloin	57
Delicious Bacon Delight	58
Squeaky Beef Stroganoff	58
Sloppiest Sloppy Joe	58
Wrapped Asparagus	59
Majestic Veal Stew	59
The Surprising No "Noodle" Lasagna	59
Worthwhile Balsamic Beef	60
Friendly Chipotle Copycat	60
Ground Beef with Beans and Tomatoes	60
Lamb Spare Ribs	61
Curry Lamb shanks	61
Moroccan Lamb Tajine	62
Quick Jalapeno Crisps	62
Crispy Egg Chips	62
Marinated beef Kebabs	62

Chapter 9: Fish and Seafood **64**

Cowboy Caviar Salad	64
Asparagus And Lemon Salmon Dish	64
Spicy Baked Shrimp	64
Shallot and Tuna	64
Brazilian Shrimp Stew	64
Heart-Warming Medi Tilapia	65
Lemon Cod	65
Lemon And Garlic Scallops	65
Cajun Snow Crab	66
Calamari Citrus	66
Lasagna	66
Shrimp And Avocado Dish	66
Fresh Calamari	67
Deep Fried Prawn And Rice Croquettes	67
Thai Pumpkin Seafood Stew	67
Blackened Tilapia	68

Shrimp Pasta Primavera	68
Brown Stewed Fish	68
Grilled Cod	69
Baked Salmon	69
Steamed Mussels	69
Creamy Seafood and Veggies Soup	69
Seafood Gumbo	70
Lemon and Spinach Trout	70
Easy Roast Salmon with Roasted Asparagus	70
Shrimp Pasta Primavera	70
Cilantro-Lime Tilapia Tacos	71
Garlic and Butter Sword Fish	71
Pressure Cooker Crab Legs	71
Delicious Tuna Sandwich	71
Easy Mussels	72
Parmesan-Crusted Fish	72
Salmon and Horseradish Sauce	72
Crunchy Topped Fish with Potato Sticks	72
Halibut and Cherry Tomatoes	73
Salmon and Cauliflower Mix	73
Salmon in Dill Sauce	73
Salmon and Potatoes Mix	73
Roasted Hake	74
Sautéed Fish Fillets	74
Coconut Cream Shrimp	74
Cinnamon Salmon	74
Scallops and Strawberry Mix	74
Cod Peas Relish	75
Baked Haddock	75
Hot Tuna Steak	75
Marinated Fish Steaks	75
Baked Tomato Hake	76
Cheesy Tuna Pasta	76
Herb-Coated Baked Cod with Honey	76
Tender Salmon in Mustard Sauce	76
Broiled White Sea Bass	76
Tuna and Shallots	77
Paprika Tuna	77

Ginger Sea Bass Mix 77
Parmesan Cod Mix 77
Linguini with Clam Sauce 77
Spicy Baked Fish 78
Smoked Trout Spread 78
Creamy Sea Bass Mix 78
Tuna Melt 78
Crab Salad 79
Spicy Cod 79
Fish Tacos 79
Lemony Scallop 79
Baked Trout 79
Moustard Savoury Salmon 80
Spinach Stuffed Sole 80
Lemon Salmon with Kaffir Lime 80
Steamed Fish Balls 81
Shrimp Quesadillas 81
Teriyaki Salmon 81
Lemon-Parsley Baked Flounder 81
Pan-Seared Scallops 82
Baked Cod Packets with Broccoli and Squash 82
Lemony Ceviche 82
Mediterranean Baked Fish 82
Garlic Salmon and Snap Peas 83

Chapter 10: Vegan and Vegetarian 84
Pesto And Goat Cheese Terrine 84
Green Crackers 84
Macaroni and Cheese 84
Springtime Pasta 84
Shitake & Snow Peas Quinoa 85
Low-Carb Zucchini Lasagna Rolls 85
Baked Pumpkin Pasta 85
Gruyere and Spinach Casserole 85
Italian Cheese Sticks 86
Broccoli Sticks 86
Halloumi Cheese Crunchy Fries 86
Special Cucumber Cups 86
Black-Bean and Vegetable Burrito 87

Black Bean and Corn Pita 87
Black Beans with Rice 87
Caribbean Pink Beans 88
Lentils with Brown Rice 88
Tortilla Pizzas 88
Beans from Tuscany - Italy 89
Veggie Tortilla Roll-Ups 89
Baked Eggs In Avocado 89
White Beans with Spinach and Tomatoes 90
Black-Eyed Peas and Greens Power Salad 90
Butternut-Squash Macaroni and Cheese 90
Pasta with Tomatoes and Peas 90
Healthy Vegetable Fried Rice 91
Portobello-Mushroom Cheeseburgers 91
Baked Chickpea-and-Rosemary Omelet 91
Black-Bean Soup 92
Loaded Baked Sweet Potatoes 92
Lemon Roasted Artichokes 92
Chocolate Aquafaba Mousse 93
Peas Feta Rice 93
Rhubarb and Strawberry Compote 93
Zucchini Cakes 94
Vegan Rice Pudding 94
Couscous from Middle-East 94
Kasha with Bell Pepper 94
Easy Chickpea Veggie Burgers 95
Cinnamon-Scented Quinoa 95
Thyme Mushrooms 95
Rosemary Endives 95
Roasted Beets 95
Dates and Cabbage Sauté 96
Baked Squash Mix 96
Garlic Mushrooms and Corn 96
Cilantro Broccoli 96
Paprika Carrots 97
Mashed Cauliflower 97
Spinach Spread 97
Mustard Greens Sauté 97

Cauliflower with Breadcrumbs 97
Chayotes Stuffed with Cheese 98
Rotelle Pasta with Sun-Dried Tomato 98

Chapter 11: Side Dishes and Appetizers 99
Garlic Steamed Squash 99
Grilled Asparagus 99
Apple Glazed Sweet Potatoes 99
Cauliflower and Potato Mash 99
Mexican Cauliflower Rice 100
Asparagus with Lemon Sauce 100
Autumn Salad 100
Broccoli and Cheese 100
Caribbean Casserole 101
Avocado Garden Salad 101
Oven-Fried Yucca 101
Celery with Cheese Mousse 101
Chicken Tomatillo Salad 101
Green Beans Sauté 102
Romaine Lettuce With Dressing 102
Corn and Green Chili Salad 102
Avocado appetizer 102
Cabbage and Tomato Salad 103
Creole Green Beans 103
Mango and Blackeye Pea Salsa 103
Garden Potato Salad 103
Oven Fries 104
Parmesan Rice and Pasta 104
Potato Sauté with Onions 104
Garlic Mashed Potatoes 104
Red Hot Fusilli 105
Egg and Beans 105
Glazed Carrots 105
Fresh Cabbage and Tomato Salad 105
Garlic Mashed Potatoes 106
Corn and Green Chili Salad 106
Cheddar and Apple Sandwich 106
Herbed Potato Salad 106
Herbed Vegetable Mix 107

Limas and Spinach 107
Oriental Rice 107
Parmesan Rice and Pasta Pilaf 107
Roasted Carrots 108
Turkey and Cheese Sandwich 108
Crunchy Mashed Sweet Potatoes 108
Special Roast Potatoes 108
Crazy Eggs 109
Potato, Onions and Bell Peppers 109
Green Pea Purée 109
Green Beans with Nuts 109
Beets Stewed with Apples 110
Cabbage Quiche 110
Baked Tomatoes 110
Cabbage Rolls with Dried Apricots 110
Herbed Green Beans 110
Chickpea Meatballs 111
Lemon Roasted Radishes 111
Green Beans with Nuts 111
Beets Stewed with Apples 111
Cabbage Quiche 111
Rice and Chicken Stuffed Tomatoes 112
Berry Soufflé 112
Stuffed Turnips 112
Roasted Asparagus 112
Brussels Sprouts with Walnuts 113
Grilled Pesto Shrimps 113
Rosemary Potato Shells 113
Basil Tomato Crostini 113
Cranberry Spritzer 113
Penne with Broccoli 114
White Sponge Cake 114
Pan Seared Acorn Squash and Pecans 114
Squash Pancakes 114
Apples Stuffed with Quark 114
Meringue Cookies 115
Rose Hip Jelly 115
Easy Broccoli and Pasta 115

Chapter 12: Snacks and Desserts 116

- Hearty Chia And Blackberry Pudding 116
- Special Cocoa Brownies 116
- Gentle Blackberry Crumble 116
- Nutmeg Nougats 116
- Apple And Almond Muffins......................... 117
- Sweet Potatoes and Apples Mix 117
- Sautéed Bananas with Orange Sauce 117
- Caramelized Apricot 117
- Rhubarb Pie... 118
- Berry Bars... 118
- Chocolate Avocado Pudding 118
- Ginger Peach Pie...................................... 118
- Pomegranate Mix 119
- Blueberry Cream 119
- Mocha Ricotta Cream 119
- Mango Sweet Mix 119
- Ginger Peach Pie...................................... 119
- Berries Mix 120
- Coconut Cream 120
- Coconut Figs.. 120
- Cinnamon Apples...................................... 120
- Green Apple Bowls.................................... 120
- Pecan Granola.. 120
- Banana Sashimi 121
- Creamy Peanuts with Apples 121
- Maple Malt 121
- Walnut Green Beans 121
- Cheese Stuffed Apples............................... 121
- Green Tea Cream 121
- Fresh Figs With Walnuts And Ricotta............ 122
- Coconut Mousse 122
- Rice Pudding with Oranges......................... 122
- Chickpeas and Pepper Hummus 122
- Tortilla Chips... 122
- Kale Popcorn 123
- Peas and Parsley Hummus 123
- White Beans Hummus 123
- Peanuts Snack Bar 123
- Chickpeas Dip.. 123
- Special Raspberry Chocolate Bombs 123
- Cranberry Muffins 124
- Broad Bean Hummus 124
- Carrot Cake 124
- Hearty Almond Bread 125
- Apple Coffee Cake 125
- Baked Apple Slices 125
- Frosted Cake 125
- Fruit Skewers with Yogurt Dip 126
- Fudgy Fruit.. 126
- Mousse Vanilla Banana.............................. 126
- Oatmeal Cookies...................................... 127
- Oven Fried Plantains................................. 127
- Mixed Fruits Freeze 127
- Peach Apple Crisp 127
- Peach Crumble 128
- Peachy Pita 128
- Peanut Butter Hummus.............................. 128
- Rainbow Salad... 129
- Savory Grilled Fruit................................... 129
- Southern Banana Pudding 129
- Tropical Fruit and Nut Snack Mix................. 129
- Fruit Compote 130
- Winter/Summer Crisp................................ 130

Chapter 13: Breads 131

- Apricot Breads 131
- Banana & Pecans Breads........................... 131
- Carrots Bread 131
- Easy Cornbread 132
- Classical Homemade Biscuits 132
- Soft Bread... 132
- Savory Muffins 133
- Cherry Tomatoes Muffins 133

Chapter 14: 4 Weeks MEAL PLAN 134

Conclusion 137

Introduction

The DASH diet is no ordinary diet. It's not just a diet. It's a lifestyle. The DASH way of eating is a lifestyle, which means the end of yoyo dieting for you. All we're going to do is just clean up your usual diet. It's a plan based on simple common sense. We're going to move you away from all the bad stuff - refined sugar cholesterol saturated fat. But it doesn't end there. On the DASH diet, we'll have you focused on eating food that makes your body feel good. You can have fish, low-fat dairy, fruits, vegetables, lean meat, poultry, and whole grains as well. See? No restrictions and a lot of choices!

Above all else, on the DASH diet, you will reduce your sodium intake. This is a great thing if you've got high blood pressure, kidney diseases, diabetes, and osteoporosis. Slashing your salt intake is also something your heart will thank you for – heartily. You probably want to know why you should bother with this diet. Well, that's what this book will cover. I'm going to help you understand how the DASH diet is crazy easy to follow. More than that, I'm going to show you just how much fat you can burn following this diet and as an added bonus how you can reduce your blood pressure while you're at it.

If you're going to make the DASH diet work, then you need to understand meal planning is key. Once you know what you're going to eat over the coming week, it becomes easier to just automatically eat the right things. You're less likely to cheat since you don't have any room for poor decisions and choices. What this means for you is there will always be lovely delicious meals on hand whenever you're hungry. Plus! You can eat them while watching the fat melt away. I don't know about you, but I think that's a pretty sweet deal.

The fact that you are here shows that you have taken a bold step to do something about your health – the most important thing in your life. Congratulations.

Some things are indeed genetic and your family history might loom large. Even then, taking control of your diet and Nutrition: will go a long way toward promoting your overall health. You are not a victim and the fact that you've chosen to read this book indicates you're ready to take charge of your own health!

So, why is the DASH Diet important and something you should consider trying? The answer is simple. DASH was originally developed specifically to deal with high blood pressure or hypertension, but it turns out that multiple health issues such as being overweight, developing diabetes and many of the other issues that we've already mentioned are all related. At their root, they at least in part, have a common cause. So while DASH had a specific intent – to lower blood pressure – it also improves health across the board, promoting weight loss, improving blood sugar, and reducing cholesterol. In addition, in recent years, evidence has linked high blood sugars to cancer (lots of insulin in your bloodstream contributes as well). Since DASH helps you lose weight, it may even lessen chances of cancer.

While the DASH diet primarily focuses on increasing the intake of fruits, vegetables, and low-fat dairy items, you are still allowed to go for meat-based recipes, although in small quantities.

Keeping that in mind, the recipes found in this book are a combination of all sorts of recipes, ranging from simple vegetarian to exquisite meat recipes, to ensure that you have a plethora of options to choose from!

It's time to get started. Let's find out what the DASH Diet is all about, how and why it was developed, and how you can use it to improve your health!

Chapter 1: What is the Dash Diet

Salt is perhaps one of the most commonly used and controversial ingredient in the pantry of any chef or cook worldwide. Too little of it will simply turn your dish into a bland and tasteless mess fit for a horse! Too much of it, and you might just create a dish suitable for the open sea.

Finding the perfect balance of salt in any meal is always a challenge for new chefs who just began their journey into the culinary world.

However, here's the thing; table salt or "Sodium Chloride" to be more exact has an infamous reputation of being a "Silent Killer" to anyone who consumes it more than the suggested level for a human body.

Why Should Someone Follow Dash Diet?

Because an over exposure of salt (over 500mg per day) easily wrecks-havoc inside your body and negatively affects your health by inducing hypertension and high blood pressure (both of which greatly contribute and increase the risk of suffering from a number of cardiovascular diseases).

The saddest part is that despite being aware of the negative impacts of salt, today's Americans are exposed to more salt in their foods than ever! Processed cold cuts, fast foods, taste enhancers and similar edibles, all contribute in catapulting the daily salt intake to a substantially risky level. In fact, at the time of writing, statistics estimated that every one out of three Americans are bound to develop high blood pressure due to increased salt intake. So, are you doomed for life? Of course not!

What exactly is a Dash Diet?

There are many different kinds of diets which help to tackle concepts of weight loss. There is a Ketogenic Diet, the Paleo Diet...the list goes on. However, none of them addresses the issue of high "Sodium" intake.

This is where Dash Diet (Dietary Approach to Stop Hypertension) is unique. Unlike other diets, the core objective of a Dash Diet is not to trim you down, but rather to help you lower your blood pressure and prevents hypertension and other cardiovascular diseases.

What is even more interesting is the fact that positive results can be experienced just after two weeks after starting the diet!

The key thing to remember with a Dash Diet is to strike the perfect balance where your maximum sodium intake is limited to 1500mg per day. To put that into perspective, a typical American diet consists of more than 3,400 mg per day!

Brief History of the Dash Diet

The National Heart, Lung and Blood Institute is estimates that at this very moment, around 50 million people in the U.S and 1 billion worldwide suffer from some form of hypertension.

Research is continuous and seamlessly establishes the relation between high blood pressure and other various diseases such as CVD.

Higher blood pressure is also linked to a higher chance of having a heart attack, stroke, heart failure, kidney disease and so on.

Despite having such a large impact, the issue of hypertension didn't come into the spot light prior to 1992, when the U.S National Institute of Health took a stand to fund research specially designed to study the link between dietary patterns and blood pressure.

The NHLBI worked with five of the most well respected medical research centers of that time to conduct one of the largest and most intricate studies to date!

The DASH study is the result of that particular research.

The DASH study used a rigorous design known as "Randomized Controlled Trial", which involved multiple teams of physicians, Nutrition:ists, nurses, statistician and research co-coordinators who co-operated to monitor the participants of the study.

With everyone involved, two DASH trials were conducted, both were in multi-centers and randomized, and focused on testing the effects of dietary patterns on blood pressure.

Perhaps the most distinctive feature of this diet was the fact that the chosen foods were based on traditional and every-day food items to make certain that the study was fair.

It began in August 1993and ended in July 1997 with the dawning of the DASH meal plan!

Advantages of Dash Diet

Let's have a look at the advantages you will enjoy with a DASH Diet!

- Lowers blood pressure
- Helps to lower cholesterol levels
- Helps in weight loss (discussed later)
- A healthier heart
- Helps to prevent Osteoporosis
- Improves Kidney health
- Helps to prevent cancer
- Controls Diabetes
- Helps to prevent depression
- These are just the tip of the iceberg!

Understanding the food requirements

The DASH diet is relatively simple when compared to other "Big Shot" diets! Aside from cutting down on salt, there are other types of food the DASH diet recommends. To maintain your DASH diet accurately, you should:

- Consume more fruits, low-fat dairy products and vegetables
- Cut back on foods that are high in cholesterol, saturated fat and trans fat

- Eat more whole grain foods, nuts, poultry and fish
- Try to limit sodium, sugary drinks, sweets and red meat such as beef/ pork etcup

Research has shown you will see results within 2 weeks!

Alternatively, a different form of diet known as the DASH Sodium calls for cutting sodium down to about 1,500 mg per day (about 2/3 tsp per day).

Generally speaking, the suggested DASH routine includes:

Daily 7-8 servings of Grains

Daily 4-5 servings of vegetables

Daily 4-5 servings of fruits

Daily 2-3 servings of Low-Fat/ Fat-Free dairy products

2 or less daily servings of Meat/ Fish/ Poultry

4-5 servings per week of nuts, dry beans and seeds

2-3 daily servings of Fats and Oil

Less than 5 servings per week of sweets

Moreover, to give you an idea of what "Each" serving means, here are a few pointers.

The following quantities are to be considered as 1 Servings:

½ a cup of cooked rice/pasta

1 slice of bread

1 cup of raw fruits of veggies

½ a cup of cooked fruit or veggies

8 oz of milk

3 oz of cooked meat

1 tsp of olive oil/ or any healthy oil

3 oz of tofu

Does it help to lose weight?

Despite the fact it is not specifically designed for weight loss, the Dash Diet indeed helps to trim your weight by various indirect means.

While the DASH diet does not focus on reducing calories, it fills up your diet with very nutrient dense foods as opposed to ones that are rich in calories, this helps to shed off a few lbs!

Being on a diet full of veggies and fruits, you will consume lots of fiber, which is also believed to help in weight loss.

Apart from that, the diet also controls your appetite since cleaner and Nutrition: dense foods will keep you satisfied throughout the whole day. Lowering the food intake will further contribute to weight loss.

Does it help lower blood pressure?

This is perhaps the main reason why the DASH diet was even invented.

Salt is believed to be closely related to increasing blood pressure. The purpose of the DASH diet is to monitor the intake of salt and lower it to minute levels, and improve your blood pressure.

Beside the salt itself, the DASH diet also helps control the levels of potassium, magnesium and calcium, which altogether plays a great role in lowering blood pressure as well.

The balanced diet controls your system's cholesterol and fat levels, which prevents atherosclerosis that keeps arteries healthy and strain free.

Does it help control Diabetes?

Since the Dash Diet eliminates empty carbohydrates and starchy foods while avoiding simple sugars; a fine balance between the glucose and insulin levels is created that helps to thwart diabetes.

Amazing Tips for Success!

With all this information, you are ready to jump into the diet itself and explore the DASH compatible recipes in this book.

Before you do that, however, allow me to share a number of tips to help you reach the full potential of your DASH journey.

Increase the amount of fresh/frozen fruits and vegetables you consume daily. While you will find a plethora of fruit and veggie based recipes on this book, it is advised that you develop a habit of munching on fruits for breakfast or a snack. Make sure that you have a "Balanced" plate, which includes about a half plate of veggies.

When creating your meal plan, replace the meat-based dishes with various legumes or fish. This helps to ensure that you fully take advantage of this diet.

Go for whole grain products as much as possible. Therefore, Whole Wheat bread, pasta, oats, quinoa, brown rice etcup are all extremely fine options.

When consuming dairy, use the low-fat milk or yogurt. Keep in mind that milk is a nutritious and healthy alternative to other sugary beverages.

Have a variety of unsalted nuts, and seeds a few times per week.

Develop a habit of reading Nutrition:al facts on food labels and find ones that contain the lowest amount of saturated and Trans fat.

Add a serving of veggies at dinner and lunch

Add a serving of fruit to your meals or such as snacks

If you wish, go for low-fat/ skim dairy products instead of full-fat/cream

Craving for snacks? Try to go for unsalted pretzels, raisins or nuts instead of chips or sweets.

Chapter 2: Blood pressure and general health

Hypertension is an alternative name for high blood pressure. It can lead to severe health problems and increase the risk of heart disease, stroke, and sometimes even death. Keeping blood pressure under control is vital for preserving health and reducing the risk of these dangerous conditions. In this chapter, we examine factors that can cause high blood pressure.

Up to a billion people are estimated to have high blood pressure. It's more acute in developed countries and when we examine possible causes of high blood pressure, the reasons why become clear. In the United States, it is estimated that about half of all adults are suffering from high blood pressure, but many are not aware of this fact. The actual number is unknown and it's often called "the silent killer" as someone can appear to be completely healthy and yet have high blood pressure. Their body may look fine from the outside, but internally, it's being destroyed, minute by minute.

If we assume that high blood pressure exists in your family and then you adopt an unhealthy lifestyle of smoking or not maintaining a healthy weight through diet and exercise, then the chances are high that you are staring down the barrel of hypertension.

Roosevelt died from a cerebral hemorrhage, which basically means a blood vessel in your brain bursts and it fills with blood, killing off your brain cells. He had multiple health problems – and most of them could be traded to his high blood pressure. We measure blood pressure in mm of mercury, which is abbreviated mm Hg. The reason this is done is that historically (and often still today) scientists measure pressure by seeing how far a thin column of mercury will rise inside a narrow glass tube, or capillary. Mercury is metal but its liquid at room temperature. The properties of mercury made it ideal for measuring pressure.

Blood pressure has 2 parts, the systolic and diastolicup Systolic blood pressure is the number at the top and diastolic blood pressure is the lower or the one at the bottom. So your blood pressure is given like this:

Blood pressure = systolic/diastolic

Systolic and diastolic blood pressures are measured in units of mm Hg, and not to get into a mathematics lesson, but we need to know this to understand what we're reading - the units cancel since we have a ratio. So you can simply refer to the ratio when describing overall blood pressure while understanding that individually each number is measured in mm Hg.

Systolic blood pressure measures the pressure in your blood vessels when the heart is contracted. In other words, it's the pressure when the pump is forcing blood through the arteries. That's why it's a larger number.

Diastolic blood pressure measures the blood vessels when the heart is at rest. While it's a smaller number, a high pressure when the heart isn't pumping can indicate serious health problems!

FDR's blood pressure was routinely above 200/100, and may have been as high as 300/195! Have you checked your blood pressure lately? It's probably not nearly that high.

If you're so inclined, you can read more detail about FDR's blood pressure and health problems in a scientifically published article here:

https://www.ncbi.nlm.nih.gov/pmc/articles/PMC1071503/

If your blood pressure reached 200/100 or 300/195, it would be considered an emergency. Back in those days, FDR was allowed to continue his usual routine in daily life. Today, 200/100 would be considered an emergency requiring a visit to the emergency room while 300/195 would be considered absolutely catastrophicup And of course, it was – when his blood pressure got that high he ended up dying.

Let's briefly talk about pipes and pumps so that we have some understanding of how blood pressure works. You can imagine a water pumping system with a pump that pushes the water through the pipes. Different pipes will lead to different conditions. Without getting into the physics and engineering behind it, you can understand that pressure will go up if the pipes are narrow, compared to pipes with a wider or larger diameter. Also, to get the same amount of water through, the pump has to work harder or expend more energy to get that water through narrow pipes than it does through larger pipes. The water also travels at a higher velocity and what happens if you break open the pipes? The more narrow the pipes the more forceful the water gushing out would be.

Your circulatory system – and we are focusing on arteries and veins in this case – is pretty analogous to this. Actually, its more than an analogy, your heart is a pump and your arteries are pipes. However, there is a key difference when comparing this to your basic water pumping system described above. Your arteries have some flexibility that metal or PVC pipes found in your plumbing don't have. They can contract and expand, based on many factors. Some of these factors are related to the immediate environment. Remember how narrow pipes help push fluid faster and more forcefully. What happens when you're exercising? Your body tissues and muscle need more oxygen –and hence more blood. So your arteries are going to contract to help get that blood where it needs to go as quickly as possible so you can run or whatever effectively. In other words when you exercise your blood pressure goes up.

Conversely, if you're totally relaxed or meditating your blood pressure goes down.

Many things can lead your blood pressure to go up or down, not just exercise or relaxation. Some people are simply pre-disposed toward high blood pressure because of their genetics, or as we say in common language their family history. As you age, your bodily functions are not as efficient as they were when you were young, and this impacts your circulatory system as well, so the blood vessels may not relax as well as they used to and your blood pressure may creep up as you get older.

But there are many environmental factors that influence blood pressure. In particular, drugs or substances that are stimulants tend to raise blood pressure. A stimulant can be thought of as something that puts your body in a fight or flight state, and so it tightens up your blood vessels. Some over the counter drugs like Sudafed which work in part by tightening the blood vessels in your sinus and nasal passages can cause higher blood pressure in certain sensitive people. Illegal drugs like cocaine and meth can raise blood pressure to dangerous levels and as a result, cause massive damage to the circulatory system if used regularly over extended periods. The New York Times reports that many people who indulged in cocaine use during the 1980s are now showing up with major cardiovascular problems, including a high risk for a brain hemorrhage and also bursting of a major artery in your gut area, which is known as an abdominal aneurysm (before it bursts).

On the legal front, the use of tobacco products is also associated with high blood pressure and the resulting damage to the cardiovascular system that tightening of those pipes we call the arteries can lead to. This is largely due to the presence of nicotine, which like cocaine and meth is a stimulant (though it's of a milder variety). Cigarette smoking, in particular, is tightly linked to a higher risk of high blood pressure, abdominal aneurysm, and cerebral hemorrhage. If you're a smoker, one of the best things you can do for your health is to quit now – and the elevated risk of lung cancer isn't the only reason for doing so.

Even drinking caffeine, in the form of coffee, tea, or energy drinks, can impact the blood pressures of some people. Some folks are more susceptible than others, and it also depends on how much you drink and how rapidly. For most people, coffee and tea will have no impact, or only temporarily raise their blood pressure mildly. But others will be more susceptible. Some energy drinks, which might have more concentrated levels of caffeine, may be more of a problem. There have been reports of some people even having bleeding in the brain and nearly dying after consuming large amounts of energy drinks.

Of course, drugs and stimulants are not the only environmental factors that impact blood pressure. Fluid retention can also be important. When a patient is suffering from fluid retention, this means that blood moves through the arteries at a slower pace. Remember we noted when you exercise blood moves through your arteries at a faster clip – helping to give your tissues, cells, and muscles the extra oxygen and fuel they need to function at a higher level. So you won't be surprised to learn that if you're suffering from fluid retention and blood flow is reduced, your tissues, cells, and muscles aren't going to be getting the oxygen and nutrients they need to function properly. But your body doesn't take this sitting down – it tries to adjust. Specifically, your kidneys can recognize reduced blood flow and respond in turn. The kidneys will cause the release of certain hormones that lead your body to retain sodium and fluid (so it's like a feedback cycle – retain fluid, kidneys then cause your body to retain more). One thing that happens when you've got fluid retention is the fluid in your blood increases in volume – so you're trying to pump more fluid through the same pipes. What does that do? It increases blood pressure.

Health Threats From Hypertension

Smoking

Cigarette smoking, in particular, has been strongly identified as an environmental risk factor for developing high blood pressure. This is due to the fact that people who smoke cigarettes get higher amounts of nicotine in their system.

Weight gain/obesity

Not all overweight people have high blood pressure, but it's clear that being overweight significantly increases your risk of developing it. The heavier you get, the higher the risk.

Sedentary lifestyle

Exercise counteracts hypertension. It helps keep the blood vessels flexible and responsive and helps keep the heart in shape. Someone who has good cardiovascular fitness has a lower resting heart rate and their heart pumps with a healthier level of force, so the blood pressure is reduced as compared to what it would be otherwise. In contrast, people who don't exercise raise their risk of developing high blood pressure, especially if they have a family history.

Race

Studies indicate that African Americans are more prone to high blood pressure than other groups. However, bear in mind that all racial and ethnic groups have plenty of risk of high blood pressure and its victims include people of all races and from every country across the globe.

Kidney disease

The kidneys are closely tied to the healthy maintenance of blood sugar. They help regulate the amount of fluid and salt in the body. When you are suffering from kidney disease, the kidneys may not function as well and this may lead to fluid and sodium retention, which can cause high blood pressure.

Age

Simply getting older raises risk, although we would never call high blood pressure "normal." However, as you get older, things don't work as well (you knew that, right?). If your joints are stiffening, you can bet your arteries are as well. Even though you may be reasonably healthy overall, simply getting older raises your risk of developing some level of high blood pressure. There is some debate about whether older people need to use the same standards as to what constitutes a diagnosis of hypertension or not, but a general rule applies. You're better off if your blood pressure is below 140/10

Nutrition:al deficiencies

Nutrition:al deficiencies of potassium and magnesium can lead to the development of high blood pressure, along with other health problems such as heart palpitations and muscle cramps. Salt, especially in excess causes your body to retain fluid as the body adapts to maintain a healthy balance of sugar levels. Salt also promotes the contraction of blood vessels, among other things. All of these factors can lead to high blood pressure.

The DASH Diet provides an opportunity to address several items on this list. It reduces salt in the diet and addresses Nutrition:al deficiencies of potassium and magnesium. The practice of consuming large amounts of fruit and vegetables, along with a low-fat diet reduces the risk of kidney problems. Controlling weight can also reduce the risks of developing high blood pressure.

Side effects of using Blood Pressure Drugs

Let's briefly review some of the major classes of blood pressure medications prescribed by doctors and how they work.

Diuretics

These are the oldest of blood pressure medications. Basically, they cause your body to eliminate fluid and sodium from the body, by excess urination. By reducing fluid and sodium in the body, they reduce the amount of fluid in the blood and hence reduce blood pressure. While they work, they aren't as effective as newer medications and also have some problems associated with them. For example, it's not just sodium that gets taken out of the body – all that fluid will take potassium with it too.

Beta Blockers

Remember that pressure isn't just due to the size of the pipe, the action of the pump and how forcefully it pushes fluid through the pipes can impact pressure as well. Beta Blockers work on this by acting directly on the heart, to reduce heart rate and the force with which the heart pumps.

Ace Inhibitors

ACE is angiotensin-converting enzymes. Basically, they make angiotensin, a hormone that makes blood vessels contract, or become narrow, raising blood pressure. By blocking the production of the hormone, it reduces blood pressure. It's not blocked completely, only reduced.

Angiotensin II Receptor Blockers

These drugs work on the blood vessel narrowing hormone as the ACE inhibitors but in a different way. They block some angiotensin molecules from binding to the blood vessels, to reduce the narrowing effect.

Calcium Channel Blockers

While calcium is beneficial for many aspects of health, it increases the force of contraction of the heart, and for people for which this is a problem contributes to high blood pressure. Calcium channel blockers reduce this effect.

Alpha Blockers

In short, alpha blockers help the blood vessels dilate, or relax. This reduces blood pressure.

Vasodilators

These also work to help the blood vessels dilate, but by a different mechanism than alpha blockers.

Adrenergic Inhibitors

These drugs are older and work by blocking mechanisms in the brain that tell the blood vessels to constrict. They are only used rarely these days if other medications don't work because they have a lot of side effects.

Sodium and Hypertension

Our kidneys function is to remove extra fluids from the body after filtering the blood. The extra fluid is directed to the bladder and eliminated from the body as urine. This process uses osmosis, which requires a delicate balance of potassium and sodium.

Eating excess sodium, which is basically the salt in your diet, disrupts this balance, compromising the effectiveness of your kidneys in eliminating the fluids.

Munching on salty food causes you to pee less frequently. In fact, before a long journey or when going to a function where the bathroom is not readily accessible, some people will eat a pinch of salt and this will effectively keep their bladder from filling for hours.

For these reasons, there is a specific version of the DASH Diet that pays precise attention to the amount of salt in the diet, recommending a maximum of 2,300 mg of sodium a day. If you're already suffering from hypertension, your daily limit should not exceed 1,500 mg. Note that the average American's diet consists of up to 3,400 mg of sodium in a single day.

Even when you do not add a single grain of salt to your food, there's already so much of it in processed foods. This is one of the reasons why the DASH Diet highly recommends fresh foods.

You can reduce your sodium intake by getting a substitute for table salt in your food. There are several natural spices such as ginger or garlic that have that sour tinge that you crave for in salt. Another alternative is to sprinkle fresh lemon juice, especially on meat.

Rinse canned foods before cooking. Most of them come soaked with a salty sauce which you can do away with. How about processed meat? Check the labels for sodium content. Sausages, hot dogs, bacon, ham, and the like tend to be quite salty. If you cannot find a sodium-free/low option, stay away from them altogether. Finally, remove that salt shaker from the dinner table. Sometimes the act of adding salt is purely psychological, with some people adding even before they taste the food. Even in a restaurant, ask the waiter to take it back. Once it's out of sight, chances are, you won't even need it.

For a diet that was formulated to treat hypertension and which in most cases, has successfully done so, the DASH Diet has so many additional benefits. As it is basically healthy eating, the body benefits in multiple aspects. Even if you're not suffering from high blood pressure, the DASH Diet is still highly recommended. It'll go a long way in helping you avoid the condition as well as other lifestyle diseases such as diabetes, obesity, and heart disease.

IF YOU'RE ALREADY SUFFERING FROM HYPERTENSION, THIS DIET CAN HELP YOU EASE THE SYMPTOMS WHICH INCLUDE HEADACHES, CHEST PAINS, FATIGUE, LABORED BREATHING, AND IRREGULAR HEARTBEAT. EVEN IF YOU'RE ALREADY ON MEDICATION, THE DIETARY CHANGES RECOMMENDED BY THIS DIET WILL REGULATE YOUR BLOOD PRESSURE, SO YOU DON'T HAVE TO LIVE ON MEDICATION.

Chapter 3: Benefits of Dash Diet

Hypertension affects millions of people around the world. Therefore, switching to the DASH Diet can help many people live healthier lives. It is not very difficult to follow this diet because it is not restrictive. All you need to do is consume more vegetables and fruits while having red meat and sugary foods in moderation.

More Nutritious Meals

Eliminating processed foods and incorporating more fresh foods gives you healthy meals which are beneficial for every aspect of your wellbeing. Adjusting may take some effort at first, especially if you're accustomed to fast foods, but the results will be well worth the effort. You will reduce the chances of health issues throughout your lifetime and enjoy a largely vibrant, pain-free life.

Healthier Kidneys

The nutrients found in the DASH eating plan, including potassium, calcium, magnesium, and fiber, nourish every part of the body, and the kidneys are no exception. The lower consumption of sodium as recommended, further favor the kidneys, allowing them to filter blood efficiently.

Cardiovascular Health

The DASH Diet decreases your consumption of refined carbohydrates by increasing your consumption of foods high in potassium and dietary fiber (fruits, vegetables, and whole grains). It also lessens your consumption of saturated fats. Therefore, the DASH Diet has a positive effect on your lipid profile and glucose tolerance, which reduces the prevalence of metabolic syndrome (MS) in post-menopausal women.

Reports state that a diet limited to 500 calories favors a loss of 17% of total body weight in 6 months in overweight women. This reduces the prevalence of metabolic syndrome by 15%. However, when this diet follows the patterns of the DASH Diet, while triglycerides decrease similarly, the reduction in weight and blood pressure is even greater.

It also reduces blood sugar and increases HDL (high-density lipoprotein cholesterol), which decreases the prevalence of MS in 35% of women. These results contrasted with those of other studies, which have reported that the DASH Diet alone, i.e., without caloric restriction, does not affect HDL and glycemia. This means that the effects of the DASH Diet on MS are associated mainly with the greater reduction in BP (Blood Pressure) and that, for more changes, the diet would be required to be combined with weight loss.

Helpful for Patients with Diabetes

The DASH Diet helps reduce inflammatory and coagulation factors (C-reactive protein and fibrinogen) in patients with diabetes. These benefits are associated with the contribution of antioxidants and fibers, given the high consumption of fruits and vegetables that the DASH Diet requires. In addition, the DASH Diet has been shown to reduce total cholesterol and LDL (low-density lipoprotein cholesterol), which reduces the estimated 10-year cardiovascular risk. Epidemiological studies have determined that women in the highest quintile of food consumption, according to the DASH Diet, have a 24% to 33% lower risk of coronary events and an 18% lower risk of a cerebrovascular event. Similarly, a meta-analysis of six observational studies has determined that the DASH Diet can reduce the risk of cardiovascular events by 20%.

Weight Reduction

Limited research associates the DASH Diet, in isolation, with weight reduction. In some studies, weight reduction was greater when the subject was on the DASH Diet as compared to an isocaloric controlled diet. This could be related to the higher calcium intake and lower energy density of the DASH Diet. The American guidelines for the treatment of obesity emphasize that, regardless of diet, a caloric restriction would be the most important factor in reducing weight.

However, several studies have made an association between greater weight and fat loss in diets and caloric restriction and higher calcium intake. Studies have also observed an inverse association between dairy consumption and body mass index (BMI). In obese patients, weight loss has been reported as being 170% higher after 24 weeks on a hypocaloric diet with high calcium intake.

In addition, the loss of trunk fat was reported to be 34% of the total weight loss as compared to only 21% in a control diet. It has also been determined that a calcium intake of 20 mg per gram has a protective effect in overweight middle-aged women. This would be equivalent to 1275 mg of calcium for a western diet of 1700 kcal.

Despite these reports, the effect that diet-provided calcium has on women's weight after menopause is a controversial subject. An epidemiological study has noted that a sedentary lifestyle and, to a lesser extent, caloric intake is associated with post-menopausal weight gain and calcium intake is not associated with it. The average calcium intake in this group of women is approximately 1000 mg, which would be low, as previously stated. Another study of post-menopausal women shows that calcium and vitamin D supplementation in those with a calcium intake of less than 1200 mg per day decreases the risk of weight gain by 11%.

In short, the DASH Diet has positive impacts, both in weight control and in the regulation of fatty tissue deposits, due to its high calcium content (1200 mg/day). The contribution of calcium plays a vital role in the regulation of lipogenesis.

Chapter 4: Food requirements

Both DASH diet versions include lots of low-fat dairy products, vegetables, fruits, and whole grains. The DASH diet also contains some legumes, poultry and fish, and recommends a small amount of seeds and nuts a few times per week. You can eat fats, sweets and red meat in small quantities.

Directions: Start Your DASH Diet

Keep in mind that the amount of servings depends on how many calories you need per day, which changes depending your sex, weight etcup

Once you decided on your calorie intake, start your DASH diet by making gradual changes.

A good way to start is to limit your sodium to 2,400 mg per day, and keep lowering it .

Once your body adjusted to the change, go for 1,500mg per day (which is about 2/3 of a tsp)

(Keep in mind that the sodium count includes both the sodium already present in your food as well as any additional salt you might add)

As general rules you should remember to:

- avoid to eat salty foods (potato chips, corn chips etc)
- read the label on processed food products and avoid to buy foods that contain salt as ingredient or buy the low-sodium version of them
- use different ingredients to add flavor (spices and herbs for meat, poultry and fish, grated lemon rind or vinegar for soups and stew)

The DASH diet does not have a lot of total fat, trans-fat and saturated fat.

Based on the 2,000-calorie-a-day DASH diet, below are the recommended servings for each food group.

Legumes, seeds and nuts: 4 to 5 servings per week

Lentils, peas, kidney beans, sunflower seeds, almonds and other related foods in this category are good sources of protein, potassium and magnesium.

They're also filled with fiber and phytochemicals – these are plant comlbs that might protect against some cardiovascular disease and cancer. Serving sizes are little and are meant to be eaten only a few times per week since these foods have higher calories.

Examples of a single serving include ½ cup cooked peas or beans, 2 tbsp nut butter or seeds, or 1/3 cup nuts.

Soybean-based products like tempeh and tofu, can be a good substitute to meat since they contain every amino acid needed by your body to make a full protein, just like meat.

Nuts are sometimes looked at negatively due to their fat content, however they contain healthy forms of fat — omega-3 fatty acids and monounsaturated fat. Nuts have high calories, so they should be eaten in moderate quantities. Try adding them to cereals, salads or stir-fries.

Dairy: 2 to 3 servings per day

Cheese, yogurt, milk, and other dairy items are major sources of protein, vitamin D and calcium. But it is essential that you select dairy products that are fat-free or low-fat because if not they can be a huge source of fat — mostly saturated.

Examples of a single serving include 1½ oz part-skim cheese, 1 cup low-fat yogurt, or 1 cup of skimmed milk/1 percent milk.

Use regular cheeses and even fat-free cheeses in moderation because they are usually high in sodium.

If you have difficulty digesting dairy products, select lactose-free products or consider purchasing an over-the-counter product that have the enzyme lactase, which is used to prevent or reduce the signs of lactose intolerance.

Fat-free or low-fat frozen yogurt can assist you in boosting the quantity of dairy products you consume while providing a sweet treat. You can add fruit to get a healthy twist.

Vegetables: 4 to 5 servings per day

Greens, sweet potatoes, broccoli, carrots, tomatoes and other vegetables are filled with vitamins, fibers, and such minerals like magnesium and potassium.

Examples of a single serving include ½ cup cooked/ cut-up raw vegetables or 1 cup raw leafy green vegetables.

To increase the amount of servings you get on a daily basis, be creative. For example, in a stir-fry, reduce the quantity of meat by half and increase the vegetables.

Frozen and fresh vegetables are both good options. When buying canned and frozen vegetables, select those labeled as low-sodium or with no added salt.

Don't regard vegetables as only side-dishes — a hearty mix of vegetables served on top of whole-wheat noodles or brown rice can be the main dish.

Sweets: 5 servings or less per week

You do not need to completely remove sweets while on the DASH diet — just don't overindulge.

Examples of a single serving include 1 cup lemonade, ½ cup sorbet, or 1 tbsp jam, jelly or sugar.

Reduce the amount of added sugar that doesn't provide any Nutrition:al value but can have a lot of calories.

Artificial sweeteners such as sucralose (Splenda) and aspartame (Equal, NutraSweet) may aid in satisfying your sweet tooth while limiting the sugar. But note that you should still use them reasonably. It's OK to exchange a diet soda for a regular soda, but not as a replacement of a more nutritious drink like low-fat milk or even ordinary water.

When you eat sweets, select those that are low-fat or fat-free, such as low-fat cookies, graham crackers, hard candy, jellybeans, fruit ices, or sorbets.

Fish, poultry and lean meat: 6 one-ounce servings or less per day

Meat can be an abundant source of zinc, iron, B vitamins and protein. Choose lean varieties and try for a maximum of 6 one-ounce servings per day. Reducing your meat portion will create room for additional vegetables.

Examples of a single serving include 1 ounce of cooked fish, poultry or meat, or 1 egg.

Eat heart-healthy fish, like tuna, herring and salmon. These kinds of fish have high omega-3 fatty acids that are healthy for the heart.

Trim away fat and skin from meat and poultry and then roast, grill, broil or bake rather than frying in fat.

Fruits: about 4 to 5 servings per day

Several fruits need minimal preparation in order to be a healthy aspect of a snack or meal. Like vegetables, they're filled with magnesium, potassium and fiber and are usually low in fat — one exception to this is coconut.

Examples of a single serving include 4 oz of juice, 1/2 cup canned, frozen or fresh fruit, or one medium fruit.

If you purchase juice or canned, make sure that it doesn't contain added sugar.

Remember that citrus juices and fruits, such as grapefruit, can affect certain medications, so discuss with your pharmacist or doctor to know if it is appropriate.

Make use of edible peels when possible. The peels from fruits such as pears, apples and several other fruits puts a nice texture to recipes and contain healthy fiber and nutrients.

Eat a piece of fruit during meals and eat one as a snack. Afterwards, you can complete the day with a dessert made up of fresh fruits that is topped with a tbsp of low-fat yogurt.

Grains: 6 to 8 servings per day

Grains include pasta, rice, cereal and bread.

Examples of a single serving include ½ cup cooked pasta, rice or cereal, 1-ounce dry cereal, or 1 slice whole-wheat bread.

Focus on whole grains since they have more nutrients and fiber than refined grains do. For example, use whole-grain bread rather than white bread, whole-wheat pasta rather than regular pasta or brown rice rather than white rice. Search for products labeled as "100% whole wheat" or "100% whole grain."

Grains are low in fat, by nature. Keep them like this by avoiding cheese sauces, cream and butter.

Oils and fats: 2 to 3 servings per day

Fat assists your body in absorbing essential vitamins and assists the immune system of your body. But too much fat raises your risk of obesity, diabetes and heart disease. The DASH diet pushes for a healthy balance through the restriction of total fat to a maximum of 30% of daily calories gotten from fat, with an emphasis on the beneficial monounsaturated fats.

Examples of a single serving include 2 tbsp of salad dressing, 1 tbsp of mayonnaise or 1 tsp of soft margarine.

Read the food labels on salad dressing and margarine so that you can buy foods that are free of trans-fat and have minimal saturated fat.

Avoid trans-fat, usually found in processed foods. For example: fried items, baked goods and crackers.

Trans-fat and saturated fat are the chief dietary culprits in raising the risk of coronary artery related diseases. DASH assists in keeping the daily saturated fat to a maximum of 6% of your whole calories by restricting use of eggs, cream, whole milk, cheese, butter and meat in your diet, as well as foods made from coconut oil, palm oil, solid shortenings and lard.

What Not to Eat

When you are on the DASH plan, you need to limit the amount you eat of the below foods:

Packaged snacks that are often high in sugar, salt and fat.

Foods that contain lots of saturated fats, such as deep-fried foods and whole fat dairy.

SUGAR-SWEETENED BEVERAGES. Those that consume fewer calories (individuals not physically active or smaller individuals) should try to totally avoid foods with extra sugar. This might include syrup, jelly and hard candy. Those that consume calories moderately can eat up to five treats a week, and those that are very active may eat less than two per day.

ALCOHOL. Adult beverages like spirits, wine, and beer are not completely off-limits, but it is recommended that you limit your consumption. If you consume alcoholic drinks, do within reasonable limits. Drinking moderately can be described as having a maximum of one drink a day for women and a maximum of two drinks a day for men.

Adding unnecessary salt to food or eating foods with excess salt. Before using salt substitutes (which usually contain potassium) or increasing the level of potassium in your diet, check with your doctor. People that have kidney issues or take certain medicines should be careful about the quantity of potassium they consume.

Chapter 5: Breakfast & Smoothie

Swiss Chard Omelet

Prep time: 5 mins | Servings: 2
Ingredients:
- 2 eggs, lightly beaten
- 1 tbsp almond butter
- 2 cups Swiss chard, sliced
- ½ tsp sunflower seeds
- Fresh pepper

Directions:
1. Mix the almond butter and Swiss chard and cook for 2 mins in a non-stick frying pan
2. Pour the eggs into the pan and gently stir them into the Swiss chard
3. Season with garlic sunflower seeds and pepper
4. Cook for 2 mins

Nutrition:
Calories 260, Fat 21 g, Carbs 4 g, Protein 14 g

Hearty Pineapple Oatmeal

Prep time: 10 mins | Servings: 5
Ingredients:
- 1 cup steel-cut oats
- 4 cup unsweetened almond milk
- 2 medium apples, sliced
- 1 tsp coconut oil
- 1 tsp cinnamon
- ¼ tsp nutmeg
- 2 tbsp maple syrup, unsweetened
- A drizzle of lemon juice

Directions:
1. Add listed Ingredients: to a cooking pan and mix well
2. Cook on very low flame for 8 hours/or on high flame for 4 hours
3. Gently stir
4. Add your desired toppings
5. Store in the fridge for later use

Nutrition:
Calories 180, Fat 5 g, Carbs 31 g, Protein 5 g

Sweet Potatoes with Coconut Flakes

Prep time: 10 mins | Servings: 5
Ingredients:
- 16 oz sweet potatoes
- 1 tbsp maple syrup
- ¼ cup fat-free coconut Greek yogurt
- 1/8 cup unsweetened toasted coconut flakes
- 1 chopped apple

Directions:
1. Preheat oven to 400 °F.
2. Place your potatoes on a baking sheet
3. Bake them for 45 - 60 mins or until soft.
4. Use a sharp knife to mark "X" on the potatoes and fluff pulp with a fork
5. Top with coconut flakes, chopped apple, Greek yogurt, and maple syrup

Nutrition:
Calories 321, Fat 3 g, Carbs 70 g, Protein 7 g

Banana Smoothie

Prep time: 5 mins | Servings: 1
Ingredients:
- 1 frozen banana
- ½ cup almond milk
- Vanilla extract.
- 2 tbsp Flax seed
- 1 tsp maple syrup
- 1 tbsp almond butter

Directions:
1. Add all your Ingredients: to a food processor or blender and run until smooth.
2. Pour the mixture into a glass and enjoy

Nutrition:
Calories 376, Fat 19.4 g, Carbs 48.3 g, Protein 9.2 g

Strawberry Smoothie

Prep time: 5 mins | Servings: 1
Ingredients:
- 1/2 cup 100% orange juice
- 1 large banana, peeled and sliced
- 1 cup fresh or frozen strawberries, thawed
- 1 cup low-fat vanilla yogurt
- 5 ice cubes

Directions:
1. Combine orange juice, banana, and half the strawberries into a blender container. Blend until smooth.
2. Add yogurt, remaining strawberries, and ice cubes. Blend until smooth. Serve immediately.

Nutrition:

Calories 153, Carbs 32 g, Protein 5 g, Fat 1 g

Summer Smoothie

Prep time: 5 mins | Servings: 1
Ingredients:
- 1 cup yogurt, plain nonfat
- 6 medium strawberries
- 1 cup pineapple, crushed, canned in juice
- 1 medium banana
- 1 tsp vanilla extract
- 4 ice cubes

Directions:
1. Place all Ingredients: in a blender and purée until smooth.
2. Serve in a frosted glass.

Nutrition:
Calories 121, Fat 1 g

Tropical Smoothie

Prep time: 5 mins | Servings: 1
Ingredients:
- 1 mango, peeled, seeded, and cut into chunks
- 1 large banana, peeled and sliced
- 1 cup undrained pineapple chunks
- 3/4 cup low fat vanilla frozen yogurt
- 1 cup ice cubes

Directions:
1. Cut papayas in half lengthwise. Scoop out seeds. Place each half in a medium plate.
2. Place an equal amount of banana, kiwifruit, strawberries, and oranges in each papaya half.
3. Combine yogurt, honey and mint; mix well. Spoon over fruit before serving.

Nutrition:
Calories 195, Carbs 46 g, Protein 5 g, Fat 1 g

Paradise Smoothie

Prep time: 5 mins | Servings: 1
Ingredients:
- 1/2 cup 100% orange juice
- 2/3 peeled peaches
- 1 cup low-fat vanilla yogurt
- 5 ice cubes

Directions:
Combine orange juice, peaches into a blender container. Blend until smooth. Add yogurt and ice cubes. Blend until smooth. Serve immediately.
Nutrition:

Calories 123, Carbs 22 g, Protein 5 g, Fat 1 g

Fruity Smoothie

Prep time: 5 mins | Servings: 12
Ingredients:
- 1 cup ice cold water
- 1 cup packed spinach
- ¼ cup frozen mango chunks
- ½ cup frozen pineapple chunks
- 1 tbsp chia seeds
- 1 container silken tofu
- 1 frozen banana

Directions:
1. In a powerful blender, add all ingredients and puree until smooth and creamy.
2. Evenly divide into two glasses, serve and enjoy.

Nutrition:
Calories 175, Fat 3.7 g, Carbs 33.3 g, Protein 6.0 g

Grape Shake

Prep time: 5 mins | Servings: 1
Ingredients:
- 2 cups green or red seedless grapes
- 2 bananas, peeled and sliced
- 2 oranges, peeled and quartered
- 12-16 ice cubes, crushed

Directions:
1. Place grapes, bananas, oranges, and ice in a blender container.
2. Blend until smooth. Pour into glasses and serve.

Nutrition:
Calories 139, Carbs 36 g, Protein 2 g

Melon Shake

Prep time: 5 mins | Servings: 1
Ingredients:
- 2 cups chopped melon (cantaloupe, honeydew)
- 2 cups cold water

Directions:
Place all ingredients in a blender container. Blend until smooth.
Nutrition:
Calories 27, Carbs 7 g, Protein 1 g, Fat 0 g

Mango and Pear Smoothie

Prep time: 10 mins | Servings: 1
Ingredients:

- 1 ripe mango, cored and chopped
- ½ mango, peeled, pitted and chopped
- 1 cup kale, chopped
- ½ cup plain Greek yogurt
- 2 ice cubes

Directions:
1. Add pear, mango, yogurt, kale, and mango to a blender and puree
2. Add ice and blend until you have a smooth texture

Nutrition:
Calories 345, Fat 18.4 g, Carbs 46.3 g, Protein 9.4 g

Mixed Berries Smoothie

Prep time: 5 mins | Servings: 2
Ingredients:
- ¼ cup of frozen blueberries
- ¼ cup of frozen blackberries
- 1 cup of unsweetened almond milk
- 1 tsp of vanilla bean extract
- 3 tsp of flaxseed
- 1 scoop of chilled Greek yogurt
- Stevia as needed

Directions:
1. Mix everything in a blender and emulsify them.
2. Pulse the mixture four time until you have your desired thickness.
3. Pour the mixture into a glass and enjoy!

Nutrition:

Calories 360, Fat 16.4 g, Carbs 41.3 g, Protein 9.2 g

Healthy Bagels

Prep time: 5 mins | Servings: 8
Ingredients:
- 1 ½ cup warm water
- 1 ¼ cup bread flour
- 2 tbsp Honey
- 2 cup whole wheat flour
- 2 tsp Yeast
- 1 ½ tbsp Olive oil
- 1 tbsp vinegar

Directions:
1. In a bread machine, mix all Ingredients:, and then process on dough cycle.
2. Once done, create 8 pieces shaped like a flattened ball.
3. Make a hole in the center of each ball using your thumb then create a donut shape.
4. In a greased baking sheet, place donut-shaped dough then cover and let it rise about ½ hour.
5. Prepare about 2 inches of water to boil in a large pan.
6. In a boiling water, drop one at a time the bagels and boil for 1 minute, then turn them once.
7. Remove them and return to baking sheet and bake at 350oF for about 20 to 25 mins until golden brown.

Nutrition:
Calories 228.1, Fat 3.7 g, Carbs 41.8 g, Protein 6.9 g

Watermelon Shake

Prep time: 5 mins | Servings: 1
Ingredients:
- 3 cups chopped watermelon
- 2 cups cold water

Directions:
Place all ingredients in a blender container. Blend until smooth.

Nutrition:
Calories 27, Carbs 7 g, Protein 1 g, Fat 0 g

Morning Punch

Prep time: 5 mins | Servings: 6
Ingredients:
- 4 tbsps Lemon juice
- 2 cup peeled citrus fruits
- 1 cup ice
- 8 oz cranberry juice
- 1 ½ cup chopped pineapple

Directions:
- Place all ingredients in a food blender.
- Puree until smooth.
- Serve immediately.

Nutrition:
Calories 116.6, Fat 0, Carbs 29.6 g, Protein 0

Cherries Oatmeal

Prep time: 10 mins | Servings: 6
Ingredients:
- 2 c. pitted and sliced cherries
- 6 c. water
- 1 tsp. cinnamon powder
- 1 c. almond milk
- 2 c. old-fashioned oats
- 1 tsp. vanilla flavor

Directions:

In a little pot, combine the oats while using the water, milk, cinnamon, vanilla and cherries, toss, bring to a simmer over medium-high heat, cook for quarter-hour, divide into bowls and serve in the morning.
Nutrition:
Calories 180, Fat 4 g, Carbs 9 g, Protein 6.9 g

Veggie Omelette

Prep time: 5 mins | Servings: 8
Ingredients:
- 2 tbsp Olive oil
- 2 whole eggs
- 3 cup spinach, fresh
- Cooking spray
- 10 sliced baby Bella mushrooms
- 8 tbsp Sliced red onion
- 4 egg whites
- 2 oz goat cheese

Directions:
1. Place a skillet over medium-high heat and add olive.
2. Add the sliced red onions to the pan and stir until translucent. Then, add your mushrooms to the pan and keep stirring until they are slightly brown.
3. Add spinach and stir until they wilted. Season with a tiny bit of pepper and salt. Remove from heat.
4. Spray a small pan with cooking spray and Place over medium heat.
5. Break 2 whole eggs in a small bowl. Add 4 egg whites and whisk to combine.
6. Pour the whisked eggs into the small skillet and allow the mixture to sit for a minute.
7. Use a spatula to gently work your way around the skillet's edges. Raise the skillet and tip it down and around in a circular style to allow the runny eggs to reach the center and cook around the edges of the skillet.
8. Add crumbled goat cheese to a side of the omelet top with your mushroom mixture.
9. Then, gently fold the other side of the omelet over the mushroom side with the spatula.
10. Allowing cooking for thirty seconds. Then, transfer the omelet to a plate.

Nutrition:
Calories 412, Fat 29 g, Carbs 18 g, Protein 25 g

Avocado cup

Prep time: 5 mins | Servings: 4
Ingredients:
- 4 tsps parmesan cheese
- 1 chopped stalk scallion
- 4 dashes pepper
- 4 dashes paprika
- 2 ripe avocados
- 4 medium eggs

Directions:
1. Preheat oven to 375 °F.
2. Slice avocadoes in half and discard seed. cook.
3. Slice the rounded portions of the avocado, to make it level and sit well on a baking sheet.
4. Place avocadoes on baking sheet and crack one egg in each hole of the avocado.
5. Pop in the oven and bake for 25 minutes or until eggs are cooked to your liking.
6. Serve with a sprinkle of parmesan., parika and pepper.

Nutrition:
Calories 206, Fat 15.4 g, Carbs 11.3 g, Protein 8.5 g

Eggs with Cheese

Prep time: 5 mins | Servings: 1
Ingredients:
- ¼ cup chopped tomato
- 1 egg white
- 1 chopped green onion
- 2 tbsp Fat-free milk
- 1 slice whole wheat bread
- 1 egg
- ½ oz reduced fat grated cheddar cheese

Directions:
7. Mix the egg and egg whites in a bowl and add the milk.
8. Scramble the mixture in a non-stick frying pan until the eggs cook.
9. Meanwhile, toast the bread.
10. Spoon the scrambled egg mixture onto the toasted bread and top with the cheese until it melts.
11. Add the onion and the tomato.

Nutrition:
Calories 251, Fat 11.0 g, Carbs 22.3 g, Protein 16.9 g

Quinoa Quiche

Prep time: 10 mins | Servings: 4
Ingredients:
- 1 cup fat-free ricotta cheese
- 2/3 cup grated low-fat parmesan
- 3 oz chopped spinach
- 1 ½ tsp Garlic powder
- 1 cup cooked quinoa
- 3 eggs

Directions:
1. In a bowl, combine the quinoa while using spinach, ricotta, eggs, garlic powder and parmesan, whisk well, pour into a lined pie pan, introduce inside oven and bake at 355 ⁰F for 45 mins.
2. Cool the quiche down, slice and serve enjoying.

Nutrition:
Calories 201, Fat 2 g, Carbs 12 g, Protein 7 g

Fruits Breakfast Salad

Prep time: 10 mins | Servings: 2
Ingredients:
- 1 cored and cubed Asian pear
- ½ tsp cinnamon powder
- 1 peeled and sliced banana
- 2 oz toasted pepitas
- ½ lime juice

Directions:
In a bowl, combine the banana using the pear, lime juice, cinnamon and pepitas, toss, divide between small plates and serve enjoying.
Nutrition:
Calories 188, Fat 2 g, Carbs 5 g, Protein 7 g

Mediterranean Toast

Prep time: 10 mins | Servings: 6
Ingredients:
- 1 ½ tsp. reduced-fat crumbled feta
- 3 sliced Greek olives
- ¼ mashed avocado
- 1 slice good whole wheat bread
- 1 tbsp roasted red pepper hummus
- 1 sliced hardboiled egg
- 3 sliced cherry tomatoes

Directions:
1. First, toast the bread and top it with ¼ mashed avocado and 1 tablespoon hummus.
2. Add the cherry tomatoes, olives, hardboiled egg and feta.

Nutrition:
Calories 333.7, Fat 17 g, Carbs 33.3 g, Protein 16.3 g

Italian Bruschetta

Prep time: 10 mins | Servings: 8 | Cooking: 10 mins
Ingredients:
- ½ cup chopped basil
- 2 minced garlic cloves
- 1 tbsp balsamic vinegar
- 2 tbsps Olive oil
- ½ tsp cracked black pepper
- 1 sliced whole wheat baguette
- 8 diced ripe Roma tomatoes

Directions:
1. First, preheat the oven to 375 F.
2. In a bowl, dice the tomatoes, mix in balsamic vinegar, chopped basil, garlic, salt, pepper, and olive oil, set aside.
3. Slice the baguette into 16-18 slices and for about 10 minutes, place on a baking pan to bake.
4. Serve with warm bread slices and enjoy.
5. For leftovers, store in an airtight container and put in the fridge. Try putting them over grilled chicken, it is amazing!

Nutrition:
Calories 57, Fat 2.5 g, Carbs 7.5 g, Protein 1.7 g

Quinoa Breakfast Bars

Prep time: 2 hours | Servings: 6
Ingredients:
- 1/3 cup flaked coconut
- ½ tsp cinnamon powder
- 2 tbsp Coconut sugar
- 2 tbsp Unsweetened chocolate chips
- ½ cup fat-free peanut butter
- 1 tsp vanilla flavoring
- 1 cup quinoa flakes

Directions:
In a large bowl, combine the peanut butter with sugar, vanilla, cinnamon, quinoa, coconut and chocolate chips, stir well, spread about the bottom of the lined baking sheet, press well, cut in 6 bars, keep inside fridge for just two hours, divide between plates and serve.
Nutrition:
Calories 182, Fat 4 g, Carbs 13 g, Protein 11 g

Cherries Oatmeal

Prep time: 10 mins | Servings: 6
Ingredients:
- 2 cup pitted and sliced cherries
- 6 cup water
- 1 tsp cinnamon powder
- 1 cup almond milk
- 2 cup old-fashioned oats
- 1 tsp vanilla flavor

Directions:
1. In a little pot, combine the oats while using the water, milk, cinnamon, vanilla and cherries, toss, bring to a simmer over medium-high heat, cook for quarter-hour, divide into bowls and serve in the morning.

Nutrition:
Calories 180, Fat 4g, Fiber 4g, Carbs 9g, Protein 7g

Cheese & Kale Omelette

Prep time: 10 mins | Servings: 6
Ingredients:
- 1/3 cup sliced scallions
- ¼ tsp pepper
- 1 diced red pepper
- ¾ cup non-fat milk
- 1 cup shredded sharp low-fat cheddar cheese
- 1 tsp olive oil
- 5 oz baby kale and spinach
- 12 eggs

Directions:
1. Preheat oven to 375 °F.
2. With olive oil, grease a glass casserole dish.
3. In a bowl, whisk well all Ingredients: except for cheese.
4. Pour egg mixture in prepared dish and bake for 35 mins.
5. Remove from oven and sprinkle cheese on top and broil for 5 mins.
6. Remove from oven and let it sit for 10 mins.
7. Cut up and enjoy.

Nutrition:
Calories 198, Fat 11.0 g, Carbs 5.7 g, Protein 18.7 g

Chicken Breakfast Burritos

Prep time: 5 mins | Servings: 2
Ingredients:
- 2 tbsp Italian salad dressing
- 1 whole wheat tortilla
- 1 sliced pear
- 4 oz cooked skinless chicken
- 1 cup fresh spinach

Directions:
1. Slice the chicken into small bite-sized pieces and arrange them on the tortilla.
2. Cover the meat with spinach and arrange the pear slices on top.
3. Drizzle with Italian salad dressing.
4. Wrap the tortilla around all the Ingredients: until it's a snug burrito.

Nutrition:
Calories 246, Fat 10.3 g, Carbs 23.6 g, Protein 15.6 g

Chia Seeds Breakfast Mix

Prep time: 8 hours | Servings: 4
Ingredients:
- 1 tsp grated lemon zest
- 4 tbsp Chia seeds
- 1 cup blueberries
- 4 tbsp Coconut sugar
- 2 cup old-fashioned oats
- 3 cup coconut milk

Directions:
1. In a bowl, combine the oats with chia seeds, sugar, milk, lemon zest and blueberries, stir, and divide into cups whilst within the fridge for 8 hours.

Nutrition:
Calories 283, Fat 12 g, Carbs 13 g, Protein 8 g

Apple Cinnamon Crisp

Prep time: 10 mins | Servings: 4
Ingredients:
- 1 tsp cinnamon
- 1 cup brown sugar
- 3 lbs Granny Smith apples
- 2 tbsp All-purpose flour
- 1 stick butter
- 1 cup oatmeal
- 1 tbsp granulated sugar

Directions:
1. Peel and core the apples, slice thinly.
2. Mix granulated sugar with flour and add the apples. Toss to coat.
3. Put apples into the bottom of a 5-6 quart crock pot.
4. Combine brown sugar with oatmeal and butter. Mix until mixture is crumbly.
5. Sprinkle oatmeal mixture on top of the apples.

6. Cook apples fully on high heat.

Nutrition:
Calories 549, Fat 27 g, Carbs 71 g, Protein 6 g

Strawberry Chia Breakfast Pudding

Prep time: 5 mins | Servings: 4
Ingredients:
- 1 tbsp honey
- 3 cup chopped strawberries
- 1 tsp pure vanilla extract
- 2 cup unsweetened coconut milk
- ½ cup chia seeds

Directions:
1. Combine the coconut milk and strawberries in a blender and puree until smooth.
2. Add the chia seeds, vanilla extract, and honey. Stir well.
3. Cover and refrigerate at least 6 hours or overnight.

Nutrition:
Calories 314.8, Fat 25.0 g, Carbs 22.1 g, Protein 4.5 g

Zingy Onion and Thyme Crackers

Prep time: 15 mins | Servings: 75 crackers
Ingredients:
- 1 garlic clove, minced
- 1 cup sweet onion, coarsely chopped
- 2 tsp fresh thyme leaves
- ¼ cup avocado oil
- ¼ tsp garlic powder
- Freshly ground black pepper
- ¼ cup sunflower seeds
- 1 ½ cups roughly ground flax seeds

Directions:
1. Preheat your oven to 225 degrees F
2. Line two baking sheets with parchment paper and keep it on the side
3. Add garlic, onion, thyme, oil, sunflower seeds, and pepper to a food processor
4. Add sunflower and flax seeds, pulse until pureed
5. Transfer the batter to prepared baking sheets and spread evenly, cut into crackers
6. Bake for 60 mins
7. Remove parchment paper and flip crackers, bake for another hour
8. Remove from oven and let them cool

Nutrition:
Calories 180, Fat 2.7 g, Carbs 0.8 g, Protein 0.4 g

Coffee Frappe

Prep time: 2 mins | Servings: 2
Ingredients:
- 1 tbsp unsweetened cocoa powder
- ½ cup low-fat milk
- 2 tbsps Pure maple syrup
- ½ cup brewed coffee
- 1 small ripe banana
- 1 cup low-fat vanilla yogurt

Directions:
Place the banana in a blender or food processor and purée.
Add the remaining ingredients and pulse until smooth and creamy. Serve immediately.

Nutrition:
Calories 206, Fat 2.7 g, Carbs 38 g, Protein 6 g

Sweet Corn Muffins

Prep time: 5 mins | Servings: 1
Ingredients:
- 1 tbsp. sodium-free baking powder
- ¾ cup nondairy milk
- 1 tsp pure vanilla extract
- ½ cup sugar
- 1 cup white whole-wheat flour
- 1 cup cornmeal
- ½ cup canola oil

Directions:
1. Preheat the oven to 400°F. Line a 12-muffin tin with paper liners and set aside.
2. Place the cornmeal, flour, sugar, and baking powder into a mixing bowl and whisk well to combine.
3. Add the nondairy milk, oil, and vanilla and stir just until combined.
4. Divide the batter evenly between the muffin cups. Place muffin tin on middle rack in oven and bake for 15 minutes.
5. Remove from oven and place on a wire rack to cool.

Nutrition:
Calories 203, Fat 9 g, Carbs 26 g, Protein 3 g

Banana Chocolate

Prep time: 5 mins | Servings: 4
Ingredients:
- 1 tbsp honey
- ¼ cup dark chocolate shavings

- 2 tsp Dark cocoa powder
- 1 cup sliced banana
- 2 cup low fat milk
- 1 cup uncooked quinoa

Directions:
1. In a saucepan, combine the milk with the dark cocoa powder and honey. Heat over medium to medium high heat until mixture bubbles, stirring frequently.
2. Add the quinoa and reduce heat to low. Cover and simmer for 15-20 mins, or until most of the liquid is absorbed and grain is tender.
3. Serve warm garnished with sliced banana and chocolate shavings, if desired.

Nutrition:
Calories 256.5, Fat 4.4 g, Carbs 49.4 g, Protein 7.4 g

Mexican Omelet

Prep time: 10 mins | Servings: 2
Ingredients:
- ¼ cup low-fat Mexican cheese
- 2 tbsp Water
- 1 tsp organic olive oil
- ¼ tsp black pepper
- 2 eggs
- ¼ cup chunky salsa

Directions:
1. In a bowl, combine the eggs with all the water, cheese, salsa and pepper and whisk well.
2. Heat up a pan with all the oil over medium-high heat, add the eggs mix, spread in for the pan, cook for 3 mins, flip, cook for 3 more mins, divide between plates and serve enjoying.

Nutrition:
Calories 221, Fat 4 g, Carbs 13 g, Protein 7 g

Spinach & Ham Muffins

Prep time: 10 mins | Servings: 6
Ingredients:
- 4 oz spinach
- 2 oz chopped ham
- ½ cup non-fat milk
- Cooking spray
- 6 eggs
- 1 cup crumbled low-fat cheese
- ½ cup chopped roasted red pepper

Directions:
1. In a bowl, combine the eggs using the milk, cheese, spinach, red pepper and ham and whisk well.
2. Grease a muffin tray with cooking spray, divide the muffin mix, introduce within the oven and bake at 350 °F for around 30 mins.
3. Divide between plates and serve enjoying.

Nutrition:
Calories 155, Fat 10 g, Carbs 4 g, Protein 10 g

Crunchy Flax and Almond Crackers

Prep time: 15 mins | Servings: 20-24 crackers
Ingredients:
- ½ cup ground flaxseeds
- ½ cup almond flour
- 1 tsp coconut flour
- 2 tsp shelled hemp seeds
- ¼ tsp sunflower seeds
- 1 egg white
- 2 tsp unsalted almond butter, melted

Directions:
1. Preheat your oven to 300 degrees F
2. Line a baking sheet with parchment paper, keep it on the side
3. Add flax, almond, coconut flour, hemp seed, seeds to a bowl and mix
4. Add egg white and melted almond butter, mix until combined
5. Transfer dough to a sheet of parchment paper and cover with another sheet of paper
6. Roll out dough
7. Cut into crackers and bake for 60 mins

Nutrition:
Calories 180, Fat 6 g, Carbs 1.2 g, Protein 2 g

Basil and Tomato Baked Eggs

Prep time: 10 mins | Servings: 2
Ingredients:
- ½ garlic clove, minced
- ½ cup canned tomatoes
- ¼ cup fresh basil leaves, roughly chopped
- ¼ tsp chili powder
- ¼ tsp sunflower seeds
- ½ cup canned tomatoes
- ½ tsp olive oil
- 2 whole eggs
- pepper to taste

Directions:
1. Preheat your oven to 375 degrees F

2. Take a small baking dish and grease with olive oil
3. Add garlic, basil, tomatoes chili, olive oil into a dish and stir
4. Crack eggs into a dish, keeping space between the two
5. Sprinkle the whole dish with sunflower seeds and pepper
6. Place in oven and cook for 12 mins until eggs are set and tomatoes are bubbling
7. Serve with basil on top

Nutrition:
Calories 235, Fat 16 g, Carbs 7 g, Protein 14 g

Mushroom Snacks

Prep time: 5 mins | Servings: 2
Ingredients:
- 4 Portobello mushroom caps
- 3 tbsp coconut aminos
- 2 tbsp sesame oil
- 1 tbsp fresh ginger, minced
- 1 small garlic clove, minced

Directions:
1. Set your broiler to low, keeping the rack 6 inches from the heating source
2. Wash mushrooms under cold water and transfer them to a baking sheet
3. Take a bowl and mix in sesame oil, garlic, coconut aminos, ginger and pour the mixture over the mushrooms tops
4. Cook for 10 mins

Nutrition:
Calories 196, Fat 14 g, Carbs 14 g, Protein 7 g

Delicious Pancakes

Prep time: 5 mins | Servings 4
Ingredients:
- 1 tbsp pure vanilla extract
- ¼ cup sugar
- 1 tbsp sodium-free baking powder
- 1 tbsp canola oil
- 1 1/3 cup white whole-wheat flour
- 1 ½ cup low-fat milk
- 1 egg white

Directions:
1. Measure the flour, sugar, and baking powder into a mixing bowl and whisk well to combine.
2. Add the milk, egg white, oil, and vanilla. Mix well and let sit for 1–2 mins to thicken.
3. Place nonstick griddle or skillet on stove and turn heat to medium-low. Pour batter onto heated griddle. When pancake has bubbled on top and is nicely browned on bottom approximately 2 to 4 mins, flip over. Brown on second side another 2–3 mins. If pancakes are browning too quickly, lower heat to low.
4. Repeat process with remaining batter. Serve pancakes warm.

Nutrition:
Calories 266, Fat 5 g, Carbs 46 g, Protein 9 g

French Toast

Prep time: 5 mins | Servings: 4
Ingredients:
- ½ tsp cinnamon
- 3 large eggs
- 1 tsp vanilla
- 8 whole-wheat slices bread
- 2 tbsp Low-fat milk

Directions:
1. First, preheat a griddle to 350°F.
2. Combine the vanilla, eggs, milk, and cinnamon in a small bowl and whisk until smooth.
3. Pour into a plate or flat-bottomed dish.
4. Into the egg mixture, dip the bread, flip to coat both sides and put on the hot griddle.
5. Cook for about 2 mins or until the bottom is lightly browned, then flip and cook the other side as well.

Nutrition:
Calories 281.0, Fat 10.8 g, Carbs 37.2 g, Protein 14.5 g

Scrambled Eggs

Prep time: 5 mins | Servings: 1
Ingredients:
- 1 tsp olive oil
- 1 tsp chopped fresh basil
- 1 medium chopped tomato
- ¼ cup Swiss cheese
- 2 eggs
- ½ tsp cayenne pepper
- ½ cup chopped packed spinach

Directions:
1. In a small bowl, whisk well eggs, basil, pepper, and Swiss cheese.
2. Place a medium fry pan on medium fire and heat oil.

3. Stir in tomato and sauté for 3 mins. Stir in spinach and cook for 2 mins or until starting to wilt.
4. Pour in beaten eggs and scramble for 2 to 3 mins or to desired doneness.

Nutrition:
Calories 230, Fat 14.3 g, Carbs 8.4 g, Protein 17.9 g

Green Smoothie

Prep time: 5 mins | Servings: 4
Ingredients:
- 4 cup frozen mango
- 2 tsp Ginger root
- 4 tbsp Fresh lemon juice
- 2 cup fresh baby spinach, fresh
- 20 fresh peppermint leaves
- 2 cup English cucumber
- 1 jalapeno pepper
- 1½ cup water or unsweetened iced green tea

Directions:
1. Cube your frozen mango and add into a blender.
2. Chop cucumber and add into the blender.
3. Add the remaining Ingredients:, cover, and blend.

Nutrition:
Calories 142, Fat 0 g, Carbs 35 g, Protein 1 g

Greens and Giger Smoothie

Prep time: 5 mins | Servings: 4
Ingredients:
- 4 whole chopped stalks celery
- 40 g raw ginger
- 2 unpeeled and sliced medium cucumbers
- Crushed ice
- 340 g mixed kale
- 1 whole lemon
- 3 medium granny smith apples
- 680 g orange juice

Directions:
1. Add ginger to jazz things up.
2. Add the greens to the blender; the kale, the sliced cucumbers, the celery and the chopped apples.
3. Let them blend for about a minute while you peel a lemon, or just juice it if you want.
4. Add the lemon peel or juice and add in the chopped ginger.
5. Blend and top with ice and you are ready!

Nutrition:

Calories 121, Fat 0.7 g, Carbs 26.64 g, Protein 4 g

Banana Bread

Prep time: 15 mins | Servings: 20
Ingredients:
- 2 ¼ g ground cinnamon
- 2 whole eggs
- 85 g coconut sugar
- 2 ¼ g baking soda
- 455 g All-purpose flour
- 75 g softened butter
- 3 mashed ripe bananas
- 1 ¼ g baking powder

Directions:
1. Preheat the oven to 400 ºF and grease two small loaf pans with a touch of butter and set aside.
1. In two separate dishes mix your dry and wet Ingredients:. Start by putting the softened butter, eggs, and mashed bananas into a bowl and slowly mix in the coconut sugar, until smooth.
2. In another bowl, shift your flour, salt, baking soda, baking powder, and a touch of cinnamon if you like the flavor. You can also use powdered cardamom for a slightly more aromatic flavor.
3. Combine the Ingredients:, and either blend or mix by hand, whichever you prefer. Add in any extra Ingredients: you want to use, pour the dough into the prepped pans, and put them in to bake for 20 mins exactly.
4. Once baked, use a knife or a toothpick to test if the loaves have cooked through, and you're all done!
5. You can easily slice and store the bread for later, so don't forget to have a container handy to store your fresh banana bread for the next week!

Nutrition:
Calories 133, Fat 3.4 g, Carbs 11 g, Protein 4.3 g

Fruits Bowls

Prep time: 10 mins | Servings: 2
Ingredients:
- 1 cup chopped pineapple
- 1 sliced banana
- 1 cup chopped mango
- 1 cup almond milk

Directions:

In a bowl, combine the mango with all the current banana, pineapple and almond milk, stir, divide into smaller bowls and serve each day.
Nutrition:
Calories 182, Fat 2 g, Carbs 12 g, Protein 6 g

Banana and Buckwheat Porridge

Prep time: 10 mins |Servings: 2
Ingredients:
- 1 cup of water
- 1 cup buckwheat groats
- 2 big grapefruits, peeled and sliced
- 1 tbsp ground cinnamon
- 3-4 cups almond milk
- 2 tbsp natural almond butter

Directions:
1. Take a medium-sized saucepan and add buckwheat and water
2. Place the pan over medium heat and bring to a boil
3. Keep cooking until the buckwheat absorbs the water
4. Reduce heat to low and add almond milk, stir gently
5. Add the rest of the Ingredients: (except the grapefruits)
6. Stir and remove from the heat
7. Transfer into cereal bowls and add grapefruit chunks

Nutrition:
Calories 223, Fat 4 g, Carbs 4 g, Protein 7 g

Delightful Berry Quinoa Bowl

Prep time: 5 mins |Servings: 4
Ingredients:
- 1 cup quinoa
- 2 cups of water
- 1 piece, 2-inch sized cinn amon stick
- 2-3 tbsp of maple syrup

Flavorful Toppings
- ½ cup blueberries, raspberries or strawberries
- 2 tbsp raisins
- 1 tsp lime
- ¼ tsp nutmeg, grated
- 3 tbsp whipped coconut cream
- 2 tbsp cashew nuts, chopped

Directions:
1. Rinse the grains under cold water thoroughly
2. Pour in the water in a medium-sized saucepan
3. Add the grains and bring the whole mixture to a boil
4. Add cinnamon sticks and cover the saucepan
5. Lower the heat and let the mixture simmer for 15 mins to allow the grain to absorb the liquid
6. Remove the heat and fluff up the mixture using a fork
7. Add maple syrup if you want additional flavor.

Nutrition:
Calories 202, Fat 5 g, Carbs 35 g, Protein 6 g

Fantastic Bowl

Prep time: 5 mins |Servings: 4
Ingredients:
- 3 ¾ cup water
- 1 ¼ cup steel-cut oats
  Flavorful Toppings
- 1 tsp cinnamon
- ½ tsp nutmeg
- ½ tsp lemon pepper
- 1 tsp Garam masala
- Mixed berries/diced mangos/sliced bananas/nuts as needed

Directions:
1. Add water in a medium-sized saucepan and allow the water to heat up
2. Add the steel-cut oats with some salt and lower the heat to medium-low
3. Let's simmer for about 25 mins, making sure to keep stirring it all the way
4. serve with some berries or nuts

Nutrition:
Calories 125, Fat 3 g, Carbs 20 g, Protein 7 g

Quinoa and Cinnamon Bowl

Prep time: 10 mins |Servings: 4 |Cooking Time: 15 mins
Ingredients:
- 1 cup uncooked quinoa
- 1½ cups water
- ½ tsp ground cinnamon
- ½ tsp sunflower seeds
- A drizzle of almond/coconut milk for serving

Directions:
1. Rinse quinoa thoroughly underwater

2. Add quinoa, water, cinnamon, and seeds in a medium-sized saucepan
3. Stir and place it over medium-high heat
4. Bring the mix to a boil
5. Reduce heat to low and simmer for 10 mins
6. Once cooked, remove from the heat and let it cool
7. Serve with a drizzle of almond or coconut milk.

Nutrition:
Calories 255, Fat 13 g, Carbs 33 g, Protein 5 g

Breakfast Parfait

Prep time: 5 mins |Servings: 2
Ingredients:
- 1 tsp sunflower seeds
- ½ cup low-fat milk
- 1 cup all-purpose flour
- 1 tsp vanilla
- 3 eggs, beaten
- 1 tsp baking soda
- 2 cups non-fat Greek yogurt

Directions:
1. Break up pretzels into small-sized portions and slice up the strawberries
2. Add yogurt to the bottom of the glass and top with pretzel pieces and strawberries
3. Add more yogurt and keep repeating until you have used up all the Ingredients:

Nutrition:
Calories 304, Fat 1 g, Carbs 58 g, Protein 15 g

Healthy Granola Bowl

Prep time: 5 mins |Servings: 6 |Cooking Time: 25 mins
Ingredients:
- 1-once Porridge oats
- 2 tsp maple syrup
- 4 medium bananas
- 4 pots of Caramel Layered Fromage Frais
- 5 oz fresh fruit salad, such as strawberries, blueberries, and raspberries
- ¼ oz pumpkin /sunflower /dry chia seeds
- ¼ oz desiccated coconut

Directions:
1. Preheat your oven to 300 degrees F
2. Take a baking tray and line with baking paper
3. Add oats, maple syrup, and seeds in a large bowl
4. Spread mix on a baking tray
5. Spray coconut oil on top and bake for 20 mins, making sure to keep stirring from time to time
6. Sprinkle coconut after the first 15 mins
7. Remove from oven and let it cool
8. Take a bowl and layer sliced bananas on top of the Fromage Fraise
9. Spread the cooled granola mix on top and serve with a topping of berries

Nutrition:
Calories 446, Fat 29 g, Carbs 37 g, Protein 13 g

Cinnamon and Pumpkin Porridge

Prep time: 10 mins |Servings: 2 |Cooking Time: 15 mins
Ingredients:
- 1 cup unsweetened almond/coconut milk
- 1 cup of water
- 1 cup uncooked quinoa
- ½ cup pumpkin puree
- 1 tsp ground cinnamon
- 2 tbsp ground flaxseed meal
- Juice of 1 lemon

Directions:
1. Take a pot and place it over medium-high heat
2. Whisk in water, almond milk and bring the mix to a boil
3. Stir in quinoa, cinnamon, and pumpkin
4. Reduce heat to low and simmer for 10 mins
5. Remove from the heat and stir in flaxseed meal
6. Transfer porridge to small bowls
7. Sprinkle lemon juice and add pumpkin seeds on top.

Nutrition:
Calories 245, Fat 1 g, Carbs 59 g, Protein 4 g

Quinoa and Date Bowl

Prep time: 10 mins |Servings: 2 |Cooking Time: 15 mins
Ingredients:
- 1 date, pitted and chopped finely
- ½ cup red quinoa, dried
- 1 cup unsweetened almond milk
- 1/8 tsp vanilla extra ct
- ¼ cup fresh strawberries, hulled and sliced
- 1/8 tsp ground cinnamon

Directions:
1. Take a pan and place it over low heat.

2. Add quinoa, almond milk, cinnamon, vanilla, and cook for about 15 mins, making sure to keep stirring from time to time
3. Garnish with strawberries and enjoy!

Nutrition:
Calories 195, Fat 4.4 g, Carbs 32 g, Protein 7 g

Crispy Tofu

Prep time: 5 mins |Servings: 8 |Cooking Time: 20-30 mins
Ingredients:
- 1 lb extra-firm tofu, drained and sliced
- 2 tbsp olive oil
- 1 cup almond meal
- 1 tbsp yeast
- ½ tsp onion powder
- ½ tsp garlic powder
- ½ tsp oregano

Directions:
1. Add all Ingredients: except tofu and olive oil in a shallow bowl and mix wel
2. Preheat your oven to 400 degrees F
3. In a wide bowl, add the almond meal and mix well
4. Brush tofu with olive oil, dip into the mix and coat well
5. Line a baking sheet with parchment paper
6. Transfer coated tofu to the baking sheet
7. Bake for 20-30 mins, making sure to flip once until golden brown

Nutrition:
Calories 282, Fat 20 g, Carbs 9 g, Protein 12 g

Pumpkin Pie Oatmeal

Prep time: 10 mins |Servings: 2 |Cooking Time: 10 mins
Ingredients:
- ½ cup canned pumpkin, low sodium
- Mashed banana as needed
- ¾ cup unsweetened almond milk
- ½ tsp pumpkin pie spice
- 1 cup oats

Directions:
1. Mash banana using a fork and mix in the remaining Ingredients: (except oats) and mix well
2. Add oats and finely stir
3. Transfer mixture to a pot and let the oats cook until it has absorbed the liquid and is tender

Nutrition:
Calories 264, Fat 4 g, Carbs 52 g, Protein 7 g

Powerful Oatmeal

Prep time: 10-15 mins |Servings: 2 |Cooking Time: 5 mins
Ingredients:
- ¼ cup quick-cooking oats
- ¼ cup almond milk
- 2 tbsp low fat Greek yogurt
- ¼ banana, mashed
- 2-1/4 tbsp flaxes oat meal

Directions:
1. Whisk in all of the Ingredients: in a bowl
2. Transfer the bowl to your fridge and let it refrigerate for 15 mins
3. Serve and enjoy!

Nutrition:
Calories: 260, Fat 11 g, Carbs 27 g, Protein 10 g

Chia Porridge

Prep time: 10 mins |Servings: 2 | Cooking Time: 5-10 mins
Ingredients:
- 1 tsp chia seeds
- 1 tbsp ground flaxseed
- 1/3 cup coco nut cream
- ½ cup water
- 1 tsp vanilla extract
- 1 tbsp almond butter

Directions:
1. Add chia seeds, coconut cream, flaxseed, water and vanilla to a small pot
2. Stir and let it sit for 5 mins
3. Add almond butter and place pot over low heat
4. Keep stirring as almond butter melts
5. Once the porridge is hot/not boiling, pour into bowl
6. Add a few berries or a dash of cream for extra flavor.

Nutrition:
Calories 410, Fat 38 g, Carbs 10 g, Protein 6 g

Simple Blueberry Oatmeal

Prep time: 10 mins |Servings: 4 | Cooking Time: 5-10 mins
Ingredients:
- 1 cup blueberries
- 1 cup steel-cut oats
- 1 cup coconut milk
- 2 tbsp agave nectar

- ½ tsp vanilla extract
- Coconut flakes, garnish

Directions:
1. Add blueberries, oats, milk and vanilla to a small pot
2. Stir and let it sit for 5 mins
3. Add agave nectar and place pot over low heat
4. Once the porridge is hot/not boiling, pour into bowl
5. Add a few berries or coconut flakes to garnish.

Nutrition:
Calories 202, Fat 6 g, Carbs 12 g, Protein 6 g

Apple "Porridge"

Prep time: 5 mins |Servings: 2 |Cooking Time: 5 mins
Ingredients:
- 1 large apple, peeled, cored and grated
- 1 cup unsweetened almond milk
- 1 ½ tbsp sunflower seeds
- 1/8 cup fresh blueberries
- ¼ tsp fresh vanilla bean extract

Directions:
1. Add sunflower seeds, vanilla extract, almond milk, apples in a large pan and stir
2. Place over medium-low heat and cook for 5 mins, making sure to keep the mixture stirring
3. Transfer to a serving bowl.

Nutrition:
Calories 123, Fat 1.3 g, Carbs 23 g, Protein 4 g

The Unique Smoothie Bowl

Prep time: 10 mins |Servings: 2 |Cooking Time: 10 mins
Ingredients:
- 2 cups baby spinach leaves
- 1 cup coconut almond milk
- ¼ cup low fat cream
- 2 tbsp flaxseed oil
- 2 tbsp chia seeds
- 2 tbsp walnuts, roughly chopped
- A handful of fresh berries

Directions:
1. Add spinach leaves, coconut almond milk, cream and flaxseed oil to a blender
2. Blitz until smooth and then pour smoothie into serving bowls
3. Sprinkle chia seeds, berries, walnuts on top.

Nutrition:
Calories 380, Fat 36 g, Carbs 12 g, Protein 5 g

Cinnamon and Coconut Porridge

Prep time: 5 mins |Servings: 4 |Cooking Time: 5 mins
Ingredients:
- 2 cups water
- 1 cup coconut cream
- ½ cup unsweetened dried coconut, shredded
- 2 tbsp flaxseed meal
- 1 tbsp almond butter
- 1 ½ tsp stevia
- 1 tsp cinnamon
- Toppings as blueberries

Directions:
1. Add the listed Ingredients: to a small pot, mix well
2. Transfer pot to stove and place over medium-low heat
3. Bring to mix to a slow boil
4. Stir well and remove from the heat
5. Divide the mix into equal servings and let them sit for 10 mins.

Nutrition:
Calories 171, Fat 16 g, Carbs 6 g, Protein 2 g

Morning Porridge

Prep time: 15 mins |Servings: 2 |Cooking Time: 8 mins
Ingredients:
- 2 tbsp coconut flour
- 2 tbsp vanilla protein powder
- 3 tbsp Golden Flaxseed meal
- 1 ½ cups almond milk, unsweetened
- Powdered erythritol

Directions:
1. Take a bowl and mix in flaxseed meal, protein powder, coconut flour and mix well
2. Add mix to the saucepan (place over medium heat)
3. Add almond milk and stir, let the mixture thicken
4. Add your desired amount of sweetener and serve.

Nutrition:
Calories 259, Fat 13 g, Carbs 5 g, Protein 16 g

Sweet Potato Porridge

Prep time: 15 mins |Servings: 2 |Cooking Time: 8 mins

Ingredients:
- 6 sweet potatoes, peeled and cut into 1-inch cubes
- 1 ½ cups light coconut milk
- 1 tsp ground cinnamon
- 1 tsp ground cardamom
- 1 tsp pure vanilla extract
- 1 cup raisins

Directions:
1. Add the listed Ingredients: to a small pot, mix well
2. Transfer pot to stove and place over medium-low heat
3. Bring to mix to a slow boil
4. Stir well and remove from the heat
5. Divide the mix into equal servings and let them sit for 10 mins.

Nutrition:
Calories 317, Fat 4g, Carbs 71g, Protein 4g

German Oatmeal

Prep time: 10 mins |Servings: 2 |Cooking Time: 8 mins

Ingredients:
- 1 cup steel-cut oats
- 3 cups water
- 6 oz coconut milk
- 2 tbsp cocoa powder
- 1 tbsp brown sugar
- 1 tbsp coconut, shredded

Directions:
1. Add all the Ingredients: in a small pot
2. Stir and let it sit for 5 mins
3. Add agave nectar and place pot over low heat
4. Once the porridge is hot/not boiling, pour into bowl

Nutrition:
Calories 200, Fat 4g, Carbs 11g, Protein 5g

Banana Oatmeal

Prep time: 10 mins |Servings: 2 |Cooking Time: 8 mins

Ingredients:
- 1 cup steel-cut oats
- 1 ripe banana, mashed
- 2 cups unsweetened almond milk
- 1 cup water
- 1 ½ tbsp honey
- ½ tsp vanilla extract
- ¼ cup almonds, chopped
- 1 tsp ground cinnamon
- ¼ tsp ground nutmeg

Directions:
5. Grease the Slow Cooker well.
6. Add the listed Ingredients: to your Slow Cooker and stir.
7. Cover with lid and cook on LOW for 7-9 hours.
8. Serve and enjoy!

Nutrition:
Calories 230, Fat 7g, Carbs 40g, Protein 5g

Chapter 6: Soups and Salads

Tofu Soup

Prep time: 10 mins | Servings: 8 | Cooking Time: 10 mins

Ingredients:
- 1 lb. cubed extra-firm tofu
- 3 diced medium carrots
- 8 cup low-sodium vegetable broth
- ½ tsp freshly ground white pepper
- 8 minced garlic cloves
- 6 sliced and divided scallions
- 4 oz sliced mushrooms
- 1-inch minced fresh ginger piece

Directions:
2. Pour the broth into a stockpot. Add all of the Ingredients: except for the tofu and last 2 scallions. Bring to a boil over high heat.
3. Once boiling, add the tofu. Reduce heat to low, cover, and simmer for 5 mins.
4. Remove from heat, ladle soup into bowls, and garnish with the remaining sliced scallions. Serve immediately.

Nutrition:
Calories 91, Fat 3 g, Carbs 8 g, Protein 6 g

Tomato Soup

Prep time: 10 mins | Servings: 3 | Cooking Time: 6 hours

Ingredients:
- 4 cups water or vegetable broth
- 7 large tomatoes, ripe
- ½ cup macadamia nuts, raw
- 1 medium onion, chopped
- Sunflower seeds and pepper, to taste

Directions:
1. Take a nonstick skillet and put the onion.
2. Brown the onion for 5 mins.
3. Add all the Ingredients: to a crockpot.
4. Cook for 6-8 hours on low.
5. Make a smooth puree by using a blender.
6. Serve it warm and enjoy!

Nutrition:
Calories 91, Fat 3 g, Carbs 8 g, Protein 6 g

Vichyssoise

Prep time: 10 mins | Servings: 6 | Cooking Time: 25 mins

Ingredients:
- 1lb leeks, finely sliced
- 8 oz potatoes, peeled and sliced
- 1 tbsp olive oil
- 2 cup water
- 1 cup milk
- ¾ cup natural yoghurt

Directions:
1. Heat up a pot using the oil over medium heat, add the leeks and potatoes for 10 mins.
2. Add the water, bring to the boil and simmer for about 20 mins, Cool and put in a blender. Stir in the milk and chill very well. Serve garnished with yoghurt.

Nutrition:
Calories 131, Fat 8 g, Carbs 8 g, Protein 5 g

Pumpkin and Rosemary Soup

Prep time: 10 mins | Servings: 4 | Cooking Time: 25 mins

Ingredients:
- 1lb pumpkin flesh
- 3 oz pumpkin seeds
- 5 garlic clove
- 2 onions
- 1 tbsp freshly chopped rosemary
- ½ cup olive oil
- 3 cup vegetable stock

Directions:
5. Cut the pumpkin in cubes. Peel the cloves of garlic and chop finely.
6. Mix the pumpkin, garlic, onions, pumpkin seeds, rosemary, and olive oil and put everything on a baking tray on a baking sheet.
7. Bake in a preheated oven (350 °F) for approx. 25 mins, stirring every 10 mins
8. Then put everything in a large saucepan, mix roughly if necessary.
9. Add broth little by little, bring back to boil and cook in small broths for another 5 mins.

Nutrition:
Calories 125, Fat 8 g, Carbs 8 g, Protein 5 g

Mangetout Soup

Prep time: 10 mins | Servings: 6 | Cooking Time: 25 mins

Ingredients:
- 1 onion finely chopped
- 4 oz yellow spli peas, soaked for 1 hour
- 1 tbsp olive oil
- 4 cup vegetable stock
- 9 oz mangetout

Directions:
1. Heat up a pot using the oil over medium heat, add the onions and cook for 5 mins. Add the split peas and stir to coat in the oil.
2. Add the stock and bring to boil and simmer for 30 mins
3. add the mangetout and continue to simmer for 5 mins. Cool a little and serve.

Nutrition:
Calories 111, Fat 7 g, Carbs 8 g, Protein 4 g

Nicoise Salad

Prep time: 10 mins | Servings: 4 | Cooking Time: 25 mins

Ingredients:
- Mesclun
- 1 big can of tuna
- Some anchovies
- 4 tomatoes
- Radish
- 2 peppers
- 1 cucumber (optional)
- 1 cup green beans (optional)
- 2 hard-boiled eggs
- 2 onions
- Black olives
- Basil
- Olive oil

Directions:
1. Wash and drain the mesclun.
2. Wash and cut peppers into small cubes and mince the onions
3. Wash and cut the tomatoes in quarters.
4. Add tomatoes to salad, olives, boiled eggs, tuna, and anchovies.
5. Make the vinaigrette with oil and basil and serve

Nutrition:
Calories 125, Fat 9 g, Carbs 8 g, Protein 4 g

Zucchini Soup

Prep time: 10 mins | Servings: 5 | Cooking Time: 25 mins

Ingredients:
- 1/3 cup packed basil leaves
- ¾ cup chopped onion
- ¼ cup olive oil
- 2 lbs trimmed and sliced zucchini
- 2 chopped garlic cloves
- 4 cup divided water

Directions:
1. Peel and julienne the skin from half of zucchini; toss with 1/2 tsp salt and drain in a sieve until wilted, at least 20 mins. Coarsely chop remaining zucchini.
2. Cook onion and garlic in oil in a saucepan over medium-low heat, stirring occasionally, until onions are translucent. Add chopped zucchini and 1 tsp salt and cook, stirring occasionally.
3. Add 3 cups water and simmer with the lid ajar until tender. Pour the soup in a blender and purée soup with basil.
4. Bring remaining cup water to a boil in a small saucepan and blanch julienned zucchini. Drain.
5. Top soup with julienned zucchini. Season soup with salt and pepper and serve.

Nutrition:
Calories 169.3, Fat 13.7 g, Carbs 12 g, Protein 2 g

Black Bean Soup

Prep time: 10 mins | Servings: 4 | Cooking Time: 20 mins

Ingredients:
- 1 tsp. cinnamon powder
- 32 oz. low-sodium chicken stock
- 1 chopped yellow onion
- 1 chopped sweet potato
- 38 oz. no-salt-added, drained and rinsed canned black beans
- 2 tsps. organic olive oil

Directions:
3. Heat up a pot using the oil over medium heat, add onion and cinnamon, stir and cook for 6 mins.
4. Add black beans, stock and sweet potato, stir, cook for 14 mins, puree utilizing an immersion blender, divide into bowls and serve for lunch.

Nutrition:

Calories 221, Fat 3 g, Carbs 15 g, Protein 7 g

Chicken and Dill Soup

Prep time: 10 mins | Servings: 6 | Cooking Time: 1 hour
Ingredients:
- 1 cup chopped yellow onion
- 1 whole chicken
- 1 lb. sliced carrots
- 6 cup low-sodium veggie stock
- ½ cup chopped red onion
- 2 tsps. chopped dill

Directions:
1. Put chicken in a pot, add water to pay for, give your boil over medium heat, cook first hour, transfer to a cutting board, discard bones, shred the meat, strain the soup, get it back on the pot, heat it over medium heat and add the chicken.
2. Also add the carrots, yellow onion, red onion, a pinch of salt, black pepper and also the dill, cook for fifteen mins, ladle into bowls and serve.

Nutrition:
Calories 202, Fat 6 g, Carbs 8 g, Protein 12 g

Cheese Soup with crispy bacon

Prep time: 10 mins | Servings: 6 | Cooking Time: 35 mins
Ingredients:
- 1 garlic clove
- 1 tsp olive oil
- 1 lb potatoes peeles and chopped
- 4 cup vegetable stock
- 6 rashers bacon, diced
- 4 oz cheddar cheese grated
- 1 large onion finely chopped

Directions:
In a pan, heat the oil and cook garlic and onion. Add potatoes, stoxk and bring to the boil. Simmer for about 20 mins. To garnish add crispy bacon.
Nutrition:
Calories 257, Fat 15g, Carbs 11g, Protein 12g

Cherry Stew

Prep time: 10 mins | Servings: 6
Ingredients:
- 2 cup water
- ½ cup powered cocoa
- ¼ cup coconut sugar
- 1 lb pitted cherries

Directions:
In a pan, combine the cherries with all the water, sugar plus the hot chocolate mix, stir, cook over medium heat for ten mins, divide into bowls and serve cold.
Nutrition:
Calories 207, Fat 1 g, Carbs 8 g, Protein 6 g

Raspberry and cranberry soup

Prep time: 10 mins | Servings: 6 | Cooking Time: 15 mins
Ingredients:
- 1 lb fresh or frozen raspberries
- 3 cup cranberry juice
- 3 tsp arrowroot
- 1 tbsp sugar

Directions:
Combine 2/3 of he raspberries with the cranberry juice. Bring to the boil in a saucepan . In a separate bowl mix the arrowroot and the tbsp of cranberry juice until smooth. Mix together and stir over a gentle heat until the soup has thickened.
Nutrition:
Calories 157, Fat 1 g, Carbs 6 g, Protein 6 g

Sirloin Carrot Soup

Prep time: 30-35 mins | Servings: 4 | Cooking Time: 20 mins
Ingredients:
- 1 lb. chopped carrots and celery mix
- 32 oz. low-sodium beef stock
- 1/3 cup whole-wheat flour
- 1 lb. ground beef sirloin
- 1 tbsp olive oil
- 1 chopped yellow onion

Directions:
1. Heat up the olive oil in a saucepan over medium-high flame; add the beef and the flour.
2. Stir well and cook to brown for 4-5 mins.
3. Add the celery, onion, carrots, and stock; stir and bring to a simmer.
4. Turn down the heat to low and cook for 12-15 mins.
5. Serve warm.

Nutrition:
Calories 140, Fat 4.5 g, Carbs 16 g, Protein 9 g

Classical Wonton Soup

Prep time: 5 mins | Servings: 8 | Cooking Time: 15 mins
Ingredients:

- 4 sliced scallions
- ¼ tsp. ground white pepper
- 2 cup sliced fresh mushrooms
- 4 minced garlic cloves
- 6 oz. dry whole-grain yolk-free egg noodles
- ½ lb. lean ground pork
- 1 tbsp minced fresh ginger
- 8 cup low-sodium chicken broth

Directions:
1. Place a stockpot over medium heat. Add the ground pork, ginger, and garlic and sauté for 5 mins. Drain any excess fat, then return to stovetop.
2. Add the broth and bring to a boil. Once boiling, stir in the mushrooms, noodles, and white pepper. Cover and simmer for 10 mins.
3. Remove pot from heat. Stir in the scallions and serve immediately.

Nutrition:
Calories 143, Fat 4 g, Carbs 14 g, Protein 12 g

Pumpkin and Coconut Soup

Prep time: 10 mins |Servings: 3 |Cooking Time: 30 mins
Ingredients:
- 1 cup pumpkin, canned
- 6 cups chicken broth
- 1 cup low fat coconut almond milk
- 1 tsp sage, chopped
- 3 garlic cloves, peeled
- Sunflower seeds and pepper to taste

Directions:
1. Take a stockpot and add all the Ingredients: except coconut almond milk into it.
2. Place stockpot over medium heat.
3. Let it bring to a boil.
4. Reduce heat to simmer for 30 mins.
5. Add the coconut almond milk and stir.

Nutrition:
Calories 144.3, Fat 15.7 g, Carbs 15 g, Protein 3 g

Kale And Spinach Soup

Prep time: 5 mins |Servings: 4 |Cooking Time: 10 mins
Ingredients:
- 3 oz coconut oil
- 8 oz kale, chopped
- 2 avocado, diced
- 4 and 1/3 cups coconut almond milk
- Sunflower seeds and pepper to taste

Directions:
1. Take a skillet and place it over medium heat
2. Add kale and Saute for 2-3 mins
3. Add kale to blender
4. Add water, spices, coconut almond milk and avocado to blender as well
5. Blend until smooth and pour mix into bowl

Nutrition:
Calories 145.3, Fat 13.7 g, Carbs 14 g, Protein 3 g

Onion Soup

Prep time: 10 mins |Servings: 4 | Cooking Time: 1 hour
Ingredients:
- 2 tbsps avocado oil
- 5 yellow onions, cut into halved and sliced
- Black pepper to taste
- 5 cups beef stock
- 3 thyme sprigs
- 1 tbsp tomato paste

Directions:
1. Take a pot and place it over medium high heat
2. Add onion and thyme and stir
3. Lower down heat to low and cook for 30 mins
4. Uncover pot and cook onions for 1 hour, stirring often
5. Add tomato paste, stock and stir
6. Simmer for 30 mins more
7. Ladle soup into bowls and enjoy!

Nutrition:
Calories 86, Fat 4 g, Carbs 7 g, Protein 5 g

Vegetarian Soup in a Crock Pot

Prep: 10 mins | Servings: 8 | Cooking Time: 4 hours
Ingredients:
- 2 chopped ribs celery
- 2 cubes low-sodium bouillon
- 8 cup water
- 2 cup uncooked green split peas
- 3 bay leaves
- 2 carrots
- 2 chopped potatoes

Directions:
1. In your Crock-Pot, put the bouillon cubes, split peas, and water. Stir a bit to break up the bouillon cubes.
2. Next, add the chopped potatoes, celery, and carrots followed with bay leaves.

3. Stir to combine well.
4. Cover and cook for at least 4 hours on your Crock-Pot's low setting or until the green split peas are soft.
5. Add a bit salt and pepper as needed.
6. Before serving, remove the bay leaves and enjoy.

Nutrition:
Calories 149, Fat1 g, Carbs 30 g, Protein 7 g

Rhubarb Stew

Prep time: 10 mins | Servings: 3 | Cooking Time: 5 mins
Ingredients:
- 1 tsp. grated lemon zest
- 1 ½ cup coconut sugar
- Juice of 1 lemon
- 1 ½ cup water
- 4 ½ cup roughly chopped rhubarbs

Directions:
1. In a pan, combine the rhubarb while using water, fresh lemon juice, lemon zest and coconut sugar, toss, bring using a simmer over medium heat, cook for 5 mins, and divide into bowls and serve cold.

Nutrition:
Calories 108, Fat 1 g, Carbs 8 g, Protein 5 g

Gazpacho

Prep time: 10 mins | Servings: 6
Ingredients:
- 4 cups tomato juice
- 1/2 medium onion, peeled and coarsely chopped
- 1 small green pepper, peeled, cored, seeded, and coarsely chopped
- 1 small cucumber, peeled, pared, seeded, and coarsely chopped
- 1/2 tsp Worcestershire sauce
- 1 clove garlic, minced
- 1 drop hot pepper sauce
- 1/8 tsp cayenne pepper
- 2 tbsps olive oil
- 1 large tomato, finely diced
- 2 tbsps minced chives or scallion tops
- 1 lemon, cut in 6 wedges

Directions:
1. Put 2 cups of tomato juice and all other ingredients except diced tomato, chives, and lemon wedges in the blender. Puree.
2. Slowly add the remaining 2 cups of tomato juice to pureed mixture. Add chopped tomato. Chill.
3. Serve icy cold in individual bowls garnished with chopped chives and lemon wedges.

Nutrition:
Calories 87, Fat 5 g, Carbs 8 g, Protein 5 g

Mixed Beans Soup

Prep time: 10 mins | Servings: 8 | Cooking Time: 1 hour
Ingredients:
- 1/2 cup each dried pink beans, dried lentils, dried black beans, yellow split peas, dried kidney beans, and dried blackeye peas
- 8 cups water
- 1 smoked ham hock (about 1/2 lb)
- 1 tsp each dried basil, dried rosemary, dried marjoram, and crushed red chilies
- 1 bay leaf
- 1 cup chopped onion 1/2 cup chopped carrots 1/2 cup chopped celery
- 2 (141/2-ounce) cans no salt added diced tomatoes, undrained
- 1 (8-ounce) can tomato sauce

Directions:
1. Rinse dried beans and lentils under cold running water. Place them in a large bowl, then cover with water to 2 inches above the mixture. Cover and let stand 8 hours, then drain.
2. Combine drained bean, lentil and pea mixture, water, and ham hock in a large pot; bring to a boil. Add spices, onion, carrots, celery, tomatoes, and tomato sauce. Uncover and cook 1 hour.
3. Discard bay leaf. Remove ham hock from soup. Remove meat from bone; shred meat with 2 forks. Return meat to soup and serve.

Nutrition:
Calories 346, Carbs 50 g, Fiber 16 g, Protein 22 g, Fat 9 g

Beef Stew

Prep time: 10 mins | Servings: 6 | Cooking Time: 1 hour and 30 mins
Ingredients:
- 1 shredded green cabbage head
- 4 chopped carrots
- 2 ½ lbs. non-fat beef brisket

- 3 chopped garlic cloves
- Black pepper
- 2 bay leaves
- 4 cup low-sodium beef stock

Directions:
1. Put the beef brisket in a pot, add stock, pepper, garlic and bay leaves, provide your simmer over medium heat and cook for an hour.
2. Add carrots and cabbage, stir, cook for a half-hour more, divide into bowls and serve for lunch.

Nutrition:
Calories 271, Fat 8 g, Carbs 16 g, Protein 9 g

Homemade Turkey Soup

Prep time: 10 mins | Servings: 4 | Cooking Time: 1 hour and 30 mins
Ingredients:
- 6 lbs turkey breast. It should have some meat (at least 2 cups) remaining on it to make a good, rich soup.
- 2 medium onions
- 3 stalks of celery
- 1 tsp dried thyme
- 1/2 tsp dried rosemary and sage
- 1 tsp dried basil
- 1/2 tsp dried tarragon
- 1/2 lb Italian pastina or pasta

Directions:
1. Place turkey breast in a large 6-quart pot. Cover with water, at least 3/4 full.
2. Peel onions, cut in large pieces, and add to pot. Wash celery stalks, slice, and add to pot also.
3. Simmer covered for about 1 hour.
4. Remove carcass from pot. Divide soup into smaller, shallower containers for quick cooling in the refrigerator.
5. While soup is cooling, remove remaining meat from turkey carcass. Cut into pieces.
6. Add turkey meat to skimmed soup along with herbs and spices.
7. Bring to a boil and add pastina. Continue cooking on low boil for about 20 mins until pastina is done. Serve at once or refrigerate for later reheating.

Nutrition:
Calories 226, Fat 5 g, Carbs 19 g, Protein 9 g

Meatball Soup

Prep time: 10 mins | Servings: 4 | Cooking Time: 1 hour and 30 mins
Ingredients:
- 6 cups water
- 1/3 cup brown rice
- 3 low-sodium beef- or chicken-flavored bouillon cubes or 1 tbsp low-sodium bouillon powder
- 4 sprigs fresh oregano, finely chopped or 1 tbsp dried oregano
- 8 oz lean ground beef, turkey, or chicken
- 1 tomato, finely chopped
- 1/2 onion, peeled and finely chopped
- 1 large egg
- 2 cups chopped fresh vegetables (carrots, celery, and broccoli)

Directions:
1. In a large pot, combine water, rice, bouillon cubes, and oregano. Bring to a boil over high heat. Stir to dissolve bouillon. Reduce heat to low and simmer.
2. Meanwhile, in a large bowl, mix ground meat, tomato, onion, egg. Form into 12 large meatballs.
3. Add meatballs to broth mixture and simmer 30 mins.
4. Add vegetables. Cook 10 to 15 mins or until meatballs are cooked and rice and vegetables are tender. Serve hot.

Nutrition:
Calories 196, Carbs 20 g, Fiber 4 g, Protein 16 g, Fat 6 g

Sorrel Soup

Prep time: 5 mins | Servings: 6 | Cooking Time: 15 mins
Ingredients:
- 4 cup vegetable stock 1 tbsp olive oil
- 1 large onion, chopped
- 1 clove garlic finely chopped
- 80 oz fresh sorrel leaves
- 1 cup single cream

Directions:
1. In a large pot, heat oil and cook onion.
2. Add the stock and bring to boil. Stir in the sorrel, cover and cook for 1 min. Put in a blinder . Srve hot or chilled.

Nutrition:
Calories 68, Fat 6 g, Carbs 9,2 g, Protein 4g

Mexican Pozole

Prep time: 10 mins | Servings: 10 | Cooking Time: 35 mins

Ingredients:
- 2 lbs lean beef, cubed
- 1 tbsp olive oil
- 1 large onion, chopped
- 1 clove garlic finely chopped
- 1/4 cup cilantro
- 1 can (15 ounce) stewed tomatoes
- 2 oz tomato paste
- 1 can (1 lb 13 ounce) hominy

Directions:
1. In a large pot, heat oil. Sauté beef.
2. Add onion, garlic, salt, pepper, cilantro, and enough water to cover the meat. Cover pot and cook over low heat until meat is tender.
3. Add tomatoes and tomato paste. Continue cooking for about 20 mins.
4. Add hominy and continue cooking another 15 mins, stirring occasionally, over low heat. If too thick, add water for desired consistency.

Nutrition:
Calories 253, Fat 10 g, Carbs 7 g, Protein 5 g

Carrot and Ginger Soup

Prep time: 15 mins | Servings: 4 | Cooking Time: 40 mins

Ingredients:
- 6 cups chicken broth
- ¼ cup full fat coconut milk, unsweetened
- ¾ lb carrots, peeled and chopped
- 1 tsp turmeric, ground
- 2 tsps ginger, grated
- 1 yellow onion, chopped
- 2 garlic cloves, peeled
- Pinch of pepper

Directions:
1. Take a stockpot and add all the Ingredients: except coconut milk into it.
2. Place stockpot over medium heat.
3. Let it bring to a boil.
4. Reduce heat to simmer for 40 mins.
5. Remove the bay leaf.
6. Blend the soup until smooth by using an immersion blender.
7. Add the coconut milk and stir.
8. Serve immediately and enjoy!

Nutrition:
Calories 80, Fat 6 g, Carbs 7 g, Protein 5 g

Cauliflower Soup

Prep time: 10 mins | Servings: 6 | Cooking Time: 40 mins

Ingredients:
- 3 cups cauliflower, riced
- 1 bay leaf
- 1 tsp herbs de Provence
- 2 garlic cloves, peeled and diced
- ½ cup coconut milk
- 2 and ½ cups vegetable stock
- 1 tbsp coconut oil
- ½ tsp cracked pepper
- 1 leek, chopped

Directions:
1. Take a pot, heat oil into it
2. Sauté the leeks in it for 5 mins
3. Add in the garlic and then stir cook for another minute
4. Add all the remaining Ingredients: and mix them well
5. Cook for 30 mins
6. Stir occasionally
7. Blend the soup until smooth by using an immersion blender.
8. Serve hot and enjoy!

Nutrition:
Calories 68, Fat 6 g, Carbs 9,2 g, Protein 4g

Minestrone Soup

Prep time: 10 mins | Servings: 6 | Cooking Time: 50 mins

Ingredients:
- 1/4 cup olive oil
- 1 clove garlic, minced or 1/8 tsp garlic powder
- 1-1/3 cups coarsely chopped onion
- 1-1/2 cups coarsely chopped celery and leaves
- 1 can (6 oz) tomato paste
- 1 tbsp chopped fresh parsley
- 1 cup sliced carrots, fresh or frozen
- 4-3/4 cups shredded cabbage
- 1 can (1 lb) tomatoes, cut up
- 1 cup canned red kidney beans, drained and rinsed
- 1-1/2 cups frozen peas
- 1-1/2 cups fresh green beans
- dash hot sauce
- 11 cups water

- 2 cups uncooked, broken spaghetti

Directions:
- Heat oil in a 4-quart saucepan.
- Add garlic, onion, and celery and sauté about 5 mins.
- Add all remaining ingredients except spaghetti, and stir until ingredients are well mixed.
- Bring to a boil. Reduce heat, cover, and simmer about 45 mins or until vegetables are tender.
- Add uncooked spaghetti and simmer 2-3 mins only.

Nutrition:
Calories 153, Carbs 9,2 g, Protein 4g

Brussels Soup

Prep time: 10 mins |Servings: 4 |Cooking Time: 20 mins
Ingredients:
- 2 tbsps olive oil
- 1 yellow onion, chopped
- 2 lbs Brussels sprouts, trimmed and halved
- 4 cups chicken stock
- ¼ cup coconut cream

Directions:
1. Take a pot and place it over medium heat
2. Add oil and let it heat up
3. Add onion and stir cook for 3 mins
4. Add Brussels sprouts and stir, cook for 2 mins
5. Add stock and black pepper, stir and bring to a simmer
6. Cook for 20 mins more
7. Use an immersion blender to make the soup creamy
8. Add coconut cream and stir well
9. Ladle into soup bowls and serve

Nutrition:
Calories 66, Fat 4 g, Carbs 7 g, Protein 5 g

Crab and Watermelon Soup

Prep time: 10 mins |Servings: 4
Ingredients:
- ¼ cup basil, chopped
- 2 lbs tomatoes
- 5 cups watermelon, cubed
- ¼ cup wine vinegar
- 2 garlic cloves, minced
- 1 zucchini , chopped
- Pepper to taste
- 1 cup crabmeat

Directions:
1. Take your blender and add tomatoes, basil, vinegar, 4 cups watermelon, garlic, 1/3 cup oil, pepper and pulse well
2. Transfer to fridge and chill for 1 hour
3. Divide into bowls and add zucchini, crab and remaining watermelon

Nutrition:
Calories 321, Fat 5 g, Carbs 28.1 g, Protein 3g

Garlic Tomato Soup

Prep time: 15 mins |Servings: 4 |Cooking: 15 mins
Ingredients:
- 8 Roma tomatoes, chopped
- 1 cup tomatoes, sundried
- 2 tbsps coconut oil
- 5 garlic cloves, chopped
- 14 oz coconut milk
- 1 cup vegetable broth
- Pepper to taste
- Basil, for garnish

Directions:
1. Take a pot, heat oil into it.
2. Sauté the garlic in it for ½ minute.
3. Mix in the Roma tomatoes and cook for 8-10 mins.
4. Stir occasionally.
5. Add in the rest of the Ingredients: except the basil and stir well.
6. Cover the lid and cook for 5 mins.
7. Let it cool.
8. Blend the soup until smooth by using an immersion blender.
9. Garnish with basil.

Nutrition:
Calories 315, Fat 5 g, Carbs 25.1 g, Protein 5g

Lobster Bisque

Prep time: 10 mins |Servings: 4 |Cooking: 15 mins
Ingredients:
- ¾ lb lobster, cooked and lobster
- 4 cups chicken broth
- 2 garlic cloves, chopped
- ¼ tsp pepper
- ½ tsp paprika
- 1 yellow onion, chopped
- 14 and ½ oz tomato , diced
- 1 tbsp coconut oil

- 1 cup low fat cream

Directions:
10. Take a stockpot and add the coconut oil over medium heat.
11. Then sauté the garlic and onion for 3 to 5 mins
12. Add diced tomatoes, spices and chicken broth then bring them to boil.
13. Reduce to a simmer then simmer for about 10 mins.
14. Add the warmed heavy cream to the soup.
15. Blend the soup till creamy by using an immersion blender.
16. Stir in cooked lobster

Nutrition:
Calories 315, Fat 8 g, Carbs 27.1 g, Protein 8g

Eggplant Soup

Prep time: 10 mins | Servings: 4 |Cooking: 30 mins
Ingredients:
- 2 tbsp no-salt-added tomato paste
- 1 tbsp olive oil
- 1 quart low-sodium veggie stock
- ¼ tsp. black pepper
- 1 chopped red onion
- 2 roughly cubed big eggplants
- 1 tbsp chopped cilantro

Directions:
1. Heat up a pot with the oil over medium heat, add the onion, stir and sauté for 5 mins.
2. Add the eggplants and the other Ingredients:, bring to a simmer over medium heat, cook for 25 mins, divide into bowls and serve.

Nutrition:
Calories 335, Fat 14.4 g, Carbs 16.1 g, Protein 8.4 g

Sweet Potato Soup

Prep time: 10 mins | Servings: 6 | Cooking: 1 hour and 40 mins
Ingredients:
- 28 oz. veggie stock
- 4 big sweet potatoes
- ¼ tsp. black pepper
- 1/3 cup low-sodium heavy cream
- ¼ tsp. ground nutmeg

Directions:
1. Arrange the sweet potatoes around the lined baking sheet, bake them at 350 ⁰F for 60 mins and 30, cool them down, peel, roughly chop them and put them inside the pot.
2. Add stock, nutmeg, cream and pepper, pulse effectively utilizing an immersion blender, heat the soup over medium heat, cook for 10 mins, ladle into bowls and serve.

Nutrition:
Calories 235, Fat 4 g, Carbs 16 g, Protein 18 g

Organic Chicken Thigh Soup

Prep time: 5 mins | Servings: 4 | Cooking: 50 mins
Ingredients:
- 1 cup fresh pineapple chunks
- 1 tsp. cinnamon
- ½ cup chopped up green onion
- 2 tbsp coconut aminos
- 2 lbs. organic chicken thigh
- 1/8 tsp. flavored vinegar
- ½ cup coconut cream

Directions:
1. Set your pot to Sauté mode and add ghee
2. Allow the ghee to melt and add diced up onion, cook for about 5 mins until the onions are caramelized
3. Add pressed garlic, ham, broth and simmer for 2-3 mins
4. Add thyme and asparagus and lock up the lid
5. Cook on SOUP mode for 45 mins
6. Release the pressure naturally and enjoy!

Nutrition:
Calories 161, Fat 8 g, Carbs 16 g, Protein 6 g

Butternut Squash Soup

Prep time: 10 mins | Servings: 6 |Cooking: 20 mins
Ingredients:
- 2 cup diced apple
- 1/8 tsp. ground allspice
- 6 cup diced butternut squash
- 6 cup water
- ½ tsp. ground cinnamon
- 2 cup unsweetened apple juice

Directions:
1. Place diced squash and apple into a stockpot, add the water and apple juice, and bring to a boil over high heat. Once boiling, reduce heat to medium-low, cover, and simmer until tender, roughly 20 mins.

2. Remove from heat. Add spices and stir to combine. Purée in a blender or food processor.

Nutrition:
Calories 150, Fat 0 g, Carbs 38 g, Protein 3 g

Soup a la Kiev

Prep time: 31 mins | Servings: 8 | Cooking: 20 mins
Ingredients:
- 1 cup brown sugar
- 1 cup favorite red wine
- 3 cup chopped strawberries
- 1 cup sour cream
- 4 c cold water

Directions:
1. In a food processor, blend the strawberries.
2. Pour the mixture in a medium sauce pan.
3. Stir in the brown sugar, sour cream, wine and water.
4. Cook over low heat. Stir gently for 20 mins. Do not allow the soup to boil, just serve it warm.

Nutrition:
Calories 37, Fat 0.9 g, Carbs 19 g, Protein 8 g

Summer Strawberry Stew

Prep time: 10 mins | Servings: 6 | Cooking: 10 mins
Ingredients:
- 2 tbsp water
- ¼ tsp. almond extract
- 2 tbsp fresh lemon juice
- 16 oz. halved strawberries
- 2 tbsp coconut sugar
- 2 tbsp cornstarch

Directions:
In a pot, combine the strawberries because of the water, sugar, fresh lemon juice, cornstarch and almond extract, toss well, cook over medium heat for ten mins, divide into bowls and serve.

Nutrition:
Calories 160, Fat 2 g, Carbs 6 g, Protein 6 g

Blueberry Stew

Prep time: 10 mins | Servings: 4 | Cooking: 10 mins
Ingredients:
- 1 cup water
- 2 tbsp lemon juice
- 12 oz. blueberries
- 3 tbsp coconut sugar

Directions:
1. In a pan, combine the blueberries with the sugar and the other Ingredients:, bring to a gentle simmer and cook over medium heat for 10 mins.
2. Divide into bowls and serve.

Nutrition:
Calories 122, Fat 0.4 g, Carbs 26.7 g, Protein 1.5 g

Chipotle Chicken Chowder

Prep time: 10 mins | Servings: 4 | Cooking: 23 mins
Ingredients:
- 1 medium onion, chopped
- 2 garlic cloves, minced
- 6 bacon slices, chopped
- 4 cups jicama, cubed
- 3 cups chicken stock
- 2 cups low-fat, cream
- 1 tbsp olive oil
- 2 tbsps fresh cilantro, chopped
- 1 and ¼ lbs chicken, thigh boneless, cut into 1 inch chunks
- ½ tsp pepper
- 1 chipotle pepper, minced

Directions:
1. Heat olive oil over medium heat in a large sized saucepan, add bacon.
2. Cook until crispy, add onion, garlic, and jicama.
3. Cook for 7 mins, add chicken stock and chicken.
4. Bring to a boil and lower temperature to low.
5. Simmer for 10 mins
6. Add heavy cream and chipotle, simmer for 5 mins.
7. Sprinkle chopped cilantro and serve, enjoy!

Nutrition:
Calories 203, Fat 0.9 g, Carbs 51 g, Protein 2 g

Peach Stew

Prep time: 10 mins | Servings: 6 | Cooking: 10 mins
Ingredients:
- 3 tbsp coconut sugar
- 5 cup peeled and cubed peaches
- 2 cup water
- 1 tsp grated ginger

Directions:
In a pot, combine the peaches while using the sugar, ginger and water, toss, provide a boil over medium

heat, cook for 10 mins, divide into bowls and serve cold
Nutrition:
Calories 142, Fat 1.4 g, Carbs 7.7 g, Protein 2.5 g

Summer Tomato Soup

Prep time: 10 mins | Servings: 6 | Cooking: 20 mins
Ingredients:
- 1 tbsp olive oil
- 1 medium onion, finely chopped
- 1 garlic clove
- a pinch of paprika
- 2 lb ripe tomatoes
- 1 tsp leom juice
- 1 cup water
- 1 tbsp mil

Directions:
1. In a pot, heat olive oil and cook onion and garlic.
2. Add paprika and tomatoes and cook for 10 mins
3. Add lemon juice and water and simmer for 5 mins
4. Cool a little and then put in a blinder. Serve garnished with basil leaves.

Nutrition:
Calories 142, Fat 1.4 g, Carbs 7.7 g, Protein 2.5 g

Summer Tomato Sorbet

Prep time: 10 mins | Servings: 4 | Cooking: 10 mins
Ingredients:
- 2 cups summer tomato soup
- 4 tbsp vodka
- 2 tsp sugar

Directions:
In a pot, mix together soup, vodka, sugar and seasoning. Put in a blender until is a soft-scoop consistency. Place in a freezer for 10 mins and then serve.
Nutrition:
Calories 142, Fat 1.4 g, Carbs 7.7 g, Protein 2.5 g

Carrot and Coriander Soup

Prep time: 10 mins | Servings: 6 | Cooking: 30 mins
Ingredients:
- 1 tbsp olive oil
- 1 medium onion, finely chopped
- 1 garlic clove
- 1 lb carrots roughly chopped
- 1 tbsp chopped fresh coriander
- fresh ground pepper
- 4 cup vegetable stock

Directions:
1. In a pot, heat olive oil and cook onion and garlic.
2. Add the chopped carrots and stock and cover. Bring to the boil.
3. Once the vegetables are tender cool a little and then put in a blender. Taste and serve.

Nutrition:
Calories 121, Fat 1.4 g, Carbs 4.7 g, Protein 2.5 g

Pappa al pomodoro

Prep time: 10 mins | Servings: 6 | Cooking: 30 mins
Ingredients:
- 1 cup olive oil
- 5 cup peeled and cubed peaches
- 4 garlice cloves
- 9 lb ripe tomatoes, skinned quarted and seeded
- bread
- 1 large bunch fresh basil
- 2 cup water

Directions:
1. In a pot, warm the oil and cook the garlic few mins. Add the tomatoes and simmer for 20 mins.
2. Add water and bring to the boil
3. Brake the bread in large pieces and add it to the tomato mixture and stir until the bread absorb the liquid.
4. Add the basil leaves and the olive oil and serve

Nutrition:
Calories 122, Fat 1.5 g, Carbs 9.7 g, Protein 2.5 g

Zucchini Cream Soup

Prep time: 10 mins | Servings: 4 | Cooking: 20 mins
Ingredients:
- 1 tbsp chopped dill
- 1 tbsp olive oil
- 32 oz. low-sodium chicken stock
- 1 tsp. grated ginger
- 1 lb. chopped zucchinis
- 1 cup coconut cream
- 1 chopped yellow onion

Directions:
1. Heat up a pot with the oil over medium heat, add the onion and ginger, stir and cook for 5 mins.

2. Add the zucchinis and the other Ingredients:, bring to a simmer and cook over medium heat for 15 mins.
3. Blend using an immersion blender, divide into bowls and serve.

Nutrition:
Calories 293, Fat 12.3 g, Carbs 11.2 g, Protein 6.4 g

Salmon and Vegetable Soup

Prep time: 10 mins | Servings: 4 | Cooking: 22 mins
Ingredients:
- 2 tbsps extra-virgin olive oil
- 1 leek, chopped
- 1 red onion, chopped
- Pepper to taste
- 2 carrots, chopped
- 4 cups low stock vegetable stock
- 4 oz salmon, skinless and boneless, cubed
- ½ cup coconut cream
- 1 tbsp dill, chopped

Directions:
1. Take a pan and place it over medium heat, add leek, onion, stir and cook for 7 mins
2. Add pepper, carrots, stock and stir
3. Boil for 10 mins
4. Add salmon, cream, dill and stir
5. Boil for 5-6 mins
6. Ladle into bowls and serve

Nutrition:
Calories 200, Fat 3 g, Carbs 51 g, Protein 3 g

Mango Salad

Prep time: 5 mins | Servings: 2
Ingredients:
- ½ seeded and minced jalapeño pepper
- 2 tbsp chopped fresh cilantro
- Juice of 1 lime
- 3 pitted and cubed ripe mangos
- 1 tsp minced red onion

Directions:
1. Combine all Ingredients: in a salad bowl.
2. Toss well.

Nutrition:
Calories 331, Fat 5 g, Carbs 28.1 g, Protein 1g

Tomato and Cucumber Salad

Prep time: 10 mins | Serving: 4
Ingredients:
- 1 minced garlic clove
- ¼ tsp freshly ground black pepper
- 1 tbsp olive oil
- 1 thinly sliced small onion
- 2 medium cucumbers
- 4 quartered ripe medium tomatoes
- ¼ cup chopped fresh basil
- 3 tbsp red wine vinegar

Directions:
1. Peel the cucumbers, slice in half lengthwise, and then use a spoon to gently scrape out the seeds.
2. Slice the cucumber halves and place in a bowl. Add the tomatoes, onion, and basil.
3. Place the remaining Ingredients: into a small bowl and whisk well to combine.
4. Pour the dressing over the salad and toss to coat. Serve immediately or cover and refrigerate until ready to serve.

Nutrition:
Calories 66, Fat 4 g, Carbs 7 g, Protein 1 g

Fresh Fruit Salad

Prep time: 15 mins | Servings: 3
Ingredients:
- 1 halved and sliced ripe banana
- 170 g sliced and halved strawberries,
- 170 g julienned granny smith apples
- 340 g chopped ripe pineapple
- 170 g sliced and quartered kiwi
- 340 g chopped ripe mango

Directions:
1. Cut the mangoes and kiwis into small cubes to get that full burst of flavor.
2. Slice the bananas about a centimeter thick and then halve them.
3. Once you have all the fruits cut up, put them in a bowl, and top with salt.
4. Stir it all together and you are ready to serve!

Nutrition:
Calories 203, Fat 0.9 g, Carbs 51 g, Protein 2 g

Green Papaya Salad

Prep Time: 10 mins | Servings: 6
Ingredients:
- 10 small shrimps, dried
- 2 small red Thai Chilies
- 1 garlic clove, peeled
- ¼ cup tamarind juice
- 1 tbsp Thai fish sauce, low sodium
- 1 lime, cut into 1 inch pieces
- 4 cherry tomatoes, halved

- 3 long beans, trimmed into 1 inch pieces
- 1 carrot, coarsely shredded
- ½ English cucumber, coarsely chopped and seeded
- 1/6 a small green cabbage, cored and thinly sliced
- 1 lb unripe green papaya, quartered, seeded and shredded using mandolin
- 3 tbsps unsalted roasted peanuts

Directions:
- Take a mortar and pestle and crush your shrimp alongside garlic, chills
- Add tamarind juice, fish sauce and palm sugar
- Squeeze 3 quarts of lime pieces over the mortar
- Grind to make a dressing, keep the dressing on the side
- Take a bowl add the remaining Ingredients: (excluding the peanut), making sure to add the papaya last
- Use a spoon and stir in the dressing
- Mix the vegetable and fruit and coat them well
- Transfer to your serving dish
- Garnish with some peanuts and lime pieces

Nutrition:
Calories 183, Fat 0.9 g, Carbs 51 g, Protein 2 g

Quinoa And Fruit Salad

Prep time: 5 mins | Servings: 5 | Cooking: 10 mins
Ingredients:
- 3 and ½ oz Quinoa
- 3 peaches, diced
- 1 and ½ oz toasted hazelnuts, chopped
- Handful of mint, chopped
- Handful of parsley, chopped
- 2 tbsps olive oil
- Zest of 1 lemon
- Juice of 1 lemon

Directions:
1. Take medium sized saucepan and add quinoa
2. Add 1 and ¼ cups of water and bring it to a boil over medium-high heat
3. Lower down the heat to low and simmer for 20 mins
4. Drain any excess liquid
5. Add fruits, herbs, Hazelnuts to the quinoa
6. Allow it to cool and season

7. Take a bowl and add olive oil, lemon zest and lemon juice
8. Pour the mixture over the salad and gie it a mix

Nutrition:
Calories 203, Fat 0.9 g, Carbs 51 g, Protein 2 g

Shrimp and Veggie Salad

Prep time: 10 mins | Servings: 4
Ingredients:
- 2 cup halved cherry tomatoes
- Cracked black pepper
- 12 oz trimmed fresh asparagus spears
- 16 oz frozen peeled and cooked shrimp
- Cracker bread
- 4 cup watercress
- ½ cup bottled light raspberry

Directions:
1. In a large skillet, cook asparagus, covered, in a small amount of boiling lightly salted water for 3 mins or until crisp-tender; drain in a colander. Run under cold water until cool.
2. Divide asparagus among 4 dinner plates; top with watercress, shrimp, and cherry tomatoes. Drizzle with dressing.
3. Sprinkle with cracked black pepper and serve with cracker bread.

Nutrition:
Calories 155.5, Fat 1.4 g, Carbs 15 g, Protein 22 g

Salmon and Spinach Salad

Prep time: 10 mins | Servings: 4
Ingredients:
- 1 cup canned salmon, drained and flaked
- 1 tbsp lime zest, grated
- 1 tbsp lime juice
- 3 tbsps fat-free yogurt
- 1 cup baby spinach
- 1 tsp capers, drained and chopped
- 1 red onion, chopped
- Pinch of pepper

Directions:
1. Take a bowl and add salmon, zest, lime juice and other Ingredients:
2. Toss well and serve

Nutrition:
Calories 155.5, Fat 1.4 g, Carbs 15 g, Protein 22 g

Peach Stew

Prep time: 10 mins | Servings: 6 | Cooking: 2 hours

Ingredients:
- 3 2 oz prosciutto, cut into strips
- 1 tsp olive oil
- 2 cups corn
- 1/2 cup salt –free tomato sauce

Corn Salad

Prep time: 10 mins | Servings: 6 |Cooking: 2 hours
Ingredients:
- 2 oz prosciutto, cut into strips
- 1 tsp olive oil
- 2 cups corn
- 1/2 cup salt –free tomato sauce
- 1 tsp garlic, minced
- 1 green bell pepper, chopped

Directions:
1. Grease your Slow Cooker with oil
2. Add corn, prosciutto, garlic, tomato sauce, bell pepper to your Slow Cooker
3. Stir and place lid
4. Cook on HIGH for 2 hours

Nutrition:
Calories 158.5, Fat 1.4 g, Carbs 15 g, Protein 23 g

Fattoush Salad

Prep time: 15 mins | Servings: 4 |Cooking: 2-3 mins
Ingredients:
- 1 whole wheat pita bread
- 1 large English cucumber, diced
- 2 cup grape tomatoes, halved
- ½ of a medium red onion, finely diced
- ¾ cup of fresh parsley, chopped
- ¾ cup of mint leaves, chopped
- 1 clove of garlic, minced
- ¼ cup of fat free feta cheese, crumbled
- 1 tbsp of olive oil
- 1 tsp of ground sumac
- Juice from ½ a lemon

Directions:
1. Mist pita bread with cooking spray
2. Season with salt
3. Toast until the breads are crispy
4. Take a large bowl and add the remaining Ingredients: and mix (except feta)
5. Top the mix with diced toasted pita and feta

Nutrition:
Calories 158.5, Fat 1.4 g, Carbs 15 g, Protein 23 g

Broccoli Salad

Prep time: 5 mins | Servings: 1 |Cooking: 10 mins

Ingredients:
- 10 broccoli florets
- 2 red onions, sliced
- 1 oz bacon, chopped into small pieces
- 1 cup coconut cream
- 1 tsp sesame seeds

Directions:
1. Cook bacon in hot oil until crispy
2. Cook onions in fat left from the bacon
3. Take a pan of boiling water and add broccoli florets, boil for a few mins
4. Take a salad bowl and add bacon pieces, onions, broccoli florets, coconut cream and salt
5. Toss well and top with sesame seeds

Nutrition:
Calories 158.5, Fat 1.4 g, Carbs 15 g, Protein 23 g

Baby Spinach Salad

Prep time: 10 mins |Servings: 2
Ingredients:
- 1 bag baby spinach, washed and dried
- 1 red bell pepper, cut in slices
- 1 cup cherry tomatoes, cut in halves
- 1 small red onion, finely chopped
- 1 cup black olives, pitted

For dressing
- 1 tsp dried oregano
- 1 large garlic clove
- 3 tbsps red wine vinegar
- 4 tbsps olive oil
- Sunflower seeds and pepper to taste

Directions:
1. Prepare the dressing by blending in garlic, olive oil, vinegar in a food processor
2. Take a large salad bowl and add spinach leaves, toss well with the dressing
3. Add remaining Ingredients: and toss again, season with sunflower seeds and pepper and enjoy!

Nutrition:
Calories 135.5, Fat 1.4 g, Carbs 12 g, Protein 25 g

Classic Tuna Salad

Prep time: 10 mins |Servings: 4
Ingredients:
- 12 oz white tuna, in water
- ½ cup celery, diced
- 2 tbsps fresh parsley, chopped

- 2 tbsps low-calorie mayonnaise, low fat and low sodium
- ½ tsp Dijon mustard
- ½ tsp sunflower seeds
- ¼ tsp fresh ground black pepper

Directions:
1. Take a medium sized bowl and add tuna, parsley, and celery
2. Mix well and add mayonnaise
3. Season with pepper and sunflower seeds
4. Stir and add olives, relish, chopped pickle, onion and mix well

Nutrition:
Calories 155.5, Fat 1.4 g, Carbs 15 g, Protein 22 g

Greek Salad

Prep time: 10 mins |Servings: 6
Ingredients:
- 2 cucumbers, diced
- 2 tomatoes, sliced
- 1 green lettuce, cut into thin strips
- 2 red bell peppers, cut
- ½ cup black olives pitted
- 3 and ½ oz feta cheese, cut
- 1 red onion, sliced
- 2 tbsps olive oil
- 2 tbsps lemon juice
- Sunflower seeds and pepper to taste

Directions:
1. Dice cucumbers and slice up the tomatoes
2. Tear the lettuce and cut it up into thin strips
3. De-seed and cut the peppers into strips
4. Take a salad bowl and mix in all the listed vegetables, add olives and feta cheese (cut into cubes)
5. Take a small cup and mix in olive oil and lemon juice, season with sunflower seeds and pepper. Pour mixture into the salad and toss well, enjoy!

Nutrition:
Calories 155.5, Fat 1.4 g, Carbs 15 g, Protein 22 g

Delicious Tuna Salad

Prep time: 5-10 mins |Servings: 4
Ingredients:
- 15 oz small white beans
- 6 oz drained chunks of light tuna
- 10 cherry tomatoes, quartered
- 4 scallions, trimmed and sliced
- 2 tbsps lemon juice

Directions:
1. Add all of the listed Ingredients: to a bowl and gently stir
2. Season with sunflower seeds and pepper accordingly, enjoy!

Nutrition:
Calories 135.5, Fat 2.4 g, Carbs 18 g, Protein 22 g

Yogurt And Cucumber Salad

Prep time: 5-10 mins |Servings: 4
Ingredients:
- 5-6 small cucumbers, peeled and diced
- 1 (8 oz) container plain Greek yogurt
- 2 garlic cloves, minced
- 1 tbsp fresh mint, minced
- Sea sunflower seeds and fresh black pepper

Directions:
1. Take a large bowl and add cucumbers, garlic, yogurt, mint
2. Season with sunflower seeds and pepper
3. Refrigerate the salad for 1 hour and serve

Nutrition:
Calories 135.5, Fat 1.4 g, Carbs 13 g, Protein 22 g

Tasty Eggplant Salad

Prep time: 10 mins |Servings: 3 |Cooking: 30 mins
Ingredients:
- 2 eggplants, peeled and sliced
- 2 garlic cloves
- 2 green bell paper, sliced, seeds removed
- ½ cup fresh parsley
- ½ cup mayonnaise, low fat, low sodium
- Sunflower seeds and black pepper

Directions:
1. Preheat your oven to 480 degree F
2. Take a baking pan and add eggplants and black pepper in it
3. Bake for about 30 mins
4. Flip the vegetables after 20 mins
5. Then, take a bowl and add baked vegetables and all the remaining ingredients

Nutrition:
Calories 135.5, Fat 2.4 g, Carbs 18 g, Protein 22 g

Potato & Octopus Salad

Prep time: 10 mins | Servings: 6-8 |Cooking: 30 mins
Ingredients:

- 2 lbs. octopus
- 2 crushed garlic cloves
- 1 bay leaf
- ½ tbsp peppercorns
- 2 lbs. potatoes
- 1 chopped parsley bunch
- 1 whole garlic cloves
- ½ cup olive oil
- 5 tbsp White wine vinegar

Directions:
1. Scrub the potatoes and place them in your pressure cooker. Pour in enough water to cover the potatoes halfway. Close and lock the lid of your pressure cooker. Cook on low pressure for 15 mins.
2. Release the pressure using the quick release method and take the potatoes out of the pressure cooker. Don't discard the cooking liquid.
3. Peel the hot potatoes; dice them into small cubes and place in a large mixing bowl.
4. To cook the prepared octopus in the pressure cooker, pour enough water to almost cover it.
5. Add the bay leaf, whole garlic clove, and peppercorns and bring to the boil. Then add the octopus.
6. Close and lock the lid. Cook on low pressure for 15 mins. When the time is up, release the pressure using the quick release method.
7. Once the octopus is done, take it out of the pressure cooker and remove any remaining skin.
8. Add the octopus chunks to the bowl with the potatoes and mix well.
9. To prepare the vinaigrette, combine all the Ingredients: in a jar and shake well to blend everything.
10. Flood the octopus and potato chunks with the vinaigrette, garnish with the chopped parsley and serve.

Nutrition:
Calories 119, Fat 0 g, Carbs 27 g, Protein 3 g

Balsamic Beet Salad

Prep time: 5 mins | Servings: 4 | Cooking: 30 mins
Ingredients:
- Extra virgin olive oil
- Kosher flavored vinegar
- 6 medium sized beets
- Freshly ground black pepper
- 1 cup water
- Balsamic vinegar

Directions:
1. Wash the beets carefully and trim them to ½ inch portions
2. Add 1 cup of water to the pot
3. Place a steamer on top and arrange the beets on top of the steamer
4. Lock up the lid and cook on HIGH pressure for 1 minute
5. Release the pressure naturally and allow the beet to cool
6. Slice the top of the skin carefully
7. Slice up the beets in uniform portions and season with flavored vinegar and pepper
8. Add a splash of balsamic vinegar and allow them to marinate for 30 mins
9. Add a bit of extra olive oil and serve!

Nutrition:
Calories 120, Fat 7 g, Carbs 13 g, Protein 2 g

Squash Garden Salad

Prep time: 15 mins | Servings: 2
Ingredients:
- 1 pitted and cubed avocado
- 2 tbsp lemon juice
- 2 tbsp olive oil
- 8 oz. peeled and cubed summer squash
- 1 oz. chopped watercress

Directions:
1. Arrange all the vegetables in a salad bowl and dress with olive oil and lemon juice.
2. Add the watercress leaves.

Nutrition:
Calories 326, Fat 29.6 g, Carbs 3 g, Protein 3 g

Beet and Walnut Salad

Prep time: 5 mins | Servings: 2
Ingredients:
- 1 minced garlic clove
- 2 tbsp olive oil
- 10 chopped prunes
- 2 peeled and grated small beets
- 1 cup chopped walnuts

Directions:
1. Combine all the Ingredients: in a salad bowl.
2. Dress with olive oil.

Nutrition:
Calories 296, Fat 21 g, Carbs 26 g, Protein 3.6 g

Steamed Saucy Garlic Greens

Prep time: 5 mins | Servings: 4
Ingredients:
- 1/8 tsp. flavored vinegar
- 1 peeled whole clove
- ¼ cup water
- 1 tbsp lemon juice
- 1 bunch leafy greens
- ½ cup soaked cashews
- 1 tsp. coconut aminos

Directions:
1. Make the sauce by draining and discard the soaking water from your cashew and add them cashew to blender
2. Add fresh water, lemon juice, flavored vinegar, coconut aminos, and garlic
3. Blitz until you have a smooth cream and transfer to bowl
4. Add ½ cup of water to the pot
5. Place the steamer basket to the pot and add the greens in the basket
6. Lock up the lid and steam for 1 minute
7. Quick release the pressure
8. Transfer the steamed greens to strainer and extract excess water
9. Place the greens into a mixing bowl
10. Add lemon garlic sauce and toss

Nutrition:
Calories 77, Fat 5 g, Carbs 0 g, Protein 2 g

Daikon Radish Salad

Prep time: 5 mins | Servings: 2
Ingredients:
- 2 tbsp lemon juice
- 2 peeled and grated small daikons
- 3 tbsp olive oil
- ¼ peeled and grated medium pumpkin
- 2 cup minced parsley

Directions:
1. Combine all the Ingredients: in a salad bowl.
2. Sprinkle with olive oil and lemon juice.

Nutrition:
Calories 237, Fat 2.6 g, Carbs 13.9 g, Protein 2.0 g

Calamari Salad

Prep time: 15 mins | Servings: 2
Ingredients:
- 1 peeled and sliced cucumber
- Lettuce leaves
- 3 ½ oz. washed, cleaned and sliced calamari fillets
- Fresh parsley
- 1 peeled, boiled and sliced potato
- 1 tbsp sour cream
- 1 peeled, cored and sliced apple

Directions:
1. Place the calamari into boiling salted water and cook for 5 min.
2. Arrange lettuce leaves on the bottom of a salad bowl. Mix the apple and vegetable strips with the calamari. Dress with sour cream, place on the lettuce leaves, and garnish with the parsley.

Nutrition:
Calories 468, Fat 8.5 g, Carbs 5.1 g, Protein 17.8 g

Chicken Raisin Salad

Prep time: 15-20 mins | Servings: 2
Ingredients:
- 2 tbsp lemon juice
- 2 tbsp raisins
- 1 peeled, cored and cubed apple
- ¼ cup chopped celery
- 2 tbsp olive oil
- 3 ¼ cup skinless and sliced chicken meat

Directions:
1. In a saucepan or skillet, cook the cubed chicken meat in olive oil until golden.
2. Transfer the cooked meat to a mixing bowl of medium-large size and add all other Ingredients:. Stir to combine
3. Serve while the chicken is warm.

Nutrition:
Calories 382, Fat 16 g, Carbs 41 g, Protein 25.7 g

Pickled Onion Salad

Prep time: 1 hour | Servings: 4
Ingredients:
- 4 chopped spring onions
- ½ cup chopped fresh cilantro
- 2 tbsp brown sugar
- 1 tbsp lime juice
- ½ cup cider vinegar
- 2 thinly sliced red onions
- 4 lettuce leaves
- 2 tsps. olive oil

Directions:
1. In a salad bowl combine the onions, vinegar, oil and sugar.
2. Cover and refrigerate for 1 hr.

3. Add cilantro and lime juice.
4. Serve on lettuce leaves.

Nutrition:
Calories 223, Fat 14.1 g, Carbs 20 g, Protein 1.8 g

Pickled Grape Salad with Pear, and Cheese

Prep time: 15 mins| Servings: 3
Ingredients:
- 200g sliced taleggio cheese
- 4 tbsp red wine vinegar
- 2 tbsp light brown sugar
- 2 handfuls fresh watercress
- 100g halved red grapes
- 1 wedged pear
- 50g halved walnut

Directions:
1. Heat a cast-iron skillet or frying pan and toast the walnut halves, until they are slightly brown and give off a lovely nutty aroma. Set aside to cool.
2. Stir together the red wine vinegar and light brown sugar in a bowl, and leave for 5 mins to allow the sugar to dissolve.
3. Add the grapes to this sweet and tangy mixture, and toss. Marinate for 10 mins while you work on the rest of the recipe.
4. Scatter the watercress onto 3 plates or onto one large sharing platter, and then top evenly with the taleggio cheese and pear wedges.
5. Drain the grapes from their marinade, but do not discard the marinade.
6. Whisk 2 tbsps of olive oil into the pickling marinade.
7. Scatter the pickled grapes all over the salad, and then drizzle over 3-4 tbsps of the dressing.
8. Finish with the toasted walnut halves, and enjoy immediately.

Nutrition:
Calories 421, Fat 28.4 g, Carbs 24.1 g, Protein 15.9 g

Tuna and Potato Salad

Prep time: 10 mins |Servings: 4
Ingredients:
- 1 lb baby potatoes, scrubbed, boiled
- 1 cup tuna chunks, drained
- 1 cup cherry tomatoes, halved
- 1 cup medium onion, thinly sliced
- 8 pitted black olives
- 2 medium hard-boiled eggs, sliced
- 1 head Romaine lettuce
- ¼ cup olive oil
- 2 tbsps lemon juice
- 1 tbsp Dijon mustard
- 1 tsp dill weed, chopped
- Pepper as needed

Directions:
1. Take a small glass bowl and mix in your olive oil, lemon juice, Dijon mustard and dill
2. Add in the tuna, baby potatoes, cherry tomatoes, red onion, green beans, black olives and toss everything nicely
3. Arrange your lettuce leaves on a beautiful serving dish to make the base of your salad
4. Top them up with your salad mixture and place the egg slices
5. Drizzle it with the previously prepared Salad Dressing
6. Serve hot

Nutrition:
Calories 142.5, Fat 2.4 g, Carbs 16 g, Protein 20 g

Spinach Parmesan Dip

Prep time: 45 mins |Servings: 6 |Cooking Time: 25 mins
Ingredients:
- 6 bacon slices
- 5 oz spinach
- ½ cup sour cream
- 8 oz soft cream cheese
- 1 tbsp garlic minced
- 1½ tbsp chopped parsley
- 5 oz parmesan
- 1 tbsp lemon juice

Directions:
1. Place a pan over medium heat then add bacon
2. Saute until crispy then transfer to a plate lined with a paper towel
3. Heat the leftover bacon grease and add spinach
4. Stir cook for 2 mins then keep it in a bowl
5. Whisk cream cheese, salt, pepper, parsley, sour cream and garlic in a separate bowl
6. Add bacon, spinach and lemon juice and mix well
7. Divide this mixture in the ramekins then bake for 25 mins at 350 degrees F

8. Switch the oven to broil settings and broil for 4 mins

Nutrition:
Calories 345, Fat 12g, Fiber 3g, Carbs 6g, Protein 11 g

Chapter 7: Poultry

Crispy Chicken Egg Rolls

Prep Time: 25 mins |Servings: 12 | Cooking: 15 mins
Ingredients:
- 4 oz blue cheese
- vegetable oil
- 12 egg roll wrappers
- 2 cups cooked and finely chopped chicken
- ½ cup tomato sauce
- 2 chopped green onions
- ½ tsp erythritol
- 2 finely chopped celery stalks

Directions:
1. Mix in a bowl the chicken meat with blue cheese, green onions, celery, tomato sauce and sweetener and stir well
2. Refrigerate for 2 hours
3. Arrange the egg wrappers on a working surface, divide chicken mix on them, roll and seal edges
4. Put in a pot vegetable oil and heat up to over medium-high heat
5. Include egg rolls and cook until they are golden, flip and cook on the other side as well
6. Place on a platter and serve them

Nutrition:
Calories 220, Fiber 2, Carbs 6g, Fat 7, Protein 10g

Chicken Brats

Prep Time: 10 mins |Servings: 6 | Cooking: 15 mins
Ingredients:
- 1 tsp celery seed
- 1 tsp ground mustard seed
- ¼ tsp Nutmeg
- 1 tsp minced rosemary
- ½ tsp cayenne pepper / ½ tsp white pepper
- 1 tsp paprika / 1 tsp cumin seed
- 2 tsps fennel seed
- 1 lb. ground chicken breast
- 1 cup cooked brown rice
- ½ tsp canola oil
- 4 minced garlic
- 1 cup minced yellow onion

Directions:
1. In a frying pan, sauté the canola oil, garlic, and onion until golden
2. Place the browned onion and garlic in the cooked rice and mix in all the other herbs and spices with the ground chicken breast
3. Let the mixture marinate in the fridge for about an hour
4. Preheat the oven to 350F
5. Remove from the fridge and roll the mixture into sausage shapes and place on a cooking sheet
6. Bake in the oven for about 5-10 mins, or until cooked.

Nutrition:
Calories 156, Fat 4g, Carbs 12g, Protein 18g

Italian Meatballs

Prep Time: 16 mins |Servings: 16 | Cooking: 15 mins
Ingredients:
- 1/4 cup almond flour
- 1 lb ground turkey meat
- 2 tbsp olive oil
- 2 tbsp egg
- 2 tbsp chopped basil
- ½ tsp garlic powder
- ½ cup shredded mozzarella cheese
- 2 tbsp chopped sundried tomatoes

Directions:
1. Get a bowl and mix turkey with egg, almond flour, garlic powder, sundried tomatoes, mozzarella and basil and stir properly
2. In the mixture carve out the shape of 12 meatballs
3. Heat a pot containing the oil to over medium-high heat
4. Put the meatballs into the oil and cook them for 2 mins on each side
5. Set on a platter and serve

Nutrition:
Calories 80, Fiber 3, Carbs 5g, Fat 6g, Protein 7g

Garlic Parmesan Wings

Prep Time: 34 mins |Servings: 6 | Cooking: 25 mins
Ingredients:
- ½ tsp Italian seasoning
- a pinch crushed red pepper flakes

- 6 lb chicken wings cut in halves
- 2 tbsp ghee
- 1 tsp garlic powder
- ½ cup grated parmesan cheese
- 1 egg

Directions:
1. Place the chicken wings on a lined baking sheet
2. Preheat your oven to 425F and introduce the chicken wings and bake for 17 mins
3. On the other hand; mix ghee with cheese, egg, salt, pepper, pepper flakes, garlic powder and Italian seasoning in your blender and blend until it is smooth
4. Remove the chicken wings from the oven, flip them, turn oven to broil and broil them for about 5 mins more
5. Remove the chicken pieces out of the oven again and pour the sauce over them, toss to coat thoroughly and cook for 1 min more
6. Serve them as a quick appetizer.

Nutrition:
Calories 134, Carbs 5g, Fiber 1g, Fat 8g, Protein 14g

White Chicken Chili

Prep Time: 10 mins |Servings: 8 | Cooking: 15 mins
Ingredients:
- 3 tbsp chopped cilantro
- 8 tbsp shredded Monterey jack cheese
- 1 tsp cayenne pepper
- 1 tsp dried oregano
- 1 tsp ground cumin
- 2 tsp chili powder
- 2 minced garlic cloves
- 1 sliced red pepper
- ½ sliced green pepper
- 4 cup low-sodium chicken broth
- 1 can diced tomatoes
- 2 cans white beans
- 1 can white chunk chicken

Directions:
1. Place the chicken broth, tomatoes, and chicken in a large cooking pot
2. Bring the mixture to a boil and then cover it to let it simmer
3. While the mixture is simmering, take a nonstick frying pan, cover it in cooking spray, and add the garlic, peppers, and onions
4. Fry the vegetables until golden brown or to your liking
5. Add the contents of the frying pan to the cooking pot
6. Add the cayenne pepper, oregano, cumin, and chili powder and cover the mixture again
7. Raise the heat up to medium and let it simmer for about 10 more mins
8. Ladle the chili into bowls and serve immediately.

Nutrition:
Calories 212, Fat 4g, Carbs 25g, Protein 19g

Chicken and Broccoli Stir-Fry

Prep Time: 10 mins |Servings: 4| Cooking:15 mins
Ingredients:
- 2 tbsp sesame oil (or olive oil), divided
- 3 tbsp balsamic vinegar, divided
- 2 tsps ground ginger

Directions:
1. Heat ½ tbsp of olive oil in a wok or large sauté pan over medium heat. Add the cubed chicken and cook until lightly browned and cooked through (about 5 to 7 mins). Transfer chicken to a bowl, cover, and set aside
2. Add 1½ tbsp of olive oil to the pan, along with the garlic and carrots. Cook until the carrots begin to soften (about 3 to 4 mins). Add the thawed broccoli florets and water chestnuts along with 1 tbsp of balsamic vinegar and cook for 3 to 4 mins
3. Add the remaining balsamic vinegar and ground ginger. Add the cooked chicken and stir until well combined

Nutrition:
Calories 189, Fat 9g, Carbs 12g, Fiber 3g, Protein 14g

Zucchini Tagine with Minced Meatballs

Prep Time: 10 mins |Servings: 4| Cooking:15 mins
Ingredients:
For Dumplings
- 3 cup of minced meat
- 1 egg
- 2 tbsp parsley very finely chopped
- 1/2 onion very finely cut
- 1 shredded garlic clove

For the Sauce
- 1/2 onion, finely chopped
- 6 tbsp of oil
- 1 cube of chicken broth

- Pepper and cinnamon
- 4 cup of zucchini cut to taste slightly salted and fries
- 3 cup of boiling water

Directions:
1. Put all the ingredients of the meatballs in a salad bowl.
2. Knead everything with your hand, and make balls of a size of a walnut.
3. In a small pot, heat the oil.
4. Add the onion, pepper, cinnamon and fry for 5 mins over low heat.
5. Wet with boiling water, immerse your meatballs and crumble your bouillon cube.
6. Let it cook for 40 mins
7. Remove the meatballs and brown them in a pan with 2 tbsp of oil.
8. Reduce the sauce, turn off the heat, and put the meatballs back on.
9. When serving, heat the zucchini in the pan.

Nutrition:
Calories 209, Fat 19g, Carbs 12g, Fiber 3g, Protein 14g

Quick Chicken Fajitas

Prep Time: 10 mins |Servings: 4| Cooking:15 mins
Ingredients:
- Cooking spray
- 4 cups frozen bell pepper strips
- 2 cups onion, sliced
- 1 tsp ground cumin
- 1 tsp chili powder
- 2 (10-ounce) cans no-salt diced tomatoes and green chilies (Ro-Tel brand)
- 8 (6-inch) whole-wheat flour tortillas, warmed

Directions:
1. Spray a large skillet with cooking spray. Preheat skillet to medium-high heat. Add the bell peppers and onions and cook for 7 mins or until tender, stirring occasionally. Remove from skillet and set aside
2. Add chicken to skillet. Sprinkle with cumin and chili powder. Cook for 4 mins until no longer pink and an instant-read thermometer registers 165°F
3. Return peppers and onions to skillet; add drained tomatoes and green chilies. Cook for 2 mins more or until hot

Divide mixture evenly between tortillas and serve immediately.
Nutrition:
Calories 424, Fat 8g, Carbs 51g, Fiber 26g, Protein 33g

Roasted Turkey

Prep Time: 15 mins |Servings: 6 | Cooking: 45 mins
Ingredients:
- 1 whole turkey
- 2 tsp garlic paste
- 1 tsp ginger powder
- 2 tbsp soya sauce
- 1 tsp cayenne pepper
- 3 tbsp lemon juice
- 2 tbsp red wine vinegar
- ½ tsp mustard powder
- 1 tsp cinnamon powder
- 2 tbsp sesame seeds oil

Directions:
1. In a bowl add garlic paste, ginger powder, cayenne pepper, black pepper, cinnamon powder, mustard powder, lemon juice, oil, vinegar, soya sauce and salt, mix well
2. Now pour this marinate over turkey and rub with hands all over it
3. Cover and leave to marinade for 15-20 mins
4. Preheat oven at 355 degrees
5. Spread aluminum foil in baking tray and place turkey on it
6. Bake for 40-45 mins or till nicely golden.

Nutrition:
Calories 244 , Fat 7g, Protein 44g, Carbs 3g

Honey Garlic Chicken Drumsticks

Prep Time: 25 mins |Servings: 6 | Cooking: 35 mins
Ingredients:
- 8 chicken drumsticks
- 3 tsp garlic powder
- 1 tsp ginger powder
- 3 tbsp soya sauce
- 1 tsp cayenne pepper
- 2 tbsp Barbecue sauce
- 2 tbsp lime juice
- ¼ cup apple cider vinegar
- 2 tbsp olive oil
- 3 tbsp honey

Directions:
1. In a bowl add ginger powder, garlic powder, soya sauce, honey, vinegar, lime juice,

barbecue sauce, salt, pepper and toss to combine
2. Add in chicken drumsticks and mix well, leave to marinade for 20 mins. Preheat oven at 355F
3. Transfer drumsticks in baking tray and bake for 30-35 mins or till golden brown

Nutrition:
Calories 122, Protein 1g, Carbs 15g, Fat 3g

Southwestern Chicken and Pasta

Prep Time: 10 mins |Servings: 2| Cooking: 10 mins
Ingredients:
- 1 cup uncooked whole-wheat rigatoni
- 2 boneless, skinless chicken breasts, 4 ounces each, cut into cubes
- 1/4 cup salsa

Directions:
1. Fill a pot with water up to ¾ full and boil it
2. Add pasta to water and cook until it is al dente
3. Drain the pasta while rinsing under cold water
4. Preheat a skillet with cooking oil, then cook the chicken for 10 mins until golden on both sides.
5. Add tomato sauce, salsa, cumin, garlic powder, black beans, corn, and chili powder.
6. Stir while cooking the mixture for a few mins. Add in pasta.
7. Serve with 2 tbsp cheese on top.

Nutrition:
Calories 245, Fat 16.3 g, Carbs 19.3g, Protein 33.3 g

Chicken Sliders

Prep Time: 10 mins |Servings: 4| Cooking: 10 mins
Ingredients:
- 10 oz ground chicken breast
- 1 tbsp black pepper
- 1 tbsp minced garlic
- 1 tbsp balsamic vinegar
- 1/2 cup minced onion
- 1 fresh chili pepper, minced
- 1 tbsp fennel seed, crushed
- 4 whole-wheat mini buns
- 4 lettuce leaves
- 4 tomato slices

Directions:
1. Combine all the Ingredients: except the wheat buns, tomato, and lettuce.

2. Mix well and refrigerate the mixture for 1 hour.
3. Divide the mixture into 4 patties.
4. Broil the patties on a greased baking sheet until golden brown.
5. Place the chicken patties in the whole wheat buns along with lettuce and tomato.

Nutrition:
Calories 224, Fat 4.5 g, Carbs 10.2 g, Protein 67.4 g

Buffalo Chicken Salad Wrap

Prep Time: 10 mins |Servings: 4| Cooking: 10 mins
Ingredients:
- 3-4 oz chicken breasts
- 2 whole chipotle peppers
- 1/4 cup white wine vinegar
- 1/4 cup low-calorie mayonnaise
- 2 diced stalks celery
- 2 carrots, cut into matchsticks
- 1 small yellow onion, diced (about 1/2 cup)
- 1/2 cup thinly sliced rutabaga or another root vegetable
- 4 oz spinach, cut into strips
- 2 whole-grain tortillas (12-inch diameter)

Directions:
1. Set the oven or a grill to heat at 375°F. Bake the chicken for 10 mins per side.
2. Blend chipotle peppers with mayonnaise and wine vinegar in the blender.
3. Dice the baked chicken into cubes or small chunks.
4. Mix the chipotle mixture with all the Ingredients: except tortillas and spinach.
5. Spread 2 oz of spinach over tortilla and scoop the stuffing on top.
6. Wrap the tortilla and cut it into the half.

Nutrition:
Calories 300, Fat 16.4 g, Carbs 8.7 g, Fiber 0.7 g, Protein 38.5 g

White Chicken Chili

Prep Time: 10 mins |Servings: 8 | Cooking: 15 mins
Ingredients:
- 3 tbsp chopped cilantro
- 8 tbsp shredded Monterey jack cheese
- 1 tsp cayenne pepper
- 1 tsp dried oregano
- 1 tsp ground cumin
- 2 tsp chili powder
- 2 minced garlic cloves
- 1 sliced red pepper

- ½ sliced green pepper
- 4 cup low-sodium chicken broth
- 1 can diced tomatoes
- 2 cans white beans
- 1 can white chunk chicken

Directions:
1. Place the chicken broth, tomatoes, and chicken in a large cooking pot
2. Bring the mixture to a boil and then cover it to let it simmer
3. While the mixture is simmering, take a nonstick frying pan, cover it in cooking spray, and add the garlic, peppers, and onions
4. Fry the vegetables until golden brown or to your liking
5. Add the contents of the frying pan to the cooking pot
6. Add the cayenne pepper, oregano, cumin, and chili powder and cover the mixture again
7. Raise the heat up to medium and let it simmer for about 10 more mins
8. Ladle the chili into bowls and serve immediately.

Nutrition:
Calories 212, Fat 4g, Carbs 25g, Protein 19g

Turkey Club Burger

Prep Time: 10 mins |Servings: 4 | Cooking: 15 mins
Ingredients:
For turkey burger
- 12 oz 99 percent fat-free ground turkey
- 1/2 cup scallions (green onions), rinsed and sliced
- 1/4 tsp ground black pepper
- 1 large egg
- 1 tbsp olive oil

For spread
- 2 tbsps light mayonnaise
- 1 tbsp Dijon mustard
- For toppings
- 4 oz spinach or arugula, rinsed and dried
- 4 oz portabella mushroom, rinsed, grilled or broiled, and sliced (optional)
- 4 whole-wheat hamburger buns

Directions:
1. Preheat oven broiler on high temperature (with the rack 3 inches from heat source) or grill on medium-high heat.
2. To prepare burgers, combine ground turkey, scallions, pepper, and egg, and mix well. Form into 1/2- to 3/4-inch thick patties, and coat each lightly with olive oil.
3. Broil or grill burgers for about 7–9 mins on each side (to a minimum internal temperature of 160 °F).
4. Combine mayonnaise and mustard to make a spread.
5. Assemble 3/4 tbsp spread, 1 ounce spinach or arugula, several slices of grilled portabella mushroom (optional), and one burger on each bun.

Nutrition: Information
Calories 299, Fat 11 g, Protein 29 g, Carbs 26 g

Mango Chicken Stir-Fry

Prep Time: 10 mins |Servings: 4 | Cooking: 15 mins
Ingredients:
- nonstick cooking spray
- 1 lb boneless, skinless chicken breasts, cut into bite-size chunks
- 1/4 cup pineapple juice
- 3 tbsps low-sodium soy sauce
- 1/4 tsp ground ginger
- 1 red bell pepper, cut into bite-size strips
- 2 mangos, pitted and cut into bite-size strips
- 1/4 cup toasted, slivered almonds ground black pepper to taste
- 2 cups cooked brown rice

Directions:
1. Spray a large wok or skillet with nonstick cooking spray.
2. Sauté chicken over medium-high heat until cooked through, about 10 mins.
3. In a small bowl, stir together pineapple juice, soy sauce, and ginger. Add sauce and bell pepper to the skillet.
4. Cook and stir for about 5 mins until peppers are crisp-tender.
5. Add the mango and almonds to the wok or skillet and cook until hot. Season with ground black pepper to taste.
6. Serve each cup of stir-fry over 1/2 cup of brown rice.

Nutrition:
Calories 387, Carbs 47 g, Protein 31 g, Fat 9 g

Chicken Couscous

Prep Time: 5 mins |Servings: 4 | Cooking: 30 mins
Ingredients:

- 1 tbsp olive oil
- 1 lb skinless chicken legs, split (about 4 whole legs)
- 1 tbsp Moroccan spice blend*
- 1 cup carrots, rinsed, peeled, and diced
- 1 cup onion, diced
- 1/4 cup lemon juice
- 2 cups low-sodium chicken broth
- 1/2 cup ripe black olives, sliced
- 1 tbsp chili sauce (optional)

For couscous
- 1 cup low-sodium chicken broth
- 1 cup couscous (try whole-wheat couscous)
- 1 tbsp fresh mint, rinsed, dried, and shredded thin (or 1 tsp dried)

Directions:
1. Heat olive oil in a large sauté pan. Add chicken legs, and brown on all sides, about 2–3 mins per side. Remove chicken from pan and put on a plate with a cover to hold warm.
2. Add spice blend to sauté pan and toast gently.
3. Add carrots and onion to sauté pan, and cook for about 3–4 mins or until the onions have turned clear, but not brown.
4. Add lemon juice, chicken broth, and olives to sauté pan, and bring to a boil over high heat. Add chicken legs, and return to a boil. Cover and gently simmer for about 10–15 mins (to a minimum internal temperature of 165 °F).
5. Meanwhile, prepare the couscous by bringing chicken broth to a boil in a saucepan. Add couscous and remove from the heat. Cover and let stand for 10 mins.
6. Fluff couscous with a fork, and gently mix in the mint.
7. When chicken is cooked, add salt. Serve two chicken legs over 1/2 cup couscous topped with 1/2 cup sauce in a serving bowl. Add chili sauce to taste.

Nutrition:
Calories 333, Fat 12 g, Protein 24 g, Carbs 36 g

Esotic Jerk Chicken

Prep Time: 8 mins |Servings: 10 | Cooking: 1 hour
Ingredients:
- 1/2 tsp cinnamon, ground
- 1-1/2 tsps allspice, ground
- 1-1/2 tsps black pepper, ground
- 1 tsp hot pepper, crushed, dried
- 2 tsps oregano, crushed
- 2 tsps thyme, crushed
- 6 cloves garlic, finely chopped
- 1 cup onion, pureed or finely chopped
- 1/4 cup vinegar
- 3 tbsps brown sugar
- 8 pieces chicken, skinless (4 breasts, 4 drumsticks)

Directions:
1. Preheat oven to 350 degrees F. Wash chicken and pat dry. Combine all Ingredients: except chicken in large bowl. Rub seasonings over chicken and marinate in refrigerator for 6 hours or longer.
2. Space chicken evenly on nonstick or lightly greased baking pan.
3. Cover with aluminum foil and bake for 40 mins. Remove foil and continue baking for an additional 30–40 mins or until the meat can easily be pulled away from the bone with a fork.

Nutrition:
Calories 113, Fat 3 g, Fiber 1 g, Protein 16 g, Carbs 6 g

Chicken Vegetable Creole

Prep Time: 8 mins |Servings: 6 | Cooking: 20 mins
Ingredients:
- nonstick cooking spray
- 1 lb boneless, skinless chicken breasts, cut into large chunks
- 1 large onion, chopped
- 1 (14-1/2-ounce) can diced tomatoes
- 1/3 cup tomato paste
- 2 stalks celery, chopped
- 1-1/2 tsps garlic powder
- 1 tsp onion powder
- 1/4 tsp red pepper flakes
- 1/8 tsp ground black pepper
- 1-1/2 cups broccoli florets

Directions:
1. Spray a large skillet with nonstick cooking spray and heat over medium heat.
2. Add chicken and onion; cook, stirring frequently, for 10 mins.
3. Stir in all remaining Ingredients: except broccoli and cook for 5 mins, stirring occasionally.

4. Stir in broccoli, cook for 5 mins more. Serve while hot.

Nutrition:
Calories 143, CarbS 11 g, Protein 19 g, Fat 3 g

Crispy Oven-Fried Chicken

Prep Time: 5 mins |Servings: 4 | Cooking: 1 hour
Ingredients:
- 1/2 cup fat-free milk or buttermilk
- 1 tsp poultry seasoning
- 1 cup cornflakes, crumbled
- 1-1/2 tbsps onion powder
- 1-1/2 tbsps garlic powder
- 2 tsps black pepper
- 2 tsps dried hot pepper, crushed
- 1 tsp ginger, ground
- 8 pieces chicken, skinless (4 breasts, 4 drumsticks)
- a few shakes paprika
- 1 tsp vegetable oil

Directions:
1. Preheat oven to 350 degrees F.
2. Add 1/2 tsp of poultry seasoning to milk.
3. Combine all other spices with cornflake crumbs, and place in plastic bag.
4. Wash chicken and pat dry. Dip chicken into milk and shake to remove excess. Quickly shake in bag with seasonings and crumbs, and remove the chicken from the bag.
5. Refrigerate chicken for 1 hour.
6. Remove chicken from refrigerator and sprinkle lightly with paprika for color.
7. Space chicken evenly on greased baking pan.
8. Cover with aluminum foil and bake for 40 mins. Remove foil and continue baking for another 30–40 mins or until meat can easily be pulled away from the bone with fork. Drumsticks may require less baking time than breasts. Crumbs will form crispy "skin."

Nutrition:
Calories 117, Fat 3 g, Protein 17 g, Carbs 6 g

Turkey Stir-Fry

Prep Time: 5 mins |Servings: 4 | Cooking: 12 mins
Ingredients:

- 1 chicken bouillon cube
- 1/2 cup hot water
- 2 tbsps soy sauce
- 1 tbsp cornstarch
- 2 tbsps vegetable oil
- 1/2 tsp garlic powder
- 1 lb turkey, cubed
- 1-3/4 cups carrots, thinly sliced
- 1 cup zucchini, sliced
- 1/2 cup onions, thinly sliced
- 1/4 cup hot water

Directions:
1. Combine chicken bouillon cube and hot water to make broth; stir until dissolved. Combine broth, soy sauce, and cornstarch in small bowl. Set aside
2. Heat oil in skillet over high heat. Add garlic and turkey. Cook, stirring, until turkey is thoroughly cooked and no longer pink in color.
3. Add carrots, zucchini, onion, and water to cooked turkey. Cover and cook, stirring occasionally, until vegetables are tender-crisp, about 5 mins. Uncover; bring turkey mixture to boil. Cook until almost all liquid has evaporated.
4. Stir in cornstarch mixture. Bring to boil, stirring constantly until thickened.

Nutrition:
Calories 195, Total Fat 9 g, Carbs 47 g, Protein 31 g

Chicken and Broccoli Stir-Fry

Prep Time: 10 mins |Servings: 4| Cooking:15 mins
Ingredients:
- 2 tbsp sesame oil (or olive oil), divided
- 3 tbsp balsamic vinegar, divided
- 2 tsps ground ginger

Directions:
1. Heat ½ tbsp of olive oil in a wok or large sauté pan over medium heat. Add the cubed chicken and cook until lightly browned and cooked through (about 5 to 7 mins). Transfer chicken to a bowl, cover, and set aside
2. Add 1½ tbsp of olive oil to the pan, along with the garlic and carrots. Cook until the carrots begin to soften (about 3 to 4 mins). Add the thawed broccoli florets and water chestnuts along with 1 tbsp of balsamic vinegar and cook for 3 to 4 mins
3. Add the remaining balsamic vinegar and ground ginger. Add the cooked chicken and stir until well combined

Nutrition:
Calories 189, Fat 9g, Carbs 12g, Fiber 3g, Protein 14g

Quick Chicken Fajitas

Prep Time: 10 mins |Servings: 4| Cooking:15 mins
Ingredients:
- Cooking spray
- 4 cups frozen bell pepper strips
- 2 cups onion, sliced
- 1 tsp ground cumin
- 1 tsp chili powder
- 2 (10-ounce) cans no-salt diced tomatoes and green chilies (Ro-Tel brand)
- 8 (6-inch) whole-wheat flour tortillas, warmed

Directions:
1. Spray a large skillet with cooking spray. Preheat skillet to medium-high heat. Add the bell peppers and onions and cook for 7 mins or until tender, stirring occasionally. Remove from skillet and set aside
2. Add chicken to skillet. Sprinkle with cumin and chili powder. Cook for 4 mins until no longer pink and an instant-read thermometer registers 165°F
3. Return peppers and onions to skillet; add drained tomatoes and green chilies. Cook for 2 mins more or until hot

Divide mixture evenly between tortillas and serve immediately.
Nutrition:
Calories 424, Fat 8g, Carbs 51g, Fiber 26g, Protein 33g

Roasted Turkey

Prep Time: 15 mins |Servings: 6 | Cooking: 45 mins
Ingredients:
- 1 whole turkey
- 2 tsp garlic paste
- 1 tsp ginger powder
- 2 tbsp soya sauce
- 1 tsp cayenne pepper
- 3 tbsp lemon juice
- 2 tbsp red wine vinegar
- ½ tsp mustard powder
- 1 tsp cinnamon powder
- 2 tbsp sesame seeds oil

Directions:
1. In a bowl add garlic paste, ginger powder, cayenne pepper, black pepper, cinnamon powder, mustard powder, lemon juice, oil, vinegar, soya sauce and salt, mix well
2. Now pour this marinate over turkey and rub with hands all over it
3. Cover and leave to marinade for 15-20 mins
4. Preheat oven at 355 degrees
5. Spread aluminum foil in baking tray and place turkey on it
6. Bake for 40-45 mins or till nicely golden.

Nutrition:
Calories 244 , Fat 7g, Protein 44g, Carbs 3g

Honey Garlic Chicken Drumsticks

Prep Time: 15 mins |Servings: 6 | Cooking: 35 mins
Ingredients:
- 8 chicken drumsticks
- 3 tsp garlic powder
- 1 tsp ginger powder
- 3 tbsp soya sauce
- 1 tsp cayenne pepper
- 2 tbsp Barbecue sauce
- 2 tbsp lime juice
- ¼ cup apple cider vinegar
- 2 tbsp olive oil
- 3 tbsp honey

Directions:
1. In a bowl add ginger powder, garlic powder, soya sauce, honey, vinegar, lime juice, barbecue sauce, salt, pepper and toss to combine
2. Add in chicken drumsticks and mix well, leave to marinade for 20 mins. Preheat oven at 355 degrees
3. Transfer drumsticks in baking tray and bake for 30-35 mins or till golden brown

Nutrition:
Calories 122, Protein 1g, Carbs 15g, Fat 3g

Southwestern Chicken and Pasta

Prep Time: 10 mins |Servings: 2| Cooking: 10 mins
Ingredients:
- 1 cup uncooked whole-wheat rigatoni
- 2 boneless, skinless chicken breasts, 4 ounces each, cut into cubes
- 1/4 cup salsa

Directions:
1. Fill a pot with water up to ¾ full and boil it
2. Add pasta to water and cook until it is al dente
3. Drain the pasta while rinsing under cold water
4. Preheat a skillet with cooking oil, then cook the chicken for 10 mins until golden on both sides.

5. Add tomato sauce, salsa, cumin, garlic powder, black beans, corn, and chili powder.
6. Stir while cooking the mixture for a few mins. Add in pasta.
7. Serve with 2 tbsp cheese on top.

Nutrition:
Calories 245, Fat 16.3 g, Carbs 19.3g, Protein 33.3 g

Chicken Sliders

Prep Time: 10 mins |Servings: 4| Cooking: 10 mins
Ingredients:
- 10 oz ground chicken breast
- 1 tbsp black pepper
- 1 tbsp minced garlic
- 1 tbsp balsamic vinegar
- 1/2 cup minced onion
- 1 fresh chili pepper, minced
- 1 tbsp fennel seed, crushed
- 4 whole-wheat mini buns
- 4 lettuce leaves
- 4 tomato slices

Directions:
1. Combine all the Ingredients: except the wheat buns, tomato, and lettuce.
2. Mix well and refrigerate the mixture for 1 hour.
3. Divide the mixture into 4 patties.
4. Broil the patties on a greased baking sheet until golden brown.
5. Place the chicken patties in the whole wheat buns along with lettuce and tomato.

Nutrition:
Calories 224, Fat 4.5 g, Carbs 10.2 g, Protein 67.4 g

Buffalo Chicken Salad Wrap

Prep Time: 10 mins |Servings: 4| Cooking: 10 mins
Ingredients:
- 3-4 oz chicken breasts
- 2 whole chipotle peppers
- 1/4 cup white wine vinegar
- 1/4 cup low-calorie mayonnaise
- 2 diced stalks celery
- 2 carrots, cut into matchsticks
- 1 small yellow onion, diced (about 1/2 cup)
- 1/2 cup thinly sliced rutabaga or another root vegetable
- 4 oz spinach, cut into strips
- 2 whole-grain tortillas (12-inch diameter)

Directions:

1. Set the oven or a grill to heat at 375°F. Bake the chicken for 10 mins per side.
2. Blend chipotle peppers with mayonnaise and wine vinegar in the blender.
3. Dice the baked chicken into cubes or small chunks.
4. Mix the chipotle mixture with all the Ingredients: except tortillas and spinach.
5. Spread 2 oz of spinach over tortilla and scoop the stuffing on top.
6. Wrap the tortilla and cut it into the half.

Nutrition:
Calories 300, Fat 16.4 g, Carbs 8.7 g, Fiber 0.7 g, Protein 38.5 g

Honey-Mustard Chicken

Prep Time: 10 mins |Servings: 4| Cooking: 15 mins
Ingredients:
- ¼ cup honey
- ¼ cup yellow mustard
- ¼ cup Dijon mustard
- 1 tbsp olive oil

Directions:
1. To a medium bowl, add the honey, yellow mustard, and Dijon mustard. Whisk to combine. Taste to check for flavor balance, adding more honey and mustard if necessary. Set aside.
2. In a large skillet, add the oil and chicken.
3. Cook over medium-high heat for 3 to 5 mins, then turn over and cook for an additional 3 to 5 mins. Cooking time will vary depending on the thickness of the chicken. Chicken should be almost cooked through.
4. Add the broccoli and stir to combine, making sure the broccoli gets coated with honey mustard. Cover and cook over medium-low heat, allowing the broccoli to steam for about 3 to 5 mins or until broccoli is crisp tender and chicken is cooked through and an instant-read thermometer registers 165°F.

Serve immediately.
Nutrition:
Calories 254, Fat 8g, Carbs 21g, Fiber 2g, Protein 27g

Grilled Chicken, Avocado, and Apple Salad

Prep Time: 15 mins |Servings: 4| Cooking: 8 mins
Ingredients:

- Cooking spray
- 2 tbsp olive oil
- 3 tbsp balsamic vinegar
- 4 (4-ounce) skinless, boneless chicken-breast halves
- 8 cups mixed salad greens
- 1 cup diced peeled apple
- ¾ cup avocado, peeled and pitted
- Optional: 2 tbsp freshly squeezed lime juice

Directions:
1. Preheat grill to high heat. . Apply cooking spray to the grill rack or broil the chicken in an oven-safe skillet under the broiler element for 5 to 6 mins.
2. Combine olive oil, balsamic vinegar, and lime juice in a small bowl. Place chicken on a large plate. Spoon 2 tbsp of oil mixture over the chicken, reserving the rest for the salad dressing. Turn chicken to coat and let stand for 5 mins.
3. Place chicken on grill rack. Cook for 4 mins on each side or until an instant-read thermometer registers 165°F. Remove and put on a plate. Cut crosswise into strips.
4. Arrange greens, apple, and avocado on 4 serving plates. Arrange chicken over greens. Drizzle reserved dressing over salads.

Nutrition:
Calories 288, Fat 16g, Carbs 8g, Fiber 5g, Protein 27g

Turkey Cutlets with Herbs

Prep Time: 5 mins |Servings: 4| Cooking: 8 mins
Ingredients:
- 2 tbsp olive oil
- 2 sliced lemons
- 1 package (approx, 1 lb) turkey-breast cutlets
- ½ tsp garlic powder
- 4 cups baby spinach
- ½ cup water
- 2 tsps dried thyme

Directions:
1. In a large skillet over medium-high heat, heat the oil
2. Add about 6 lemon slices to the skillet
3. Sprinkle the turkey-breast cutlets with garlic powder and black pepper
4. Place the turkey cutlets into the skillet and cook for about 3 mins on each side until the turkey is no longer pink and is slightly browned at the edges
5. Remove from heat and divide turkey between 4 plates
6. Add the spinach to the pan along with ½ cup of water and steam, stirring frequently for about 2 mins. Remove the greens and lemons with tongs or a slotted spoon and divide between plates
7. Serve topped with dried thyme

Nutrition:
Calories 204, Fat 8g, Carbs 8g, Fiber 4g, Protein 30g

Chili Chicken Curry

Prep Time: 5 mins |Servings: 4 | Cooking: 20 mins
Ingredients:
- 14 oz kidney beans
- 3 tbsp red curry paste
- 1 lb. ground chicken
- 1 tbsp tomato paste
- 12 oz black beans
- 1 tbsp chili powder
- 2 tsp dried oregano
- 1 cup tomato sauce
- Vegetable oil

Directions:
1. Heat the oil in a rice cooker
2. Add curry paste and stir
3. Place the chicken into a heated rice cooker
4. Cook until cooked thoroughly
5. Once cooked add the beans, tomato paste, and sauce.

Nutrition:
Calories 315, Protein 39g, Carbs 25g, Fat 9g

Honey-Mustard Chicken

Prep Time: 10 mins |Servings: 4| Cooking: 15 mins
Ingredients:
- ¼ cup honey
- ¼ cup yellow mustard
- ¼ cup Dijon mustard
- 1 tbsp olive oil

Directions:
1. To a medium bowl, add the honey, yellow mustard, and Dijon mustard. Whisk to combine. Taste to check for flavor balance, adding more honey and mustard if necessary. Set aside.
2. In a large skillet, add the oil and chicken.
3. Cook over medium-high heat for 3 to 5 mins, then turn over and cook for an

additional 3 to 5 mins. Cooking time will vary depending on the thickness of the chicken. Chicken should be almost cooked through.
4. Add the broccoli and stir to combine, making sure the broccoli gets coated with honey mustard. Cover and cook over medium-low heat, allowing the broccoli to steam for about 3 to 5 mins or until broccoli is crisp tender and chicken is cooked through and an instant-read thermometer registers 165°F.

Serve immediately.
Nutrition:
Calories 254, Fat 8g, Carbs 21g, Fiber 2g, Protein 27g

Grilled Chicken, Avocado, and Apple Salad

Prep Time: 15 mins |Servings: 4| Cooking: 8 mins
Ingredients:
- Cooking spray
- 2 tbsp olive oil
- 3 tbsp balsamic vinegar
- 4 (4-ounce) skinless, boneless chicken-breast halves
- 8 cups mixed salad greens
- 1 cup diced peeled apple
- ¾ cup avocado, peeled and pitted
- Optional: 2 tbsp freshly squeezed lime juice

Directions:
1. Preheat grill to high heat. . Apply cooking spray to the grill rack. If you don't have a grill, broil the chicken in an oven-safe skillet under the broiler element for 5 to 6 mins.
2. Combine olive oil, balsamic vinegar, and lime juice in a small bowl. Place chicken on a large plate. Spoon 2 tbsp of oil mixture over the chicken, reserving the rest for the salad dressing. Turn chicken to coat and let stand for 5 mins.
3. Place chicken on grill rack. Cook for 4 mins on each side or until an instant-read thermometer registers 165°F. Remove and put on a plate. Cut crosswise into strips.
4. Arrange greens, apple, and avocado on 4 serving plates. Arrange chicken over greens. Drizzle reserved dressing over salads.

Nutrition:
Calories 288, Fat 16g, Carbs 8g, Fiber 5g, Protein 27g

Chicken and Spanish Rice

Prep Time: 10 mins |Servings: 5 | Cooking: 5 mins
Ingredients:
- 1 cup onions, chopped
- 3/4 cup green peppers
- 2 tsps vegetable oil
- 1 8 oz can tomato sauce*
- 1 tsp parsley, chopped
- 1/2 tsp black pepper
- 1-1/4 tsps garlic, minced
- 5 cups cooked brown rice (cooked in unsalted water)
- 3-1/2 cups chicken breasts, cooked, skin and bone removed, and diced

Directions:
1. In a large skillet, sauté onions and green peppers in oil for 5 mins on medium heat.
2. Add tomato sauce and spices. Heat through.
3. Add cooked rice and chicken. Heat through.

Nutrition:
Calories 428, Fat 8 g, Protein 35 g, Carbs 52 g

Turkey Cutlets with Herbs

Prep Time: 5 mins |Servings: 4| Cooking: 8 mins
Ingredients:
- 2 tbsp olive oil
- 2 sliced lemons
- 1 package (approx, 1 lb) turkey-breast cutlets
- ½ tsp garlic powder
- 4 cups baby spinach
- ½ cup water
- 2 tsps dried thyme

Directions:
1. In a large skillet over medium-high heat, heat the oil
2. Add about 6 lemon slices to the skillet
3. Sprinkle the turkey-breast cutlets with garlic powder and black pepper
4. Place the turkey cutlets into the skillet and cook for about 3 mins on each side until the turkey is no longer pink and is slightly browned at the edges
5. Remove from heat and divide turkey between 4 plates
6. Add the spinach to the pan along with ½ cup of water and steam, stirring frequently for about 2 mins. Remove the greens and lemons with tongs or a slotted spoon and divide between plates
7. Serve topped with dried thyme

Nutrition:
Calories 204, Fat 8g, Carbs 8g, Fiber 4g, Protein 30g

Chili Chicken Curry

Prep Time: 5 mins |Servings: 4 | Cooking: 20 mins
Ingredients:
- 14 oz kidney beans
- 3 tbsp red curry paste
- 1 lb. ground chicken
- 1 tbsp tomato paste
- 12 oz black beans
- 1 tbsp chili powder
- 2 tsp dried oregano
- 1 cup tomato sauce
- Vegetable oil

Directions:
1. Heat the oil in a rice cooker
2. Add curry paste and stir
3. Place the chicken into a heated rice cooker
4. Cook until cooked thoroughly
5. Once cooked add the beans, tomato paste, and sauce.

Nutrition:
Calories 315, Protein 39g, Carbs 25g, Fat 9g

Saucy Chicken

Prep Time: 15 mins |Servings: 4 | Cooking: 10 mins
Ingredients:
- 8 chicken tights
- 1 cup chicken broth
- 1 tbsp sherry vinegar
- 1½ cup roasted red peppers, chopped
- 4 crushed garlic cloves
- 1½ cup diced russet potatoes
- 2 tsp chopped thyme leaves

Directions:
1. Preheat oven to 425F
2. Heat olive oil in a pan over medium-high heat
3. Season the chicken tights with salt and pepper and place into heated oil, skin side down
4. Cook the chicken without moving around for 3 mins or until browned
5. Transfer to a plate and repeat with remaining chicken
6. Add the garlic and thyme to the same skillet. Cook until fragrant.
7. Add the potatoes, chicken broth, red peppers, and vinegar to the pan
8. Bring to boil and once boils remove from the heat
9. Return the chicken to the pan, skin side up and place in the oven
10. Braise the chicken for 30 mins or until the potatoes are tender

Nutrition:
Calories 125 Protein 17g, Carbs 17g, Fat 6g

Chicken Fried Rice

Prep Time: 6 mins |Servings: 2 | Cooking: 8 mins
Ingredients:
- 2 tbsp Oil
- 2 minced garlic cloves
- 4 oz cubed chicken breast
- 4 oz Shrimp
- 1 cup Mix vegetables-frozen
- 12 oz Overnight rice
- 1 tbsp Fish Sauce
- 1 tbsp Soy Sauce
- ¼ tsp Oyster Sauce
- ¼ tsp White Pepper
- 2 Eggs

Directions:
1. In a pan, add oil and garlic, cook, until the aroma of the garlic becomes present
2. Add shrimp, chicken, and vegetables
3. Put in in rice and stir to combine with veggies
4. Add soy sauce, fish sauce, oyster sauce, salt, and pepper and stir the rice for a few mins
5. Use a spatula to make a gap in the center of the rice
6. Dispense eggs in the center and let it sit for 30 seconds

Use rice to cover eggs and stir as egg cooks.
Add some salt and stir a bit more then serve.
Nutrition:
Calories 306 Protein 15g, Carbs 50g, Fat 5g

Mexican Chicken

Prep Time: 10 mins |Servings: 4 | Cooking: 7 hours
Ingredients:
- 4 chicken breasts, skinless and boneless
- ½ cup water
- 16 oz chunky salsa
- 1 and ½ tbsp parsley, chopped
- 1 tsp garlic powder
- ½ tbsp cilantro, chopped
- 1 tsp onion powder
- ½ tbsp oregano, dried

- ½ tsp sweet paprika
- 1 tsp chili powder
- ½ tsp cumin, ground

Directions:
1. Put the water in your slow cooker, add chicken breasts, salsa, parsley, garlic powder, cilantro, onion powder, oregano, paprika, chili powder, cumin and black pepper to the taste, toss, cover and cook on Low for 7 hours.
2. Divide the whole mix between plates and serve.

Nutrition:
Calories 200, Fat 4g, Fiber 2g, Carbs 12g, Protein 9g

Chicken Breast Stew

Prep Time: 10 mins |Servings: 4 | Cooking: 8 hours
Ingredients:
- 1 yellow onion, chopped
- 2 lbs chicken breasts, skinless and boneless
- 4 oz canned jalapenos, drained and chopped
- 1 green bell pepper, chopped
- 4 oz canned green chilies, drained and chopped
- 7 oz tomato sauce
- 14 oz canned tomatoes, chopped
- 2 tbsp coconut oil, melted
- 3 garlic cloves, minced
- 1 tbsp chili powder
- 1 tbsp cumin, ground
- 2 tsp oregano, dried
- A bunch of cilantro, chopped
- 1 avocado, pitted, peeled and sliced

Directions:
1. Grease the slow cooker with the melted oil, add onion, chicken, jalapenos, bell pepper, green chilies, tomato sauce, tomatoes, garlic, chili powder, cumin, oregano and black pepper, stir, cover and cook on Low for 8 hours.
2. Add cilantro, shred chicken breasts using 2 forks, stir the stew, divide into bowls and top with avocado slices.

Nutrition:
Calories 205, Fat 4g, Fiber 5g, Carbs 9g, Protein 11g

Vegetable Chicken Enchiladas

Prep Time: 10 mins |Servings: 4 | Cooking: 40 mins
Ingredients:
- nonstick cooking spray
- 1 large onion, peeled and chopped
- 1 green bell pepper, seeded and chopped
- 1 large zucchini, chopped
- 1 cup cooked, chopped chicken breast
- 3/4 cup red enchilada sauce
- 2 (8-ounce) cans no salt added tomato sauce
- 8 (6-inch) corn tortillas
- 2/3 cup shredded reduced fat Monterey Jack cheese

Directions:
1. Preheat oven to 375°F.
2. Spray large skillet with nonstick cooking spray. Sauté onion for 5 mins, stirring occasionally. Add bell pepper and zucchini; cook for 5 mins more. Stir in chicken; set aside.
3. Meanwhile, combine enchilada sauce and tomato sauce in a small bowl; add 1/2 cup to vegetable and chicken mixture.
4. Soften tortillas on the stovetop or in the microwave. Dip each tortilla in sauce and place equal amounts of vegetable and chicken mixture on one side. Roll up and place in a 13x9-inch baking pan. Pour remaining sauce over the top.
5. Cover loosely with foil and bake for 20 to 25 mins. Remove cover and sprinkle cheese over top; bake for 5 mins more. Serve while hot.

Nutrition:
Calories 311, Carbs 41 g, Fiber 7 g, Protein 22 g, Fat 8 g

Turkey Meatloaf

Prep Time: 5 mins |Servings: 5 | Cooking: 25 mins
Ingredients:
- 1 lb lean ground turkey
- 1/2 cup regular oats, dry
- 1 large egg, whole
- 1 tbsp onion, dehydrated flakes
- 1/4 cup ketchup*

Directions:
1. Combine all ingredients and mix well.
2. Bake in a loaf pan at 350 °F for 25 mins or to an internal temperature of 165 °F.
3. Cut into five slices and serve.

Nutrition:
Calories 191, Fat 7 g, Protein 23 g, Carbs 9 g, Fiber 1 g

Shepherd's Pie

Prep Time: 15 mins | Servings: 4 | Cooking: 40 mins
Ingredients:
For potatoes
- 1 lb Russet potatoes (or other white baking potatoes), rinsed, peeled, and cubed into 1/2-inch to 3/4-inch pieces
- 1/4 cup low-fat plain yogurt (or low-fat sour cream)
- 1 cup fat-free milk, hot
- 1/4 tsp ground black pepper
- 1 tbsp fresh chives, rinsed, dried, and chopped (or 1 tsp dried)

For filling
- 4 cups mixed cooked vegetables—such as carrots, celery, onions, bell peppers, mushrooms, or peas (or a 1-lb bag frozen mixed vegetables)
- 2 cups low-sodium chicken broth
- 1 cup quick-cooking oats
- 1 cup grilled or roasted chicken breast, diced (about 2 small breasts)
- 1 tbsp fresh parsley, rinsed, dried, and chopped (or 1 tsp dried)
- 1/4 tsp ground black pepper
- Nonstick cooking spray

Directions:
1. Place potatoes in a medium saucepan, and add enough cold water to cover by 1 inch. Bring to a boil (about 20 to 30 mins)
2. In the meanwhile combine the vegetables, chicken broth, and oats in a medium saucepan. Bring to a boil (about 5–7 mins) Add chicken, and continue to simmer until heated through. Season with parsley and pepper.
3. When potatoes have about 5 mins left to cook, preheat the oven to 450ºF.
4. When the potatoes are done, drain and dry them well, then mash with a potato masher or big fork.
5. Add the yogurt, hot milk, and salt. Stir well until smooth. Season with pepper and chives.
6. Lightly spray an 8- by 8-inch square baking dish, or four individual 4-inch ceramic bowls, with cooking spray. Place filling in the bottom of prepared dish (about 2 cups each for individual bowls). Carefully spread potato mixture on top of the chicken and vegetables (about 1 cup each for individual bowls) so they remain in two separate layers.
7. Bake in the preheated oven for about 10 mins, or until the potatoes are browned and chicken is reheated (to a minimum internal temperature of 165ºF). Serve immediately.

Nutrition:
Calories 336, Fat 4 g, Fiber 7 g, Protein 24 g, Carbs 54 g

Turkey Breast and Sweet Potato Mix

Prep Time: 10 mins | Servings: 4 | Cooking: 8 hours
Ingredients:
- 3 sweet potatoes, cut into wedges
- 1 cup dried cherries, pitted
- 2 white onions, cut into wedges
- 1/3 cup water
- 1 tsp onion powder
- 1 tsp garlic powder
- 1 tsp parsley flakes
- 1 tsp thyme, dried
- 1 tsp sage, dried
- 1 tsp paprika, dried

Directions:
1. Put the turkey breast in your slow cooker, add sweet potatoes, cherries, onions, water, parsley, garlic and onion powder, thyme, sage, paprika and pepper, toss, cover and cook on Low for 8 hours.
2. Discard bone from turkey breast, slice meat and divide between plates.
3. Serve with the veggies and the cherries on the side.

Nutrition:
Calories 220, Fat 5g, Fiber 4g, Carbs 8g, Protein 15g

Italian Chicken

Prep Time: 10 mins | Servings: 4 | Cooking: 5 hours
Ingredients:
- 4 chicken breasts, skinless and boneless
- 6 Italian sausages, sliced
- 5 garlic cloves, minced
- 1 white onion, chopped
- 1 tsp Italian seasoning
- A drizzle of olive oil
- 1 tsp garlic powder
- 29 oz canned tomatoes, chopped
- 15 oz tomato sauce, no-salt-added
- 1 cup water
- ½ cup balsamic vinegar

Directions:

1. Put chicken and sausage slices in your slow cooker, add garlic, onion, Italian seasoning, the oil, tomatoes, tomato sauce, garlic powder, water and the vinegar, cover and cook on High for 5 hours.
2. Stir chicken and sausage mix, divide between plates and serve.

Nutrition:
Calories 237, Fat 4g, Fiber 3g, Carbs 12g, Protein 13g

Chicken Breast and Cinnamon Veggie Mix

Prep Time: 10 mins |Servings: 4| Cooking: 6 hours
Ingredients:
- 2 red bell peppers, chopped
- 2 lbs chicken breasts, skinless and boneless
- 4 garlic cloves, minced
- 1 yellow onion, chopped
- 2 tsps paprika
- 1 cup low sodium chicken stock
- 2 tsps cinnamon powder
- ¼ tsp nutmeg, ground

Directions:
1. In a bowl, mix bell peppers with chicken breasts, garlic, onion, paprika, cinnamon and nutmeg, toss to coat, transfer everything to your slow cooker, add stock, cover, cook on Low for 6 hours, divide everything between plates and serve.

Nutrition:
Calories 200, Fat 3g, Fiber 5g, Carbs 13g, Protein 8g

Chapter 8: Beef, Pork and Lamb

Buffalo & Ranch Chicken Meatloaf

Prep Time: 10 mins |Servings: 6 | Cooking: 35 mins
Ingredients:
- ½ cup ranch dressing
- ¼ cup buffalo wing sauce
- 675g ground chicken
- 120g chicken stuffing mix
- ½ cup feta cheese
- 1 sliced celery stalk
- 2 chopped green onion
- 1 egg

Directions:
1. Preheat oven to 375 degrees and lightly grease a 6 x 4-inch loaf tin with olive oil
2. Mix all your egg and dry Ingredients:, along with half of your dressing Ingredients: together until fully incorporated using your hands
3. Once combined, add your meat mixture into your greased loaf tin, top with the other half of your dressing Ingredients: and set to bake until done (about 30 to 35 mins)
4. Tip: Use a thermometer to determine doneness by inserting it into the thickest part of the meatloaf. Ensure it reads 165 F.

Nutrition:
Calories 119, Protein 6g, Carbs 14g, Fat 4g

Mexican Beef Mix

Prep Time: 10 mins |Servings: 6| Cooking: 8 hours
Ingredients:
- 1 yellow onion, chopped
- 2 tbsp sweet paprika
- 15 oz canned tomatoes, no-salt-added, roasted and chopped
- 1 tsp cumin, ground
- 1 tsp olive oil
- A pinch of nutmeg, ground
- 5 lbs beef roast
- Juice of 1 lemon
- ¼ cup apple cider vinegar

Directions:
1. Heat up a pan with the oil over medium-high heat, add onions, stir, brown them for 2-3 mins, transfer them to your slow cooker, add paprika, tomato, cumin, nutmeg, lemon juice, vinegar, black pepper and beef, toss to coat, cover and cook on Low for 8 hours.
2. Slice roast, divide between plates and serve with tomatoes and onions mix on the side.

Nutrition:
Calories 250, Fat 5g, Fiber 2g, Carbs 8g, Protein 15g

Maple Beef Tenderloin

Prep Time: 10 mins |Servings: 4| Cooking: 8 hours
Ingredients:
- A pinch of nutmeg, ground
- 2 lbs beef tenderloin, trimmed
- 4 apples, cored and sliced
- 2 tbsp maple syrup

Directions:
1. Place half of the apples in your slow cooker, sprinkle the nutmeg over them, add beef tenderloin, top with the rest of the apples, drizzle the maple syrup, cover and cook on Low for 8 hours.
2. Slice beef tenderloin, divide between plates and serve with apple slices and cooking juices on top.

Nutrition:
Calories 240, Fat 4g, Fiber 5g, Carbs 14g, Protein 14g

Beef and Cabbage Stew

Prep Time: 10 mins |Servings: 6| Cooking: 8 hours
Ingredients:
- 1 tbsp olive oil
- 2 lbs beef loin, cubed
- 3 garlic cloves, minced
- 6 baby carrots, halved
- 2 onions, chopped
- Black pepper to the taste
- 1 cabbage head, shredded
- 3 cups veggie stock
- 28 oz canned tomatoes, no-salt-added, drained and chopped
- 3 big sweet potatoes, cubed

Directions:
1. Heat up a pan with the oil over medium-high heat, add meat, brown for a few mins on each side, transfer to your slow cooker, add black pepper, carrots, garlic, onion,

potatoes, cabbage, stock and tomatoes, stir well, cover, cook on Low for 8 hours, divide the stew into bowls and serve right away.

Nutrition:
Calories 270, Fat 5g, Fiber 4g, Carbs 14g, Protein 7g

Greek Beef

Prep Time: 1 day |Servings: 6| Cooking: 8 hours
Ingredients:
- 3 lbs beeg shoulder, boneless
- ¼ cup olive oil
- 2 tsps oregano, dried
- ¼ cup lemon juice
- 2 tsps mustard
- 2 tsps mint
- 6 garlic cloves, minced

Directions:
1. In a bowl, mix oil with lemon juice, oregano, mint, mustard, garlic and pepper, whisk, rub the meat with the marinade, cover and keep in the fridge for 1 day.
2. Transfer to your slow cooker along with the marinade, cover, cook on Low for 8 hours, slice the roast and serve.

Nutrition:
Calories 260, Fat 4g, Fiber 6g, Carbs 14g, Protein 8 g

Roast and Veggies

Prep Time: 10 mins |Servings: 6| Cooking: 4 hours
Ingredients:
- 1 lb sweet potatoes, chopped
- 3 and ½ lbs beef roast, trimmed
- 8 medium carrots, chopped
- 15 oz canned tomatoes, no-salt-added and chopped
- 1 yellow onion, chopped
- Zest of 1 lemon, grated
- Juice of 1 lemon
- 4 garlic cloves, minced
- Black pepper to the taste
- ½ cup kalamata olives, pitted

Directions:
1. Put potatoes in your slow cooker, carrots, tomatoes, onions, lemon juice and zest, beef, black pepper and garlic, stir, cover and cook on High for 4 hours.
2. Transfer meat to a cutting board, slice it and divide between plates.
3. Transfer the veggies to a bowl, mash, mix them with olives, and add next to the meat.

Nutrition:
Calories 250, Fat 4g, Fiber 3g, Carbs 15g, Protein 13g

Pork Medallions

Prep Time: 10 mins |Servings: 4| Cooking: 20 mins
Ingredients:
- 1 lb pork tenderloin, trimmed and cut into 1-inch-thick slices
- 2 tsps minced garlic
- 1 tsp dried rosemary
- 1½ tbsp olive oil, divided
- 1 cup low-sodium chicken stock
- 1 cup carrots, halved and thinly sliced
- 3 tbsp water
- ½ tsp freshly ground black pepper
- 2 cups frozen lima beans, thawed
- 1 cup frozen spinach, thawed

Directions:
1. Gently lb pork slices to ½-inch-thick medallions with a meat mallet or the heel of your hand.
2. Combine garlic and rosemary in a small bowl.
3. Heat a large skillet over medium heat. Add 1 tbsp of olive oil and swirl to coat. Add the pork to the pan and cook for 4 mins without turning. Turn and cook for 3 mins or until done. Remove pork from pan and keep warm.
4. Add garlic mixture; sauté for 1 minute or until fragrant. Add chicken stock and cook for 30 seconds or until reduced to ½ cup. Remove pan from heat.
5. Heat a second large nonstick skillet over medium heat. Add remaining olive oil and swirl to coat. Add carrots and cook for 2 mins. Stir in water and black pepper. Cover and cook for 2 mins until carrots are crisp tender. Stir in lima beans and spinach, Cook for 3 mins or until thoroughly heated.
6. Divide vegetable mixture among 4 plates. Top each serving with pork and sauce.

Nutrition:
Calories 317, Fat 11g, Carbs 28g, Fiber 8g, Protein 28g

Pork Salad with Walnuts and Peaches

Prep Time: 15 mins |Servings: 4| Cooking: 10 mins
Ingredients:
- 1 tbsp olive oil

- 1 lb pork tenderloin, cut into 1-in ch cubes
- 1 (10-ounce) bag fresh spinach leaves
- 1 peach, pitted and sliced
- ¼ cup walnuts
- Balsamic vinegar

Directions:
1. Heat the olive oil in a large nonstick skillet over medium-high heat. Add the pork and cook until it is browned on the outside and cooked through (3 to 4 mins per side). Remove from heat and set aside.
2. Make a bed of spinach on each individual serving plate. Arrange peach slices over the spinach. Top with the cooked pork and sprinkle with walnuts. Drizzle balsamic vinegar over the salad.
3. Enjoy immediately.

Nutrition:
Calories 230, Fat 14g, Carbs 6g, Protein 21g

Pork, White Bean, and Spinach Soup

Prep Time: 10 mins |Servings: 4| Cooking: 15 mins
Ingredients:
- 1 tbsp olive oil
- 8 oz pork tenderloin or boneless pork chops, cut into 1-inch cubes
- 4 garlic cloves, minced
- 2 tsps paprika
- 1 (14.5-ounce) can diced salt-free tomatoes
- 4 cups low-sodium chicken broth
- 1 bunch spinach, ribs removed and chopped, about 8 cups, lightly packed
- 2 (15-ounce) cans white beans, drained and rinsed

Directions:
1. Heat the oil in a Dutch oven or heavy-bottom pot over medium-high heat. Season pork with a pinch of salt. When the pan is hot, add pork and cook, stirring occasionally, for about 2 mins, or long enough to encourage a good sear and brown sides. Transfer to a plate.
2. In the same pot, add the garlic and paprika. Cook, stirring often, until fragrant (about 30 seconds). Add tomatoes and increase heat to high and stir to scrape down any browned bits. Add broth and bring to a boil.
3. Add spinach until it just wilts (about 2 to 3 mins).

Nutrition:
Calories 327, Fat 8g, Carbs 41g, Protein 26g

Orange-Beef Stir-Fry

Prep Time: 10 mins |Servings: 2| Cooking: 10 mins
Ingredients:
- 1 tbsp cornstarch
- ¼ cup cold water
- ¼ cup orange juice
- 1 tbsp reduced-sodium soy sauce
- ½ lb boneless beef sirloin steak, cut into thin strips
- 2 tsps olive oil, divided
- 3 cups frozen stir-fry vegetable blend
- 1 garlic clove, minced

Directions:
1. In a small bowl, combine cornstarch, cold water, orange juice, and soy sauce until smooth and set aside
2. In a large skillet or wok, stir-fry beef in 1 tsp of olive oil for 3 to 4 mins or until no longer pink
3. Remove with a slotted spoon and keep warm
4. Stir-fry the vegetable blend and garlic in the remaining oil for 3 mins. Stir cornstarch mixture and add to the pan. Bring to a boil
5. Cook stirring constantly, for 2 mins or until thickened. Add the beef and heat through.

Nutrition:
Calories 268, Fat 10g, Carbs 8g, Fiber 3g, Protein 26g

Steak Tacos

Prep Time: 15 mins |Servings: 4| Cooking: 13 mins
Ingredients:
- 1 lb beef flank (or round) steak
- 1 tsp chili powder
- 1 tsp olive oil
- 1 green bell pepper, cored and coarsely chopped
- 1 red onion, coarsely chopped
- 8 (6-inch) corn tortillas, warm
- 2 tbsp freshly squeezed lime juice
- Optional for Servings: 1 avocado, sliced, and coarsely chopped cilantro

Directions:
1. Rub the steak with chili powder (and salt and pepper, if desired).
2. Heat olive oil in a large skillet over medium-high heat.
3. Add steak and cook for 6 to 8 mins on each side or until it is done. Remove from heat.

4. Place steak on a plate and cover with aluminum foil. Let rest for 5 mins.
5. Add the bell pepper and onion to skillet. Cook on medium heat, stirring frequently, for 3 to 5 mins or until onion is translucent. Remove from heat.
6. Cut steak against the grain into thin slices.
7. Top tortillas evenly with beef, onion mixture, and lime juice. Garnish with avocado and cilantro, if desired.

Nutrition:
Calories 358, Fat 12g, Carbs 34g, Fiber 2g, Protein 28g

Beef-and-Bean Chili

Prep Time: 5 mins |Servings: 4| Cooking: 20 mins
Ingredients:
- 1 lb lean or extra-lean ground beef
- 1 yellow onion, diced
- 3 (15 oz) cans salt-free diced tomatoes with green chilies
- 2 (15 oz) cans beans, drained a nd rinsed (whatever you desire: black, red, pinto, kidney, etcup)
- 2 tbsp chili powder
- Optional: 1 (10-ounce) package frozen spinach

Directions:
1. In a large stockpot, cook the beef over medium-high heat until browned, stirring frequently
2. Using a slotted spoon, transfer the cooked beef to a separate plate and set aside
3. Reserve 1 tbsp of grease in the stockpot and discard the rest.
4. Add the onion to the stockpot and sauté for 4 to 5 mins until soft.
5. Add the tomatoes with green chilies, beans, chili powder, and cooked beef to the stockpot. Stir to combine. Bring to a boil and then reduce heat to medium-low. Cover and simmer for 10 mins.

Nutrition:
Calories 429, Fat 10g, Carbs 47g, Fiber 16g, Protein 38g

Asian Pork Tenderloin

Prep Time: 10 mins |Servings: 4| Cooking: 15 mins
Ingredients:
- 2 tbsp sesame seeds
- 1 tsp ground coriander
- 1/8 tsp cayenne pep per
- 1/8 tsp celery seed
- 1/2 tsp minced onion
- 1/4 tsp ground cumin
- 1/8 tsp ground cinnamon
- 1 tbsp sesame oil
- 1-lb pork tenderloin, sliced into 4 4-ounce portions

Directions:
1. Set the oven to heat at 400°F. Grease a baking dish with cooking oil.
2. Toast the sesame seeds in a dry frying pan until golden brown.
3. Transfer the sesame seeds to a bowl and set it aside.
4. Combine coriander with celery seed, cinnamon, toasted sesame seeds, cumin, sesame oil, and minced onion in a bowl.
5. Place the pork tenderloin in a baking dish and rub them with pepper mixture.
6. Bake them for 15 mins.

Nutrition:
Calories 248, Fat 13.8 g, Carbs 1.1 g, Fiber 3.1g, Protein 55.9 g

Curried Pork Tenderloin in Apple Cider

Prep Time: 6 mins |Servings: 6| Cooking: 30 mins
Ingredients:
- 16 oz pork tenderloin, cut into 6 pieces
- 1/2 tbsp curry powder
- tbsp extra-virgi n olive oil
- medium yellow onions, chopped (about 2 cups)
- cups apple cider, divided
- tart apple, peeled, seeded, and chopped into chunks
- tbsp cornstarch

Directions:
1. Rub the pork tenderloin with curry powder and let it rest for 15 mins.
2. Preheat a skillet with olive oil on medium heat.
3. Sear the tenderloin for 10 mins per side and then transfer it to a plate.
4. Add onions to the same skillet and sauté until golden and soft.
5. Stir in 1 ½ cups apple cider and cook until it is reduced to half.
6. Add chopped apples, remaining apple cider, and cornstarch.

7. Stir and then cook the mixture for 2 mins until it thickens.
8. Return the tenderloin to the sauce.
9. Let it cook for 5 mins in the sauce.

Nutrition:
Calories 244, Fat 14.8 g, Carbs 19.4 g, Fiber 1.3 g, Protein 10.2 g

New York Strip Steak

Prep Time: 15 mins |Servings: 2| Cooking: 20 mins
Ingredients:
- 2 New York strip steaks, 4 oz each, trimmed of all visible fat
- 1 tsp trans-free margarine
- 3 garlic cloves, choppe d
- 2 oz sliced shiitake mushrooms
- 2 oz button mushrooms
- 1/4 tsp thyme
- 1/4 tsp rosemary
- 1/4 cup whiskey

Directions:
1. Preheat a charcoal grill or broiler. Grease the racks with cooking spray.
2. Place the greased rack about 4 inches away from the heat source.
3. Grill the steaks in the preheated grill for 10 mins per side.
4. Sauté garlic with mushrooms, rosemary, and thyme in a greased skillet.
5. Cook for 2 mins and then stir in whiskey after removing the pan from the heat.
6. Pour this sauce over steaks.

Nutrition:
Calories 330, Fat 9.8 g, Carbs 21.1 g, Fiber 3.1 g, Protein 44 g

Mediterranean Pork Pasta

Prep Time: 15 mins |Servings: 4| Cooking: 15 mins
Ingredients:
- 2 cups dry whole-wheat penne pasta (8 oz)
- 1 tbsp olive oil
- 1 tsp garlic, minced (about 1/2 clove)
- 8 oz white button mushrooms, rinsed and cut into quarters
- 1/2 bag (8 oz bag) sundried tomato halves, cut into thin strips
- 1/2 jar (8 oz jar) artichoke hearts in water, drained, cut into quarters
- 2 cups low-sodium beef broth
- 2 tbsps cornstarch
- 12 oz stir-fry pork strips, sliced into 12 strips (or, slice 3 4-oz boneless pork chops into thin strips)
- 1/4 cup fat-free evaporated milk
- 2 tbsps fresh parsley, rinsed, dried, and chopped (or 2 tsps dried)

Directions:
1. In a 4-quart saucepan, bring 3 quarts of water to a boil over high heat.
2. Add pasta, and cook according to package Directions::s. Drain. (Set plain pasta aside for picky eaters—see Healthy Eating Two Ways suggestion below.)
3. Meanwhile, heat olive oil and garlic in a large sauté pan over medium heat. Cook until soft, but not browned (about 30 seconds).
4. Add mushrooms, and cook over medium heat until the mushrooms are soft and lightly browned.
5. Add sundried tomatoes and artichoke hearts. Toss gently to heat.
6. In a separate bowl, combine beef broth and cornstarch. Mix well.
7. Add broth mixture to the pan, and bring to a boil.
8. Add pork strips, evaporated milk, and parsley, and bring to a boil. Simmer gently for 3–5 mins (to a minimum internal temperature of 160 °F).
9. Add pasta, and toss well to mix.
10. Serve 2 cups of pasta and sauce per portion.

Nutrition:
Calories 486, Fat 11 g, Protein 33 g, Carbs 56 g

Pork Medallions with Herbs de Provence

Prep Time: 10 mins |Servings: 4| Cooking: 20 mins
Ingredients:
- 8 oz pork tenderloin, trimmed of visible fat and cut crosswise into 6 pieces
- 1/2 tsp herbs de Provence
- 1/4 cup dry white wine

Directions:
1. Season the pork with black pepper and place the meat between sheets of parchment paper.
2. Punch the pork pieces with a mallet into ¼ inch thickness.
3. Sear the seasoned pork in a greased skillet for 3 mins per side.

4. Remove it from the pan and drizzle with herbs de Provence.
5. Transfer the pork to the serving plate.
6. Add wine to the same skillet and scrape off the brown bits while stirring.
7. Pour this wine over the medallions.

Nutrition:
Calories 120, Fat 24 g, Carbs 26.4 g, Fiber 1.5 g, Protein 23.4 g

Pork and Mint Corn

Prep time: 10 mins | Servings: 4
Ingredients:
- 1 cup corn
- 1 tbsp chopped mint
- 1 cup low-sodium veggie stock
- Black pepper
- 1 tbsp olive oil
- 1 tsps. sweet paprika
- 4 pork chops

Directions:
1. Put the pork chops in a roasting pan, add the rest of the Ingredients:, toss, introduce in the oven and bake at 380 ⁰F for 1 hour.
2. Divide everything between plates and serve.

Nutrition:
Calories 356, Fat 14 g, Carbs 11.0 g, Protein 1g

Pork Chops and Snow Peas

Prep time: 10 mins | Servings: 4
Ingredients:
- 2 tbsp olive oil
- 1 cup low-sodium veggie stock
- 4 pork chops
- 1 cup snow peas
- 2 chopped shallots
- 1 tbsp chopped parsley
- 2 tbsp no-salt-added tomato paste

Directions:
1. Heat up a pan with the oil over medium heat, add the shallots, toss and sauté for 5 mins.
2. Add the pork chops and brown for 2 mins on each side.
3. Add the rest of the Ingredients:, bring to a simmer and cook over medium heat for 15 mins.
4. Divide the mix between plates and serve.

Nutrition:
Calories 357, Fat 27 g, Carbs 7.7 g, Protein 20.7 g

Pork Meatballs

Prep time: 10 mins | Servings: 4
Ingredients:
- 2 tbsp avocado oil
- 1 tbsp chopped cilantro
- 3 tbsp almond flour
- 2 whisked egg
- 10 oz. no-salt-added canned tomato sauce
- Black pepper
- 2 lbs. ground pork

Directions:
1. In a bowl, combine the pork with the flour and the other Ingredients: except the sauce and the oil, stir well and shape medium meatballs out of this mix.
2. Heat up a pan with the oil over medium heat, add the meatballs and brown for 3 mins on each side.
3. Add the sauce, toss gently, bring to a simmer and cook over medium heat for 20 mins more.
4. Divide everything into bowls and serve.

Nutrition:
Calories 332, Fat18 g, Carbs 14.3 g, Protein 25 g

Pork with Sprouts

Prep time: 10 mins | Servings: 4
Ingredients:
- 1 cup bean sprouts
- 1 cup low-sodium veggie stock
- 1 wedged yellow onion
- 2 tbsp olive oil
- 1 lb. pork chops
- Black pepper
- 2 tbsp drained capers

Directions:
1. Heat up a pan with the oil over medium-high heat, add the onion and the meat and brown for 5 mins.
2. Add the rest of the Ingredients:, introduce the pan in the oven and bake at 390 ⁰F for 30 mins.
3. Divide everything between plates and serve.

Nutrition:
Calories 324, Fat 12.5 g, Carbs 22.2 g, Protein:15.6 g

Beef Stew with Fennel and Shallots

Prep Time: 10 mins |Servings: 6 | Cooking: 1hour

Ingredients:
- 1/3 cup chopped fresh parsley
- 3 Portobello mushrooms
- 18 small boiling onions
- 4 large red-skinned potatoes
- 4 large sliced carrots
- 3 cup vegetable stock
- 1 bay leaf
- 2 fresh thyme sprigs
- ¾ tsp ground black pepper
- 3 large shallots
- ½ fennel bulb
- 2 tbsp olive oil
- 1 lb. boneless lean beef stew meat
- 3 tbsp all-purpose flour

Directions:
1. Put the flour on a place and rolling the beef cubes in the flour
2. Using a large saucepan, pour the oil in and heat at medium heat
3. Once the beef is floured, put it into the sauce pan and cook until brown on all sides
4. Remove the beef and let cook elsewhere
5. Without changing the temperature, place the shallots and the fennel in the pan and cook until they are a light brown
6. Add the lay leaf, thyme sprigs, and a quarter of the pepper to the mix and let cook for a minute or two
7. Now, add the beef back into the pan with the vegetable stock and bring the mixture to a boil. After, reduce the heat and cover it while it simmers. Leave it like this for 30 mins
8. Once the meat is tender, add the mushrooms, onions, potatoes, and carrots
9. Stir the mixture and let simmer for another 30 mins
10. Pull the bay leaf and the thyme sprigs out of the stew and stir in the parsley and remaining pepper

Nutrition:
Calories 244, Fat 8g, Carbs 22g, Protein 21g

Grilled Portobello Mushroom Burger

Prep Time: 15 mins |Servings: 4 | Cooking: 15 mins
Ingredients:
- 2 romaine lettuce leaves
- 4 slices of red onion
- 1 slices of tomato
- 4 whole-wheat toasted buns
- 2 tbsp olive oil
- ¼ tsp cayenne pepper
- 1 minced garlic clove
- 1 tbsp Sugar
- ½ cup water
- 1/3 cup balsamic vinegar
- 4 large Portobello mushroom caps

Directions:
1. The Portobello mushrooms need to be cleaned and their stems need to be removed and the caps need to be set aside
2. Now, in a small bowl the olive oil, cayenne pepper, garlic, sugar, water, and vinegar need to be mixed together and pored over top the mushroom caps
3. The caps need to be placed into a plastic container, covered, and placed into the refrigerator to marinate for an hour
4. Turn on the grill and lightly coat it in cooking spray—or, turn on the stove and coat a frying pan in the same substance
5. Fry or grill the mushrooms on medium heat, making sure to flip them often. Usually, it will take five mins on each side
6. Place the mushrooms on their own bun and top with half a lettuce leaf, one onion slice and one tomato slice.

Nutrition:
Calories 301, Fat 9g, Carbs 45g, Protein 10g

Pork and Green Onions

Prep time: 10 mins | Servings: 5 | Cooking: 10 mins
Ingredients:
- 1 tbsp avocado oil
- 4 minced garlic cloves
- 1 lb. cubed pork meat
- 1 chopped green onion bunch
- Black pepper
- 1 cup low-sodium tomato sauce
- 1 chopped yellow onion

Directions:
1. Heat up a pan with the oil over medium-high heat, add the onion and green onions, stir and cook for 5 mins.
2. Add the meat, stir and cook for 5 mins more.
3. Add the rest of the Ingredients:, toss and cook over medium heat for 30 mins more.
4. Divide everything into bowls and serve.

Nutrition:

Calories 206, Fat 8.6 g, Carbs 7.2 g, Protein 23.4 g

Chili Verde

Prep time: 10 mins | Servings: 4 | Cooking: 55 mins
Ingredients:
- 1 lb fresh tomatillos, husks removed, washed, and cut into quarters
- 3 Anaheim chilies, roasted, peeled, seeded, and diced
- 3 green onions, sliced
- 2 cloves garlic, chopped
- 1 jalapeño pepper, seeded and diced
- 2 tbsps fresh lime juice
- 1 tsp sugar
- 2 tsps oil
- 1-1/2 lbs lean pork tenderloin, cut into 3/4-inch chunks
- 1/4 cup chopped fresh cilantro

Directions:
1. Place tomatillos in a medium saucepan with a small amount of water. Cover and simmer for about 5 mins until soft.
2. Drain tomatillos and place in a blender container with the Anaheim chilies, green onions, garlic, and jalapeño pepper. Blend on low speed until fairly smooth. Stir in lime juice and sugar and pour back into saucepan; set aside.
3. Heat oil in a large skillet. Add pork to skillet; cook and stir over high heat for about 5 mins to brown; add to the pan with the sauce. Bring to a boil; reduce heat and simmer, covered, for 40 mins.
4. Remove cover and cook for 10 mins more. Stir in cilantro and salt. Serve with 1/2 cup cooked brown rice.

Nutrition:
Calories 413, Carbs 35 g, Fiber 6 g, Protein 43 g, Fat 11 g

Pork and Carrots Soup

Prep time: 10 mins | Servings: 4
Ingredients:
- 1 lb. cubed pork stew meat
- 1 tbsp chopped cilantro
- 1 tbsp olive oil
- 1 chopped red onion
- 1 cup tomato puree
- 1 quart low-sodium beef stock
- 1 lb. sliced carrots

Directions:
1. Heat up a pot with the oil over medium-high heat, add the onion and the meat and brown for 5 mins.
2. Add the rest of the Ingredients: except the cilantro, bring to a simmer, reduce heat to medium, and boil the soup for 20 mins.
3. Ladle into bowls and serve for lunch with the cilantro sprinkled on top.

Nutrition:
Calories 354, Fat 14.6 g, Carbs 19.3 g, Protein 36 g

Chili Pork

Prep time: 10 mins | Servings: 4
Ingredients:
- 1 tbsp chopped oregano
- 2 lbs. cubed pork stew meat
- 1 chopped yellow onion
- 2 tbsp chili paste
- 2 minced garlic cloves
- 2 cup low-sodium beef stock
- 1 tbsp olive oil

Directions:
1. Heat up a pot with the oil, over medium-high heat, add the onion and the garlic, stir and sauté for 5 mins.
2. Add the meat and brown it for 5 mins more.
3. Add the rest of the Ingredients:, bring to a simmer and cook over medium heat for 20 mins more.
4. Divide the mix into bowls and serve.

Nutrition:
Calories 363, Fat 8.6 g, Carbs 17.3 g, Protein 18.4 g

Asian Pork Tenderloin

Prep Time: 20 mins | Servings: 4 | Cooking: 15 mins
Ingredients:
- 1 lb. pork tenderloin
- 1 tbsp sesame seed oil
- 1/8 tsp ground cinnamon
- ¼ tsp ground cumin
- ½ tsp celery seed
- 1/8 tsp cayenne pepper
- 1 tsp ground coriander
- 2 tbsp sesame seeds

Directions:
1. Preheat the oven to four hundred degrees F
2. While the oven is preheating, grease a baking sheet with cooking spray
3. Pull out a frying pan and on low heat fry the sesame seeds while stirring contently

4. After 1 to 2 mins, or the sesame seeds are golden brown, remove the seeds from the heat and set them aside
5. In a large mixing bowl, place the toasted sesame seeds, sesame seed oil, cinnamon, cumin, celery seed, cayenne pepper, and coriander inside and stir until it is mixed evenly
6. Using the prepared baking dish, place the tenderloin on top and evenly space them out
7. Use a brush to lather the tenderloin, on both sides, with the mixture
8. Place the baking sheet inside the oven and let bake for about fifteen mins or until they are no longer pink
9. Take the tenderloin out and serve with a side dish immediately.

Nutrition:
Calories 248, Carbs 1g, Fat 16g, Protein 26g

Delicious Bacon Delight

Prep Time: 1 hour 35 mins | Servings: 16 | Cooking: 1 hour
Ingredients:
- 16 bacon slices
- 2 tbsp erythritol
- 3 oz dark chocolate
- 1 tbsp coconut oil
- ½ tbsp ground cinnamon
- 1 tsp maple extract

Directions:
1. Put the cinnamon with erythritol in a bowl, mix and stir
2. Put the bacon slices on a lined baking sheet and sprinkle cinnamon mix on one side of the slice
3. Flip bacon slices to the other side and sprinkle cinnamon mix over them again
4. Preheat an oven to 275F then introduce the bacon slices and bake for 1 hour
5. Get a pan and heat up with the oil to over medium heat
6. Add chocolate to the oil and stir until it melts
7. Add maple extract; stir, take off the heat and set aside to cool for a short time
8. Take bacon strips out of the oven and set aside to cool down, immerse each bacon strips in the chocolate mix and place them on a parchment paper and leave them to cool down completely.

Serve cold.
Nutrition:
Calories 150, Fiber 4g, Carbs 1g, Protein 3g, Fat 4g

Squeaky Beef Stroganoff

Prep Time: 10 mins | Servings: 4 | Cooking: 30 mins
Ingredients:
- 2 cups of beef strip
- 3 tbsp of olive oil
- 1 tbsp of almond flour
- 1 chopped up onion
- 2 minced up garlic cloves
- 1 cup of sliced mushroom
- 2 tbsp of tomato paste
- 3 tbsp of Worcestershire sauce
- 2 cups of beef broth
- 1 and a ½ cup of zucchini zoodles
- ¼ tsp of flavored vinegar
- ¼ tsp of pepper

Directions:
1. Take a taking a bowl and add in the flavored vinegar, pepper and flour alongside the beef strips
2. Coat up the beef with the flour and the seasoning
3. Set your instant pot on low heat and low pressure and place your meat in your inner pot and cook for 10 mins
4. Add in the rest of your Ingredients: in your pot Close up the lid and let it cook for about 18 mins at medium pressure

Once done, release the pressure naturally
Serve finally alongside a good bunch of zoodles
Nutrition:
Calories 335, Fat: 18g ,Carbs 22g, Protein 20.02g

Sloppiest Sloppy Joe

Prep Time: 10 mins | Servings: 4 | Cooking: 15 mins
Ingredients:
- ½ a cup of white quinoa
- 2 tbsp of olive oil
- 1 large sized chopped up yellow onion
- 1 large sized Italian frying pepper completely stemmed, chopped up and deseeded
- 2 lb of lean ground beef
- 2 tsp of minced up garlic
- 1 pieces of 18 oz can of crushed tomatoes
- ½ cup of old fashioned oat tolls
- ¼ cup of packed dark brown sugar
- 2 tbsp of Dijon mustard

- 2 tbsp of Worcestershire sauce
- 2 tbsp of apple vinegar
- 2 tbsp of paprika
- ¼ tsp of ground clove

Directions:
1. Open up your instant pot and add in the grains
2. Pour in as much water, as required to cover up the grains
3. Lock up the lid and let it cook at high pressure for 3 mins
4. Quick release the pressure
5. Open up and drain out the quinoa in a fine mesh sieve set in your sink
6. Heat up your cooker in sauté mode and pour some oil
7. Add in the pepper, onion and cook for 4 mins
8. Then, add in the crumbled ground beef and garlic and keep stirring them nicely
9. Let it cook for 6 mins until the beef is not pink anymore
10. Then, stir in the tomatoes, brown sugar, oats, mustard, vinegar, cloves, paprika and Worcestershire sauce alongside the nicely drained quinoa to and stir them to mix nicely
11. Close up the lid and let it cook for 8 mins at HIGH pressure
12. Quick release the pressure
13. Open it up and serve hot

Nutrition:
Calories: 212, Fat: 14g, Carbs: 11g, Protein: 12g

Wrapped Asparagus

Prep Time: 3 mins | Servings: 4 | Cooking: 5 mins
Ingredients:
- 1 lb of thick asparagus
- 80 ounce of thinly sliced prosciutto

Directions:
1. The first step here is to prepare your instant pot by pouring in about 2 cups of water
2. Take the asparagus and wrap them up in prosciutto spears.
3. Once all of the asparagus are wrapped, gently place the processed asparaguses in the cooking basket inside your pot in layers.
4. Turn up the heat to a high temperature and when there is a pressure build up, take down the heat and let it cook for about 2-3 mins at the high pressure.
5. Once the timer runs out, gently open the cover of the pressure cooker
6. Take out the steamer basket from the pot instantly and toss the asparaguses on a plate to serve
7. Eat warm or let them come down to room temperature

Nutrition:
Calories: 212, Fat: 14g, Carbohydrates: 11g, Protein: 12g

Majestic Veal Stew

Prep Time: 10 mins | Servings: 4 | Cooking: 30 mins
Ingredients:
- 2 sprigs of fresh rosemary
- 1 tbsp of olive oil
- 1 tbsp of butter
- 8 ounce of shallot
- 2 chopped up carrot
- 2 chopped up stalks of celery
- 2 tbsp of all-purpose flour
- 3 lb of veal
- Water
- 2 tsp of flavored vinegar

Directions:
1. Set your pot to Saute mode and add olive oil, allow the oil to heat up
2. Add butter and chopped up rosemary
3. Add celery, shallots, carrots and Saute until you have a nice teture
4. Shove the veggies on the side and add meat cubes, brown them. Pour stock and cover the meat slightly. Lock up the lid and cook on HIGH pressure for 15-20 mins
5. Release the pressure naturally over 10 mins
6. Open the lid and set the pot to Saute mode, simmer for 5 mins more.

Nutrition:
Calories 470, Fat 22g, Carbs 18g, Protein 47g

The Surprising No "Noodle" Lasagna

Prep Time: 10 mins | Servings: 8 | Cooking: 25 mins
Ingredients:
- 1 lb of ground beef
- 2 cloves of minced garlic
- 1 small sized onion
- 1 and a ½ cups of ricotta cheese
- ½ a cup of parmesan cheese
- 1 large sized egg

- 25 ounce of marinara sauce
- 8 ounce of sliced mozzarella

Directions:
1. Set your pot to Saute mode and add garlic, onion and ground beef
2. Take a small bowl and add ricotta and parmesan with egg and mix
3. Drain the grease and transfer the beef to a 1 and a ½ quart soufflé dish
4. Add marinara sauce to the browned meat and reserve half
5. Top the remaining meat sauce with half of your mozzarella cheese
6. Spread half of the ricotta cheese over the mozzarella layer
7. Top with the remaining meat sauce
8. Add a final layer of mozzarella cheese on top
9. Spread any remaining ricotta cheese mix over the mozzarella
10. Carefully add this mixture to your Soufflé Dish (with meat)
11. Pour 1 cup of water to your pot
12. Place it over a trivet
13. Lock up the lid and cook on HIGH pressure for 10 mins
14. Release the pressure naturally over 10 mins

Nutrition:
Calories: 607, Fat: 23g, Carbohydrates: 65g, Protein: 33g

Worthwhile Balsamic Beef

Prep Time: 5 mins | Servings: 8 | Cooking: 55 mins
Ingredients:
- 3 lb of chuck roast
- 3 cloves of thinly sliced garlic
- 1 tbsp of oil
- 1 tsp of flavored vinegar
- ½ a tsp of pepper
- ½ a tsp of rosemary
- 1 tbsp of butter
- ½ a tsp of thyme
- ¼ cup of balsamic vinegar
- 1 cup of beef broth

Directions:
1. Cut slits in the roast and stuff garlic slices all over
2. Take a bowl and add flavored vinegar, rosemary, pepper, thyme and rub the mixture over the roast. Set your pot to Saute mode and add oil, allow the oil to heat up
3. Add roast and brown both sides (5 mins each side)
4. Take the roast out and keep it on the side
5. Add butter, broth, balsamic vinegar and deglaze the pot
6. Transfer the roast back and lock up the lid, cook on HIGH pressure for 40 mins
7. Preform a quick release

Nutrition:
Calories: 393, Fat: 15g, Carbs: 25g, Protein: 37g

Friendly Chipotle Copycat

Prep Time: 5 mins | Servings: 6 | Cooking: 55 mins
Ingredients:
- 3 lb of grass-fed chuck roast large chunks
- 1 large sized onion peeled and sliced up
- 6 garlic cloves
- 2 cans of 4 ounce of green chilies
- 1 tbsp of oregano
- 1 tsp of flavored vinegar
- 1 tsp of pepper
- 3 dried chipotle peppers with the stems removed broken up into small pieces
- Juice of 3 limes
- 3 tbsp of coconut vinegar
- 1 tbsp of cumin
- ½ a cup of water

Directions:
1. Add the listed Ingredients to your Instant Pot
2. Stir and lock up the lid , cook on HIGH pressure for 50 mins
3. Release the pressure naturally over 10 mins
4. Remove the lid and shred using a fork
5. Set your pot to Saute mode and reduce for 30 mins

Nutrition:
Calories: 452, Fat: 22g, Carbs: 12g, Protein: 52g

Ground Beef with Beans and Tomatoes

Prep Time: 15 mins | Servings: 6 | Cooking: 30 mins
Ingredients:
- 1 tsp of olive oil
- 1 lb of lean ground beef
- 1 chopped medium onion
- 1 tbsp of minced garlic
- 1 tsp of dried thyme
- 1 tsp of dried oregano
- ½ a lb of green beans, ends trimmed and cut up into 1 inch pieces

- 2 can of petite diced tomatoes with juice
- 2 cans of beef broth
- Flavored vinegar and pepper as needed

Directions:
1. Set your pot to Saute mode and add oil, allow the oil to heat up. Add ground beef and stir well as it cooks
2. Once the beef is browned up, add chopped onion, dried thyme, minced garlic, dried oregano and cook for 3 mins
3. Add petite-dice tomatoes alongside the juice and beef broth
4. Allow them to heat for a while
5. Trim the beans on both ends and cut into 1 inch pieces
6. Add beans to your pot
7. Lock up the lid and cook on SOUP mode for 30 mins
8. Perform a quick release
9. Season with flavored vinegar and pepper
10. Serve freshly with a grating of parmesan

Nutrition:
Calories: 327, Fat: 24g, Carbs: 12g, Protein: 19g

Lamb Spare Ribs

Prep Time: 5 mins | Servings: 5 | Cooking: 20 mins
Ingredients:
- 2.5 lbs of pastured lamb spare ribs
- 2 tsps of kosher flavored vinegar
- 1 tbsp of curry powder

for the sauce
- 1 t tbsp of coconut oil
- 1 large sized coarsely chopped onion
- ½ a lb of minced garlic
- 1 tbsp of curry powder
- 1 tbsp of kosher flavored vinegar
- Juice from about 1 lemon
- 1 and a 1/4th cup of divided cilantro
- 4 thinly sliced scallion

Directions:
1. Take a bowl and add spare ribs
2. Season with 2 tsp of vinegar, 1 tsp of curry powder and mix well
3. Cover it up and let them freeze for at least 1 hour
4. Set your pot to Saute mode and add coconut oil
5. Add spare ribs and allow them to brown
6. Once done, transfer them to another plate
7. Take a blender and add tomatoes and onion and blend them well to a paste
8. Add the minced garlic to your instant pot (still in Saute mode)
9. Keep stiring the garlic while carefully poring the prepared paste
10. Add curry powder, chopped up cilantro, flavored vinegar and lemon juice. Allow the whole mixture to come to a boil
11. Add spare ribs and stir until it is coated well
12. Lock up the lid and cook for 20 mins at HIGH pressure
13. Allow the pressure to release naturally once done
14. Scoop out the grease and season with some flavored vinegar

Nutrition:
Calories: 165, Fats: 14g, Carbs:5g, Fiber:2g

Curry Lamb shanks

Prep Time: 35 mins | Servings: 5 | Cooking: 45 mins
Ingredients:
- 3 lb of lamb shanks
- Amount of Kosher Flavored vinegar
- Freshly ground portions of black pepper
- 2 tbsp of well divided ghee
- 2 roughly chopped up medium sized carrots
- 2 celery roughly chopped up celery stalks
- 1 roughly chopped up large sized onion
- 1 tbsp of tomato paste
- 3 cloves of peeled and smashed garlic
- 1 cup of bone broth
- 1 tsp of Red Boast Fish Sauce
- 1 tbsp of vinegar

Directions:
1. Season the shanks with pepper and flavored vinegar
2. Set your pot to Saute mode and add ghee, allow the ghee to melt and heat up
3. Add shanks and cook for 8-10 mins until a nice brown texture appears
4. In the meantime, chop the vegetables
5. Once you have a nice brown texture on your lamb, remove it from the Instant Pot and keep it on the side
6. Add vegetables and season with flavored vinegar and pepper
7. Add a tbsp of ghee and mix
8. Add vegetables, garlic clove, tomato paste and give it a nice stir

9. Add shanks and pour broth, vinegar, fish sauce
10. Sprinkle a bit of pepper and lock up the lid
11. Cook on HIGH pressure for 45 mins
12. Release the pressure naturally over 10 mins

Nutrition:
Calories: 377, Fats: 16g, Carbs:10g, Fiber:2g

Moroccan Lamb Tajine

Prep Time: 10 mins/Cooking time: 50 mins /Servings: 4

Ingredients:
- 2 and a /13 lb of lamb shoulder
- 1 tsp of cinnamon powder
- 1 tsp of ginger powder
- 1 tsp of turmeric powder
- 2 cloves of crushed garlic
- 3 tbsp of olive oil
- 10 ounce of prunes pitted and soaked
- 1 cup of vegetable stock
- 2 medium roughly sliced onion
- 1 piece of bay leaf
- 1 stick of cinnamon
- 1 tsp of pepper
- 1 and a ½ tsp of flavored vinegar
- 3 and a ½ ounce of almonds
- 1 tbsp of sesame seeds

Directions:
1. Take a bowl and add ground cinnamon, ginger, turmeric, garlic and 2 spoons of olive oil
2. Make a paste
3. Cover the lamb with the paste
4. Take a bowl and add dried prunes with boiling water and cover, keep it on the side
5. Set your pot to Saute mode and add olive oil
6. Add onion and cook for 3 mins
7. Transfer the onion to a bowl and keep it on the side
8. Add meat and brown all sides for about 10 mins
9. Deglaze using vegetable stock
10. Add onions, cinnamon stick, bay leaf
11. Lock up the lid and cook on HIGH pressure for 35 mins
12. Release the pressure naturally
13. Add rinsed and drained prunes and set the pot to Saute mode
14. Reduce the liquid by simmer for 5 mins
15. Discard the bay leaf and sprinkle toasted almonds alongside sesame seeded

Nutrition:
Protein: 6.2g , Carbs: 2.0g, Fats: 11.8g, Calories: 134

Quick Jalapeno Crisps

Prep Time: 35 mins |Servings: 20 | Cooking: 25 mins

Ingredients:
- 5 sliced jalapenos
- Tabasco sauce for serving
- ½ tsp onion powder
- 8 oz grated parmesan cheese
- 3 tbsp olive oil

Directions:
1. Mix the jalapeno slices with salt, pepper, oil and onion powder, toss to coat and arrange on a lined baking sheet
2. Preheat your oven to a temperature of 450F and introduce the mix and bake for 15 mins
3. Take jalapeno slices out of the oven, set them aside and allow them to cool down
4. In another bowl, mix pepper slices with the cheese and compress well
5. Place all the slices on another lined baking sheet and introduce into the oven again and bake for 10 mins more
6. Leave jalapenos to cool down
7. Arrange on a plate and serve with Tabasco sauce on the side

Nutrition:
Calories 50, Fat 1g, Carbs 3g, Protein 2g

Crispy Egg Chips

Prep Time: 15 mins |Servings: 2 | Cooking: 15 mins

Ingredients:
- 4 eggs whites
- 2 tbsp shredded parmesan
- ½ tbsp water

Directions:
1. Put the egg whites with water in a bowl and mix and whisk well
2. Spoon this into a muffin pan, sprinkle cheese on top
3. introduce the mix in the oven at 400 degrees F and bake for 15 mins
4. Move the egg white chips to a platter and serve with a dip on the side

Nutrition:
Calories 120, Fiber 1, Fat 2, Carbs 2g, Protein 7g

Marinated beef Kebabs

Prep Time: 30 mins |Servings: 6 | Cooking: 10 mins

Ingredients:
- 1 red/green/orange bell pepper, cut into chunks
- 2 lbs sirloin steak, cut into medium cubes
- 4 minced garlic cloves
- ¼ cup tamari sauce
- ½ cup olive oil
- 1/4 cup lemon juice
- 1 red onion, cut into chunks
- 2½ tbsp Worcestershire sauce
- 2 tbsp Dijon mustard

Directions:
1. Mix the Worcestershire sauce with garlic, mustard, tamari, lemon juice and oil and stir until even
2. Include beef, bell peppers and onion chunks to this mix, toss to coat and set aside for a few mins
3. Arrange bell pepper, meat cubes and onion chunks on skewers alternating colors
4. Place the mix on your preheated grill of over medium-high heat and cook for 5 mins on each side

Move to a platter and serve as a summer appetizer.
Nutrition:
Calories 246, Fiber 1g, Carbs 4g, Fat 12g, Protein 26g

Chapter 9: Fish and Seafood

Cowboy Caviar Salad

Prep Time: 6 mins |Servings: 16
Ingredients:
- mayonnaise-¾ cup
- 8 eggs, hardboiled, peeled and mashed with a fork
- 1 yellow onion, finely chopped
- 4 oz red caviar
- toast baguette slices for serving
- 4 oz black caviar

Directions:
1. Mix in a bowl mashed eggs with mayonnaise, salt, pepper and onion and stir well
2. Spread eggs salad on toasted baguette slices
3. Add caviar at the top of the slices.

Nutrition:
Calories 122, Fiber 1g, Carbs 4g, Protein 7g, Fat 8g

Asparagus And Lemon Salmon Dish

Prep Time: 5 mins |Servings: 3 | Cooking: 15 mins
Ingredients:
- 2 salmon fillets, 6 oz each, skin on
- Sunflower seeds to taste
- 1 lb asparagus, trimmed
- 2 cloves garlic, minced
- 3 tbsps almond butter
- ¼ cup cashew cheese

Directions:
1. Pre-heat your oven to 400F
2. Line a baking sheet with oil
3. Take a kitchen towel and pat your salmon dry, season as needed
4. Put salmon around baking sheet and arrange asparagus around it
5. Place a pan over medium heat and melt almond butter
6. Add garlic and cook for 3 mins until garlic browns slightly
7. Drizzle sauce over salmon
8. Sprinkle salmon with cheese and bake for 12 mins until salmon looks cooked all the way and is flaky

Nutrition:
Calories 131, Fiber 1g, Carbs 7g, Protein 8g, Fat 8g

Spicy Baked Shrimp

Prep Time: 10 mins |Servings: 4 | Cooking: 25 mins + 2-4 hours
Ingredients:
- ½ oz large shrimp, peeled and deveined
- Cooking spray as needed
- 1 tsp low sodium coconut aminos
- 1 tsp parsley
- ½ tsp olive oil
- ½ tbsp honey
- 1 tbsp lemon juice

Directions:
1. Pre-heat your oven to 450 degrees F
2. Take a baking dish and grease it well
3. Mix in all the Ingredients: and toss
4. Transfer to oven and bake for 8 mins until shrimp turn pink

Nutrition:
Calories 135, Fiber 1g, Carbs 8g, Protein 10g, Fat 8g

Shallot and Tuna

Prep Time: 10 mins |Servings: 4 | Cooking: 15 mins
Ingredients:
- 4 tuna fillets, boneless and skinless
- 1 tbsp olive oil
- 2 shallots, chopped
- 2 tbsps lime juice
- Pinch of pepper
- 1 tsp sweet paprika
- ½ cup low sodium chicken stock

Directions:
1. Take a pan and place it over medium heat, add shallots and Sauté for 3 mins
2. Add fish, cook for 4 mins
3. Add remaining Ingredients:, cook for 3 mins

Nutrition:
Calories 121, Fiber 1g, Carbs 8g, Protein 7g, Fat 8g

Brazilian Shrimp Stew

Prep Time: 20 mins |Servings: 4 | Cooking: 25 mins
Ingredients:
- 4 tbsps lime juice
- 1 and ½ tbsp cumin, ground

- 1 and ½ tbsp paprika
- 2 and ½ tsps garlic, minced
- 1 and ½ tsp pepper
- 2 lbs tilapia fillets, cut into bits
- 1 large onion, chopped
- 3 large bell pepper, cut into strips
- 1 can (14 oz) tomato, drained
- 1 can (14 oz) coconut milk
- Handful of cilantro, chopped

Directions:
1. Take a large sized bowl and add lime juice, cumin, paprika, garlic, pepper and mix well
2. Add tilapia and coat it up
3. Cover and allow it to marinate for 20 mins
4. Set your pot to HIGH and add olive oil
5. Add onions and cook for 3 mins until tender
6. Add pepper strips, tilapia, and tomatoes to a skillet
7. Pour coconut milk and cover, simmer for 20 mins
8. Add cilantro during the final few mins

Nutrition:
Calories 121, Fiber 1g, Carbs 8g, Protein 7g, Fat 8g

Heart-Warming Medi Tilapia

Prep Time: 15 mins |Servings: 4 | Cooking: 15 mins
Ingredients:
1. 3 tbsps sun-dried tomatoes, packed in oil, drained and chopped
2. 1 tbsp capers, drained
3. 2 tilapia fillets
4. 1 tbsp oil from sun-dried tomatoes
5. 2 tbsps kalamata olives, chopped and pitted

Directions:
1. Pre-heat your oven to 372 degrees F
2. Take a small sized bowl and add sun-dried tomatoes, olives, capers and stir well
3. Keep the mixture on the side
4. Take a baking sheet and transfer the tilapia fillets and arrange them side by side
5. Drizzle olive oil all over them
6. Bake in your oven for 10-15 mins
7. After 10 mins, check the fish for a "Flaky" texture
8. Once cooked properly, top the fish with tomato mixture and serve!

Nutrition:
Calories 131, Fiber 1g, Carbs 7g, Protein 8g, Fat 8g

Lemon Cod

Prep Time: 15 mins |Servings: 2 | Cooking: 20 mins
Ingredients:
- 4 tbsps almond butter, divided
- 4 thyme sprigs, fresh and divided
- 4 tsps lemon juice, fresh and divided
- 4 cod fillets, 6 oz each
- Sunflower seeds to taste

Directions:
1. Pre-heat your oven to 400 degrees F.
2. Season cod fillets with sunflower seeds on both side.
3. Take four pieces of foil, each foil should be 3 times bigger than fillets.
4. Divide fillets between the foils and top with almond butter, lemon juice, thyme.
5. Fold to form a pouch and transfer pouches to the baking sheet.
6. Bake for 20 mins.
7. Open and let the steam get out.

Nutrition:
Calories 122, Fiber 1g, Carbs 4g, Protein 7g, Fat 8g

Lemon And Garlic Scallops

Prep Time: 10 mins |Servings: 4 | Cooking: 5 mins
Ingredients:
6. 1 tbsp olive oil
7. 1 and ¼ lbs dried scallops
8. 2 tbsps all-purpose flour
9. ¼ tsp sunflower seeds
10. 4-5 garlic cloves, minced
11. 1 scallion, chopped
12. 1 pinch of ground sage
13. 1 lemon juice
14. 2 tbsps parsley, chopped

Directions:
1. Take a non-stick skillet and place it over medium-high heat
2. Add oil and allow the oil to heat up
3. Take a medium sized bowl and add scallops alongside sunflower seeds and flour
4. Place the scallops in the skillet and add scallions, garlic, and sage
5. Saute for 3-4 mins until they show an opaque texture
6. Stir in lemon juice and parsley
7. Remove heat and serve hot!

Nutrition:
Calories 121, Fiber 1g, Carbs 8g, Protein 7g, Fat 8g

Cajun Snow Crab

Prep Time: 10 mins |Servings: 4 | Cooking: 10 mins
Ingredients:
- 1 lemon ,fresh and quartered
- 3 tbsps Cajun seasoning
- 2 bay leaves
- 4 snow crab legs, precooked and defrosted
- Golden ghee

Directions::
1. Take a large pot and fill it about halfway with sunflower seedsed water
2. Bring the water to a boil
3. Squeeze lemon juice into pot and toss in remaining lemon quarters
4. Add bay leaves and Cajun seasoning
5. Season for 1 minute
6. Add crab legs and boil for 8 mins (make sure to keep them submerged the whole time)
7. Melt ghee in microwave and use as dipping sauce, enjoy!

Nutrition:
Calories 142, Fiber 4g, Carbs 10g, Protein 9g, Fat 8g

Calamari Citrus

Prep Time: 10 mins |Servings: 4 | Cooking: 5 mins
Ingredients:
- 1 lime, sliced
- 1 lemon, sliced
- 2 lbs calamari tubes and tentacles, sliced
- Pepper to taste
- ¼ cup olive oil
- 2 garlic cloves, minced
- 3 tbsps lemon juice
- 1 orange, peeled and cut into segments
- 2 tbsps cilantro, chopped

Directions:
1. Take a bowl and add calamari, pepper, lime slices, lemon slices, orange slices, garlic , oil, cilantro, lemon juice and toss well
2. Take a pan and place it over medium-high heat
3. Add calamari mix and cook for 5 mins
4. Divide into bowls and serve

Nutrition:
Calories 121, Fiber 1g, Carbs 8g, Protein 7g, Fat 8g

Lasagna

Prep Time: 15 mins |Servings: 8 | Cooking: 25 mins
Ingredients:
- 3 cup shredded mozzare lla cheese
- 1 cup cottage cheese
- ¾ lb. lasagna noodles
- 3 ½ cup Water
- 8 oz unsalted tomato sauce
- 6 oz unsalted tomato paste
- ¾ tsp garlic powder
- ¾ tsp Oregano
- 1½ tsp dried basil
- 1 sliced onion
- 1 lb. extra-lean ground beef

Directions:
1. Lightly coat a 10-14 cooking pan with cooking spray. Also, preheat the oven to 325 F
2. Now, for the sauce, put a large saucepan on the stove and place the ground beef and onion in it and cook until the meet is golden brown
3. Once brown, drain the pan and then add the water, tomato sauce, tomato paste, garlic powder, oregano, and basil and stir until it comes to a boil. Reduce the heat and simmer for 10 mins
4. In the cooking pan, place a half cup of the mixture on the bottom of the pan.
5. On top of the mixture, place a layer of the uncooked lasagna noodles and then add another layer of the mixture, as well as a cup of mozzarella cheese and a third of a cup of cottage cheese.
6. Do the same for the remaining mixture.
7. Place aluminum foil on top of the lasagna and put it into the oven.
8. Bake the lasagna for an hour and fifteen mins or until the cheese is brown
9. Let the lasagna cool before serving.

Nutrition:
Calories 425, Carbs 42g, Fat 13g, Protein 33g

Shrimp And Avocado Dish

Prep Time: 10 mins |Servings: 8
Ingredients:
- 2 green onions, chopped
- 2 avocados, pitted, peeled and cut into chunks
- 2 tbsps cilantro, chopped
- 1 cup shrimp, cooked, peeled and deveined
- Pinch of pepper

Directions:

1. Take a bowl and add cooked shrimp, avocado, green onions, cilantro, pepper
2. Toss well and serve

Nutrition:
Calories 121, Fiber 1g, Carbs 8g, Protein 7g, Fat 8g

Fresh Calamari

Prep Time: 10 mins +1 hour marinating | Servings: 4 | Cooking: 8 mins
Ingredients:
- 2 tbsp extra virgin olive oil
- 1 tsp chili powder
- ½ tsp ground cumin
- Zest of 1 lime
- Juice of 1 lime
- Dash of sea sunflower seeds
- 1 and ½ lbs squid, cleaned and split open, with tentacles cut into ½ inch rounds
- 2 tbsps cilantro, chopped
- 2 tbsps red bell pepper, minced

Directions:
1. Take a medium bowl and stir in olive oil, chili powder, cumin, lime zest, sea sunflower seeds, lime juice and pepper
2. Add squid and let it marinade and stir to coat, coat and let it refrigerate for 1 hour
3. Pre-heat your oven to broil
4. Arrange squid on a baking sheet, broil for 8 mins turn once until tender
5. Garnish the broiled calamari with cilantro and red bell pepper

Nutrition:
Calories 121, Fiber 1g, Carbs 8g, Protein 7g, Fat 8g

Deep Fried Prawn And Rice Croquettes

Prep Time: 25 mins | Servings: 4 | Cooking: 13 mins
Ingredients:
- 2 tbsps almond butter
- ½ onion, chopped
- 4 oz shrimp, peeled and chopped
- 2 tbsps all-purpose flour
- 1 tbsp white wine
- ½ cup almond milk
- 2 tbsps almond milk
- 2 cups cooked rice
- 1 tbsp parmesan, grated
- 1 tsp fresh dill, chopped
- 1 tsp sunflower seeds
- Ground pepper as needed
- Vegetable oil for frying
- 3 tbsps all-purpose flour
- 1 whole egg
- ½ cup breadcrumbs

Directions:
1. Take a large skillet and place it over medium heat, add almond butter and let it melt
2. Add onion, cook and stir for 5 mins
3. Add shrimp and cook for 1-2 mins
4. Stir in 2 tbsps flour, white wine, pour in almond milk gradually and cook for 3-5 mins until the sauce thickens
5. Remove white sauce from heat and stir in rice, mix evenly
6. Add parmesan, cheese, dill, sunflower seeds, pepper and let it cool for 15 mins
7. Heat oil in large saucepan and bring it to 350 degrees F
8. Take a bowl and whisk in egg, spread bread crumbs on a plate
9. Form rice mixture into 8 balls and roll 1 ball in flour, dip in egg and coat with crumbs, repeat with all balls
10. Deep fry balls for 3 mins

Nutrition:
Calories 180, Fiber 1g, Carbs 10g, Protein 12g, Fat 10g

Thai Pumpkin Seafood Stew

Prep Time: 5 mins | Servings: 4 | Cooking: 35 mins
Ingredients:
- 1 and ½ tbsps fresh galangal, chopped
- 1 tsp lime zest
- 1 small kabocha squash
- 32 medium sized mussels, fresh
- 1 lb shrimp
- 16 thai leaves
- 1 can coconut milk
- 1 tbsp lemongrass, minced
- 4 garlic cloves, roughly chopped
- 32 medium clams, fresh
- 1 and ½ lbs fresh salmon
- 2 tbsp coconut oil
- Pepper to taste

Directions:
1. Add coconut milk, lemongrass, galangal, garlic, lime leaves in a small-sized saucepan, bring to a boil.
2. Let it simmer for 25 mins.
3. Strain mixture through fine sieve into the large soup pot and bring to a simmer.

4. Add oil to a pan and heat up, add Kabocha squash.
5. Saute for 5 mins.
6. Add mix to coconut mix.
7. Heat oil in a pan and add fish shrimp, season with salt and pepper, cook for 4 mins.
8. Add mixture to coconut milk mix alongside clams and mussels.
9. Simmer for 8 mins, garnish with basil and enjoy!

Nutrition:
Calories 121, Fiber 1g, Carbs 8g, Protein 7g, Fat 8g

Blackened Tilapia

Prep Time: 9 mins |Servings: 2 |Cooking: 9 mins
Ingredients:
- 1 cup of cauliflower, chopped
- 1 tsp of red pepper flakes
- 1 tbsp of Italian seasoning
- 1 tbsp of garlic, minced
- 6 ounce of tilapia
- 1 cup of English cucumber, chopped with peel
- 2 tbsp of olive oil
- 1 sprig dill, chopped
- 1 tsp of stevia
- 3 tbsp of lime juice
- 2 tbsp of Cajun blackened seasoning

Directions:
1. Take a bowl and add the seasoning Ingredients: (except Cajun).
2. Add a tbsp of oil and whip.
3. Pour dressing over cauliflower and cucumber.
4. Brush the fish with olive oil on both sides.
5. Take a skillet and grease it well with 1 tbsp of olive oil.
6. Press Cajun seasoning on both sides of fish.
7. Cook fish for 3 mins per side

Nutrition:
Calories 121, Fiber 1g, Carbs 8g, Protein 7g, Fat 8g

Shrimp Pasta Primavera

Prep Time: 15 mins |Servings: 6 | Cooking: 15 mins
Ingredients:
- 1¼ cup sliced Asparagus
- 12 oz whole wheat Penne
- 1 cup Green peas
- 2 tsp Olive oil
- 1 tbsp minced Garlic
- 1/8 tsp crushed Red pepper
- 1 lb. Shrimp
- ½ cup sliced green onion
- 2 tsp Lemon juice
- 1 tbsp chopped Parsley
- 1/3 cup grated Parmesan cheese

Directions:
1. Set a large saucepan over high heat, and allow to come to a boil.
2. Once boiling, add asparagus then cook until fork tender (about 4 mins) Carefully remove the asparagus from the hot water using a slotted spoon then add your pasta to the same pot.
3. Cook until done based on the instructions on the package. When the pasta was 2 mins out add peas
4. When fully cooked, drain, and add to a large bowl with the asparagus
5. Set a skillet with olive oil over medium heat, then add red pepper, and garlic, then cook, while stirring for about a minute
6. Add shrimp and cook until it becomes opaque (about 4 mins), stirring
7. Add your remaining Ingredients: to the skillet on top of shrimp and toss to coat.

Nutrition:
Calories 440, Protein 31g ,Carbs 31g, Fat 18g

Brown Stewed Fish

Prep Time: 10 mins |Servings: 4| Cooking: 10 mins
Ingredients:
- 2 lbs fish
- 1 diced large onion
- 2 small tomatoes
- 3 stalks scallion
- 1 cup Vegetables
- ¾ cup fish stock
- 2 slices hot pepper
- ¼ cup oil

Directions:
1. Scale, clean and prepare fish for frying
2. Allow oil to cool, strain nearly all of it from frying pan, put aside Sauté seasonings and vegetables in frying pan
3. Add water or stock to frying pan with sautéed vegetables and simmer until all flavors blend

4. Add fish, cover and cook for five mins.
Nutrition:
Calories 352, Protein 36g, Carbs 14g, Fat 17g

Grilled Cod

Prep Time: 15 mins |Servings: 2| Cooking: 15 mins
Ingredients:
- 2 cod fillets
- ½ tsp garlic paste
- 3 tbsp lemon juice
- ½ tsp black pepper
- ½ tsp oregano
- 1 tsp fish sauce
- ¼ tsp turmeric powder
- 2 tbsp olive oil

Directions:
1. Sprinkle turmeric powder on fish and rub all over
2. Leave it for 10-15 mins then wash out fish well
3. Take a bowl add vinegar, lemon juice, pepper, salt, fish sauce and oregano, toss to combine
4. Spread this mixture on fish fillets and rub on it with hands

Nutrition:
Calories 138, Protein 271g, Carbs 46g, Fat 7g

Baked Salmon

Prep Time: 10 mins |Servings: 6 | Cooking: 10 mins
Ingredients:
- 1½ lbs salmon fillets
- ½ sliced onion
- 1 cup chopped grape tomatoes
- 1 tsp dried basil
- 1 tbsp chopped chives
- 1 tsp dried rosemary
- 1 tsp garlic powder
- 1/3 cup soy sauce
- 1/3 cup brown sugar
- 1/3 cup Water
- ¼ cup vegetable oil

Directions:
1. Preheat oven to 350 F
2. Season salmon fillets with onion, basil, rosemary, garlic powder, and salt
3. Combine brown sugar, soy sauce, water, and vegetable oil until sugar is dissolved
4. Place fillets in a Ziploc bag or airtight container with soy sauce mixture and place in refrigerator for 2 hours to marinate
5. Preheat grill at medium heat. Lightly oil grill grate. Place fillets on the preheated grill and cook for 6 to 8 mins per side.

Nutrition:
Calories: 274, Protein 24g, Carbs 1g, Fat 19g

Steamed Mussels

Prep Time: 5 mins |Servings: 4 | Cooking: 10 mins
Ingredients:
- 6 oz chorizo
- 1 cup white wine
- 2 tbsp olive oil
- 1 sliced onion
- 4 lbs Mussels
- 3 sprigs thyme
- 1 tsp smoked paprika
- 15 oz diced tomatoes
- 4 sliced garlic cloves

Directions:
1. over medium heat, warm olive oil
2. Add the onion, season to taste and cook until softened for 3-4 mins
3. Add garlic and cook for an additional 1 minute
4. Stir in the smoked paprika and cook for 30 seconds or until fragrant
5. Add the chorizo, wine, and tomatoes
6. Add the fresh thyme and bring to a simmer
7. Stir in the mussels and coat with sauce
8. Cover and cook until mussels are opened
9. Discard all unopened ones
10. Serve mussels while still hot with toasted bread slices.

Nutrition:
Calories 256, Protein 34g, Carbs 198g, Fat 66g

Creamy Seafood and Veggies Soup

Prep Time: 10 mins |Servings: 12 | Cooking: 3 hours
Ingredients:
- 10 oz coconut cream
- 2 cups low-sodium veggie stock
- 2 cups no-salt-added tomato sauce
- 12 oz canned crab meat, no-salt-added and drained
- 1 and ½ cups water
- 1 and ½ lbs jumbo shrimp, peeled and deveined
- 1 yellow onion, chopped
- 1 cup carrots, chopped
- 4 tilapia fillets, skinless, boneless and cubed

- 2 celery stalks, chopped
- 3 kale stalks, chopped
- 1 bay leaf
- 2 garlic cloves, minced
- ½ tsp cloves, ground
- 1 tsp rosemary, dried
- 1 tsp thyme, dried

Directions:
1. In your slow cooker, mix coconut cream with stock, tomato sauce and water and stir.
2. Add shrimp, fish, onion, carrots, celery, kale, garlic, bay leaf, cloves, thyme and rosemary, cover, cook on Low for 3 hours, stir, ladle into bowls and serve.

Nutrition:
Calories 220, Fat 3g, Fiber 3g, Carbs 8g, Protein 7g

Seafood Gumbo

Prep Time: 10 mins |Servings: 4 | Cooking: 6 hours
Ingredients:
- 1 lb shrimp, peeled and deveined
- 2 lbs mussels, cleaned and debearded
- 28 oz canned clams, no-salt-added and drained
- 1 yellow onion, chopped
- 10 oz canned tomato paste, no-salt-added

Directions:
In your slow cooker, mix shrimp with mussels, clams, onion and tomato paste, stir, cover, cook on Low for 6 hours, divide into bowls and serve.
Nutrition:
Calories 200, Fat 3g, Fiber 2g, Carbs 7g, Protein 5g

Lemon and Spinach Trout

Prep Time: 10 mins |Servings: 4 | Cooking: 2 hours
Ingredients:
- 2 lemons, sliced
- ¼ cup low sodium chicken stock
- 2 tbsp dill, chopped
- 12 oz spinach
- 4 medium trout

Directions:
1. Put the stock in your slow cooker and add the fish inside
2. Season with black pepper to the taste, top with lemon slices, dill and spinach, cover and cook on High for 2 hours.
3. Divide fish, lemon and spinach between plates and serve

Nutrition:
Calories 240, Fat 5g, Fiber 4g, Carbs 9g, Protein 14g

Easy Roast Salmon with Roasted Asparagus

Prep Time: 5 mins |Servings: 4| Cooking: 15 mins
Ingredients:
- 2 (5-ounce) salmon fillets with skin
- 2 tsps olive oil, plus extra for drizzling
- 1 bunch asparagus, trimmed
- 1 tsp dried chives
- 1 tsp dried tarragon
- Fresh lemon wedges for serving

Directions:
1. Preheat the oven to 425°F.
2. Rub salmon completely with 1 tsp of olive oil per fillet. Season with salt and pepper.
3. Place asparagus spears on a foil lined baking sheet and lay the salmon fillets skin-side down on top. Put pan in upper-third of oven and roast until fish is just cooked through (about 12 mins). Roasting time will vary depending on the thickness of your salmon. Salmon should flake easily with a fork when it's ready and an instant-read thermometer should register 145°F.
4. When cooked, remove from the oven, cut fillets in half crosswise, then lift flesh from skin with a metal spatula and transfer to a plate.
5. Discard the skin. Drizzle salmon with oil, sprinkle with herbs, and serve with lemon wedges and roasted asparagus spears.

Nutrition:
Calories 220, Fat 3g, Fiber 3g, Carbs 8g, Protein 7g

Shrimp Pasta Primavera

Prep Time: 5 mins |Servings: 2| Cooking: 15 mins
Ingredients:
- 2 tbsp olive oil
- 1 tbsp garlic, minced
- 2 cups assorted fresh vegetables, chopped coarsely (zucchini, broccoli, asparagus or whatever you prefer)
- 4 oz frozen shrimp, cooked, peeled, and deveined
- Freshly ground black pepper
- Juice of ½ lemon
- 4 oz whole-wheat angel-hair pasta, cooked per package instructions
- 2 tbsp grated Parmesan cheese

Directions:

1. Heat the oil in a large nonstick skillet over medium heat. Add the garlic and sauté for 1 minute.
2. Add vegetables and sauté until crisp tender (about 3 to 4 mins)
3. Add the shrimp and sauté until just heated through. Season lightly with salt and pepper and squeeze lemon juice over the shrimp and vegetables. Continue to cook for about 2 mins until the juices have been reduced by about half. Remove from heat
4. Toss shrimp and vegetables with pasta. Serve topped with Parmesan cheese

Nutrition:
Calories 439, Fat 17g, Carbs 50g, Fiber 8g, Protein 23g

Cilantro-Lime Tilapia Tacos

Prep Time: 10 mins |Servings: 4| Cooking: 10 mins
Ingredients:
- 1 tsp olive oil
- 1 lb tilapia fillets, rinsed and dried
- 3 cups diced tomatoes
- ½ cup fresh cilantro, chopped, plus additional for serving
- 3 tbsp freshly squeezed lime juice
- Freshly ground black pepper
- 8 (5-inch) white-corn tortillas
- 1 avocado sliced into 8 wedges
- Optional: lime wedges and fat-free sour cream for serving

Directions:
1. Heat the oil in a large skillet, add the tilapia and Cook until the flesh starts to flake (about 5 mins per side).
2. Add the tomatoes, cilantro, and lime juice. Sauté over medium-high heat for about 5 mins, breaking up the fish and mixing well
3. Heat tortillas in a skillet for a few mins on each side to warm.
4. Serve ¼ cup of fish mixture on each warmed tortilla with two slices of avocado.
5. Serve immediately with optional toppings.

Nutrition:
Calories 286, Fat 12g, Carbs 22g, Fiber 4g, Protein 28g

Garlic and Butter Sword Fish

Prep time: 10 mins | Servings: 4| Cooking:2 hours and 30 mins
Ingredients:
- ½ cup melted butter
- 6 chopped garlic cloves
- 1 tbsp black pepper
- 5 sword fish fillets

Directions:
1. Take a mixing bowl and toss in all of your garlic, black pepper alongside the melted butter
2. Take a parchment paper and place your fish fillet in that paper
3. Cover it up with the butter mixture and wrap up the fish
4. Repeat the process until all of your fish are wrapped up
5. Let it cook for 2 and a half hours and release the pressure naturally
6. Serve

Nutrition:
Calories 379, Fat 26 g, Carbs 1 g, Protein 34 g

Pressure Cooker Crab Legs

Prep time: 5 mins | Servings: 4 | Cooking: 17 mins
Ingredients:
- 1 sliced lemon piece
- 1 cup water
- 1 cup melted butter
- 2 lbs. crab legs
- 1 cup white wine

Directions:
1. Add water to your Instant Pot alongside wine
2. Add crab legs
3. Lock up the lid and cook on HIGH pressure for 7 mins
4. Release the pressure naturally over 10 mins
5. Open the lid and add melted butter and a dash of lemon
6. Enjoy

Nutrition:
Calories 191, Fat 1 g, Carbs 0 g, Protein 41 g

Delicious Tuna Sandwich

Prep time: 15 mins | Servings: 2 | Cooking: 17 mins
Ingredients:
- 30 g olive oil
- 1 peeled and diced medium cucumber
- 2 ½ g pepper
- 4 whole wheat bread slices
- 85 g diced onion
- 1 can flavored tuna

- 85 g shredded spinach

Directions:
- Grab your blender and add the spinach, tuna, onion, oil, salt and pepper in, and pulse for about 10 to 20 seconds.
- In the meantime, toast your bread and add your diced cucumber to a bowl, which you can pour your tuna mixture in. Carefully mix and add the mixture to the bread once toasted.
- Slice in half and serve, while storing the remaining mixture in the fridge.

Nutrition:
Calories 302, Fat 5.8 g, Carbs 36.62 g, Protein 28 g

Easy Mussels

Prep time: 10 mins | Servings: 4 | Cooking: 17 mins
Ingredients:
- 2 lbs. cleaned mussels
- 4 minced garlic cloves
- 2 chopped shallots
- Lemon and parsley
- 2 tbsp Butter
- ½ cup broth
- ½ cup white wine

Directions:
1. Clean the mussels and remove the beard
2. Discard any mussels that do not close when tapped against a hard surface
3. Set your pot to Sauté mode and add chopped onion and butter
4. Stir and sauté onions
5. Add garlic and cook for 1 minute
6. Add broth and wine
7. Lock up the lid and cook for 5 mins on HIGH pressure
8. Release the pressure naturally over 10 mins
9. Serve with a sprinkle of parsley and enjoy!

Nutrition:
Calories 286, Fat 14 g, Carbs 12 g, Protein 28 g

Parmesan-Crusted Fish

Prep time: 5 mins | Servings: 4 | Cooking: 7-8 mins
Ingredients:
- ¾ tsp. ground ginger
- 1/3 cup panko bread crumbs
- Mixed fresh salad greens
- ¼ cup finely shredded parmesan cheese
- 1 tbsp butter
- 4 skinless cod fillets
- 3 cup julienned carrots

Directions:
1. Preheat oven to 450 °F. Lightly coat a baking sheet with nonstick cooking spray.
2. Rinse and pat dry fish; place on baking sheet. Season with salt and pepper.
3. In small bowl stir together crumbs and cheese; sprinkle on fish.
4. Bake, uncovered, 4 to 6 mins for each 1/2-inch thickness of fish, until crumbs are golden and fish flakes easily when tested with a fork.
5. Meanwhile, in a large skillet bring 1/2 cup water to boiling; add carrots. Reduce heat.
6. Cook, covered, for 5 mins. Uncover; cook 2 mins more. Add butter and ginger; toss.
7. Serve fish and carrots with greens.

Nutrition:
Calories 216.4, Fat 10.1 g, Carbs 1.3 g, Protein 29.0 g

Salmon and Horseradish Sauce

Prep time: 10 mins | Servings: 4 | Cooking: 7 mins
Ingredients:
- ½ cup coconut cream
- 1 tbsp Prepared horseradish
- 4 de-boned medium salmon fillets
- 2 tbsp Chopped dill
- 1 ½ tbsp Organic olive oil
- ¼ tsp. black pepper

Directions:
1. Heat up a pan while using the oil over medium-high heat, add salmon fillets, season with black pepper and cook for 5 mins one each side.
2. In a bowl, combine the cream with the dill and horseradish and whisk well.
3. Divide the salmon between plates and serve with all the horseradish cream for the top.

Nutrition:
Calories 275, Fat 12 g, Carbs 14 g, Protein 27 g

Crunchy Topped Fish with Potato Sticks

Prep time: 5 mins | Servings: 4 | Cooking: 7 mins
Ingredients:
- 2 tbsp Melted margarine
- Nonstick spray coating
- ¾ cup crushed herb-seasoned stuffing mix
- 12 oz. sliced medium baking potatoes

- 2 tsps. Melted cooking oil
- 16 oz. fresh catfish fillets
- Garlic salt

Directions:
1. Rinse fish and pat dry with paper towels; set aside.
2. Line a large baking sheet with foil. Spray foil with nonstick spray coating.
3. Arrange potato sticks in a single layer over half of the baking sheet. Brush potatoes with oil or the 2 tsps melted margarine. Sprinkle with garlic salt.
4. Bake in a 450 degree F oven for 10 mins.
5. Meanwhile, stir together stuffing mix and the 2 tbsps melted margarine.
6. Place fish on baking sheet next to potatoes. Sprinkle stuffing mix over fish. Return pan to oven and bake 9 to 12 mins more or until fish flakes easily when tested with a fork and potatoes are tender.

Nutrition:
Calories 94, Fat 6.19g, Carbs 9.6 g, Protein 1.2 g

Halibut and Cherry Tomatoes

Prep time: 10 mins | Servings: 4 | Cooking: 8 mins
Ingredients:
- 3 minced garlic cloves
- 4 skinless halibut fillets
- 2 cup cherry tomatoes
- 2 tbsp Chopped basil
- ¼ tsp. black pepper
- 1 ½ tbsp Organic olive oil
- 2 tbsp Balsamic vinegar

Directions:
1. Heat up a pan with 1 tbsp organic essential olive oil, add halibut fillets, cook them for 5 mins on both sides and divide between plates.
2. Heat up another pan because of the rest within the oil over medium-high heat, add the tomatoes, garlic, vinegar and basil, toss, cook for 3 mins, add next on the fish and serve.

Nutrition:
Calories 221, Fat 4 g, Carbs 6 g, Protein 21 g

Salmon and Cauliflower Mix

Prep time: 10 mins | Servings: 4 | Cooking: 20 mins
Ingredients:
- 4 boneless salmon fillets
- 2 tbsp Coconut aminos
- 1 sliced big red onion
- ¼ cup coconut sugar
- 1 head separated cauliflower florets
- 2 tbsp Olive oil

Directions:
1. In a smaller bowl, mix sugar with coconut aminos and whisk.
2. Heat up a pan with half the oil over medium-high heat, add cauliflower and onion, stir and cook for 10 mins.
3. Put the salmon inside baking dish, drizzle the remainder inside oil, add coconut aminos, toss somewhat, season with black pepper, introduce within the oven and bake at 400 ºF for 10 mins.
4. Divide the salmon along using the cauliflower mix between plates and serve.

Nutrition:
Calories 220, Fat 3 g, Carbs 12 g, Protein 9 g

Salmon in Dill Sauce

Prep time: 10 mins | Servings: 6 | Cooking: 1 hours and 30 mins
Ingredients:
- 6 salmon fillets
- 1 cup low-fat, low-sodium chicken broth
- 1 tsp. cayenne pepper
- 2 tbsp Fresh lemon juice
- 2 cup water
- ¼ cup chopped fresh dill

Directions:
1. In a slow cooker, mix together water, broth, lemon juice, lemon juice and dill.
2. Arrange salmon fillets on top, skin side down.
3. Sprinkle with cayenne pepper.
4. Set the slow cooker on low.
5. Cover and cook for about 1-2 hours.

Nutrition:
Calories 360, Fat 8 g, Carbs 44 g, Protein 28 g

Salmon and Potatoes Mix

Prep time: 10 mins | Servings: 4 | Cooking: 3-4 mins
Ingredients:
- 4 oz. chopped smoked salmon
- 1 tbsp essential olive oil
- Black pepper
- 1 tbsp chopped chives
- ¼ cup coconut cream
- 1 ½ lbs. chopped potatoes
- 2 tsps. Prepared horseradish

Directions:
1. Heat up a pan using the oil over medium heat, add potatoes and cook for 10 mins.
2. Add salmon, chives, horseradish, cream and black pepper, toss, cook for 1 minute more, divide between plates and serve.

Nutrition:
Calories 233, Fat 6 g, Carbs 9 g, Protein 11 g

Roasted Hake

Prep time: 20 mins | Servings: 4 | Cooking: 3-4 mins
Ingredients:
- ½ cup tomato sauce
- 2 sliced tomatoes
- Fresh parsley
- ½ cup grated cheese
- 4 lbs. deboned hake fish

Directions:
1. Season the fish with salt. Pan-fry the fish until half-done.
2. Shape foil into containers according to the number of fish pieces.
3. Pour tomato sauce into each foil dish; arrange the fish, then the tomato slices, again add tomato sauce and sprinkle with grated cheese.
4. Bake in the oven at 400 F until there is a golden crust.
5. Serve with fresh parsley.

Nutrition:
Calories 421, Fat 48.7 g, Carbs 2.4 g, Protein 17.4 g

Sautéed Fish Fillets

Prep time: 5 mins | Servings: 4 | Cooking: 3-4 mins
Ingredients:
- 1 tbsp extra-virgin olive oil
- 1 lb. sliced haddock
- 1/3 cup all-purpose flour
- Freshly ground pepper

Directions:
1. Combine flour, salt and pepper in a shallow dish; thoroughly dredge fillets
2. Heat oil in a large nonstick skillet over medium-high heat.
3. Add the fish, working in batches if necessary, and cook until lightly browned and just opaque in the center, 3 to 4 mins per side.
4. Serve immediately.

Nutrition:
Calories 111, Fat 11 g, Carbs 15 g, Protein 13 g

Coconut Cream Shrimp

Prep time: 10 mins | Servings: 2
Ingredients:
- 1 tbsp coconut cream
- ½ tsp. lime juice
- ¼ tsp. black pepper
- 1 tbsp parsley
- 1 lb. cooked, peeled and deveined shrimp
- ¼ tsp. chopped jalapeno

Directions:
In a bowl, mix the shrimp while using cream, jalapeno, lime juice, parsley and black pepper, toss, divide into small bowls and serve.

Nutrition:
Calories 183, Fat 5 g, Carbs 12 g, Protein 8 g

Cinnamon Salmon

Prep time: 10 mins | Servings: 2
Ingredients:
- 1 tbsp organic essential olive oil
- Black pepper
- 1 tbsp cinnamon powder
- 2 de-boned salmon fillets

Directions:
1. Heat up a pan with the oil over medium heat, add pepper and cinnamon and stir well.
2. Add salmon, skin side up, cook for 5 mins on both sides, divide between plates and serve by using a side salad.

Nutrition:
Calories 220, Fat 8 g, Carbs 11 g, Protein 8 g

Scallops and Strawberry Mix

Prep time: 20 mins | Servings: 2
Ingredients:
- 1 tbsp lime juice
- ½ cup Pico de gallo
- Black pepper
- 4 oz. scallops
- ½ cup chopped strawberries

Directions:
1. Heat up a pan over medium heat, add scallops, cook for 3 mins on both sides and take away heat,
2. In a bowl, mix strawberries with lime juice, Pico de gallo, scallops and pepper, toss and serve cold.

Nutrition:
Calories 169, Fat 2 g, Carbs 8 g, Protein 13 g

Cod Peas Relish

Prep time: 18-20 mins | Servings: 4-5 | Cooking: 5 mins

Ingredients:
- 1 cup peas
- 2 tbsp Capers
- 4 de-boned medium cod fillets
- 3 tbsp Olive oil
- ¼ tsp. black pepper
- 2 tbsp Lime juice
- 2 tbsp Chopped shallots
- 1 ½ tbsp Chopped oregano

Directions:
1. Heat up 1 tbsp olive oil in a saucepan over medium flame
2. Add the fillets, cook for 5 mins on each side; set aside.
3. In a bowl of large size, thoroughly mix the oregano, shallots, lime juice, peas, capers, black pepper, and 2 tbsp olive oil.
4. Toss and serve with the cooked fish.

Nutrition:
Calories 224, Fat 11 g, Carbs 7 g, Protein 24 g

Baked Haddock

Prep time: 10 mins | Servings: 4 | Cooking: 35 mins
Ingredients:
- 1 tsp. chopped dill
- 3 tsps. Water
- Cooking spray
- 1 lb. chopped haddock
- 2 tbsp Fresh lemon juice
- 2 tbsp Avocado mayonnaise

Directions:
1. Spray a baking dish with a few oil, add fish, water, freshly squeezed lemon juice, salt, black pepper, mayo and dill, toss, introduce inside the oven and bake at 350 °F for the half-hour.
2. Divide between plates and serve.

Nutrition:
Calories 264, Fat 4 g, Carbs 7 g, Protein 12 g

Hot Tuna Steak

Prep time: 10 mins | Servings: 6
Ingredients:
- 2 tbsp Fresh lemon juice
- Roasted orange garlic mayonnaise
- ¼ cup whole black peppercorns
- 6 sliced tuna steaks
- 2 tbsp Extra-virgin olive oil

Directions:
1. Place the tuna in a bowl to fit. Add the oil, lemon juice, salt and pepper. Turn the tuna to coat well in the marinade. Let rest 15 to 20 mins, turning once.
2. Place the peppercorns in a double thickness of plastic bags. Tap the peppercorns with a heavy saucepan or small mallet to crush them coarsely. Place on a large plate.
3. When ready to cook the tuna, dip the edges into the crushed peppercorns. Heat a nonstick skillet over medium heat. Sear the tuna steaks, in batches if necessary, for 4 mins per side for medium-rare fish, adding 2 to 3 tbsps of the marinade to the skillet if necessary to prevent sticking.
4. Serve dolloped with roasted orange garlic mayonnaise

Nutrition:
Calories 124, Fat 0.4 g, Carbs 0.6 g, Protein 28 g

Marinated Fish Steaks

Prep time: 10 mins | Servings: 4 | Cooking: 12 mins
Ingredients:
- 4 lime wedges
- 2 tbsp Lime juice
- 2 minced garlic cloves
- 2 tsps. Olive oil
- 1 tbsp snipped fresh oregano
- 1 lb. fresh swordfish
- 1 tsp. lemon-pepper seasoning

Directions:
1. Rinse fish steaks; pat dry with paper towels. Cut into four serving size pieces, if necessary.
2. In a shallow dish combine lime juice, oregano, oil, lemon-pepper seasoning, and garlicup Add fish; turn to coat with marinade.
3. Cover and marinate in refrigerator for 30 mins to 1-1/2 hours, turning steaks occasionally. Drain fish, reserving marinade.
4. Place fish on the greased unheated rack of a broiler pan.
5. Broil 4 inches from the heat for 8 to 12 mins or until fish begins to flake when tested with a fork, turning once and brushing with reserved marinade halfway through cooking. Discard any remaining marinade.

6. Before serving, squeeze the juice from one lime wedge over each steak.

Nutrition:
Calories 240, Fat 6 g, Carbs 19 g, Protein 12 g

Baked Tomato Hake

Prep time: 35-40 mins | Servings: 4-5
Ingredients:
- ½ cup tomato sauce
- 1 tbsp olive oil
- Parsley
- 2 sliced tomatoes
- ½ cup grated cheese
- 4 lbs. de-boned and sliced hake fish

Directions:
1. Preheat the oven to 400 ºF.
2. Season the fish with salt.
3. In a skillet or saucepan; stir-fry the fish in the olive oil until half-done.
4. Take four foil papers to cover the fish.
5. Shape the foil to resemble containers; add the tomato sauce into each foil container.
6. Add the fish, tomato slices, and top with grated cheese.
7. Bake until you get a golden crust, for approximately 20-25 mins.
8. Open the packs and top with parsley.

Nutrition:
Calories 265, Fat 15 g, Carbs 18 g, Protein 22 g

Cheesy Tuna Pasta

Prep time: 5-8 min | Servings: 3-4
Ingredients:
- 2 cup arugula
- ¼ cup chopped green onions
- 1 tbs. red vinegar
- 5 oz. drained canned tuna
- ¼ tsp. black pepper
- 2 oz. cooked whole-wheat pasta
- 1 tbsp olive oil
- 1 tbsp grated low-fat parmesan

Directions:
1. Cook the pasta in unsalted water until ready. Drain and set aside.
2. In a bowl of large size, thoroughly mix the tuna, green onions, vinegar, oil, arugula, pasta, and black pepper.
3. Toss well and top with the cheese.

Nutrition:
Calories 566.3, Fat 42.4 g, Carbs 18.6 g, Protein 29.8 g

Herb-Coated Baked Cod with Honey

Prep time: 5 mins | Servings: 2 | Cooking: 10 mins
Ingredients:
- 6 tbsp Herb-flavored stuffing
- 8 oz. cod fillets
- 2 tbsp Honey

Directions:
1. Preheat your oven to 375 ºF.
2. Spray a baking pan lightly with cooking spray.
3. Put the herb-flavored stuffing in a bag and close. Squash the stuffing until it gets crumbly.
4. Coat the fishes with honey and get rid of the remaining honey. Add one fillet to the bag of stuffing and shake gently to coat the fish completely.
5. Transfer the cod to the baking pan and repeat the process for the second fish.
6. Wrap the fillets with foil and bake until firm and opaque all through when you test with the tip of a knife blade, about ten mins.
7. Serve hot.

Nutrition:
Calories 185, Fat 1 g, Carbs 23 g, Protein 21 g

Tender Salmon in Mustard Sauce

Prep time: 10 mins | Servings: 2 | Cooking: 20 mins
Ingredients:
- 5 tbsp Minced dill
- 2/3 cup sour cream
- 2 tbsp Dijon mustard
- 1 tsp. garlic powder
- 5 oz. salmon fillets
- 2-3 tbsp Lemon juice

Directions:
1. Mix sour cream, mustard, lemon juice and dill.
2. Season the fillets with pepper and garlic powder.
3. Arrange the salmon on a baking sheet skin side down and cover with the prepared mustard sauce.
4. Bake for 20 mins at 390°F.

Nutrition:
Calories 318, Fat 12 g, Carbs 8 g, Protein 40.9 g

Broiled White Sea Bass

Prep time: 5 mins | Servings: 2 | Cooking: 10 mins
Ingredients:
- 1 tsp. minced garlic

- 1 tbsp lemon juice
- 8 oz. white sea bass fillets
- ¼ tsp. salt-free herbed seasoning blend

Directions:
1. Preheat the broiler and position the rack 4 inches from the heat source.
2. Lightly spray a baking pan with cooking spray. Place the fillets in the pan. Sprinkle the lemon juice, garlic, herbed seasoning and pepper over the fillets.
3. Broil until the fish is opaque throughout when tested with a tip of a knife, about 8 to 10 mins.

Nutrition:
Calories 114, Fat 2 g, Carbs 2 g, Protein 21 g

Tuna and Shallots

Prep time: 10 mins | Servings: 4 | Cooking: 10 mins
Ingredients:
- ½ cup low-sodium chicken stock
- 1 tbsp olive oil
- 4 boneless and skinless tuna fillets
- 2 chopped shallots
- 1 tsp. sweet paprika
- 2 tbsp lime juice

Directions:
1. Heat up a pan with the oil over medium-high heat, add shallots and sauté for 3 mins.
2. Add the fish and cook it for 4 mins on each side.
3. Add the rest of the Ingredients:, cook everything for 3 mins more, divide between plates and serve.

Nutrition:
Calories 404, Fat 34.6 g, Carbs 3 g, Protein 21.4 g

Paprika Tuna

Prep time: 4 mins | Servings: 4 | Cooking: 5 mins
Ingredients:
- ½ tsp. chili powder
- 2 tsps. sweet paprika
- ¼ tsp. black pepper
- 2 tbsp olive oil
- 4 boneless tuna steaks

Directions:
Heat up a pan with the oil over medium-high heat, add the tuna steaks, season with paprika, black pepper and chili powder, cook for 5 mins on each side, divide between plates and serve with a side salad.
Nutrition:
Calories 455, Fat 20.6 g, Carbs 0.8 g, Protein 63.8 g

Ginger Sea Bass Mix

Prep time: 10 mins | Servings: 4 | Cooking: 10 mins
Ingredients:
- 4 boneless sea bass fillets
- 2 tbsp olive oil
- 1 tsp. grated ginger
- 1 tbsp chopped cilantro
- Black pepper
- 1 tbsp balsamic vinegar

Directions:
1. Heat up a pan with the oil over medium heat, add the fish and cook for 5 mins on each side.
2. Add the rest of the Ingredients:, cook everything for 5 mins more, divide everything between plates and serve.

Nutrition:
Calories 267, Fat 11.2 g, Carbs 1.5 g, Protein 23 g

Parmesan Cod Mix

Prep time: 10 mins | Servings: 4 | Cooking: 11 mins
Ingredients:
- 1 tbsp lemon juice
- ½ cup chopped green onion
- 4 boneless cod fillets
- 3 minced garlic cloves
- 1 tbsp olive oil
- ½ cup shredded low-fat parmesan cheese

Directions:
1. Heat up a pan with the oil over medium heat, add the garlic and the green onions, toss and sauté for 5 mins.
2. Add the fish and cook it for 4 mins on each side.
3. Add the lemon juice, sprinkle the parmesan on top, cook everything for 2 mins more, divide between plates and serve.

Nutrition:
Calories 275, Fat 22.1 g, Carbs 18.2 g, Protein 12 g

Linguini with Clam Sauce

Prep time: 10 mins | Servings: 4 | Cooking: 11 mins
Ingredients:
- 12 oz whole-wheat linguini
- 1 tbsp olive oil
- 1 tbsp garlic, minced (about 2–3 cloves)
- 1 tbsp lemon juice
- 1 cup low-sodium chicken broth

- 2 cups canned whole clams, undrained
- 2 tbsps fresh parsley, minced (or 2 tsps dried)
- 1 tbsp butter

Directions:
1. In a 4-quart saucepan, bring 3 quarts of water to a boil over high heat.
2. Add linguini, and cook according to package Directions::s for the shortest recommended time, about 9 mins.
3. Heat olive oil in a large saucepan. Add garlic, and cook gently until it begins to soften, about 30 seconds. Do not brown.
4. Add lemon juice and chicken broth. Bring to a boil.
5. Add clams, along with liquid, parsley, salt, pepper, and butter. Simmer just until heated through, about 1–2 mins. Do not overcook.
6. Strain the linguini, then add the pasta to the saucepan with the clams and mix well.
7. Divide into four equal portions (each about 2-1/2 cups), and serve.

Nutrition:
Calories 476, Fat 9 g, Fiber 11 g, Protein 34 g, Carbs 66 g

Spicy Baked Fish

Prep time: 5 mins | Servings: 5 | Cooking: 15 mins
Ingredients:
- 1 tbsp olive oil
- 1 tsp. spice salt free seasoning
- 1 lb. salmon fillet

Directions:
1. Preheat the oven to 350F.
2. Sprinkle the fish with olive oil and the seasoning.
3. Bake for 15 min uncovered.
4. Slice and serve.

Nutrition:
Calories 192, Fat 11 g, Carbs 14.9 g, Protein 33.1 g

Smoked Trout Spread

Prep time: 5 mins | Servings: 2
Ingredients:
- 2 tsps. Fresh lemon juice
- ½ cup low-fat cottage cheese
- 1 diced celery stalk
- ¼ lb. skinned smoked trout fillet,
- ½ tsp. Worcestershire sauce
- 1 tsp. hot pepper sauce
- ¼ cup coarsely chopped red onion

Directions:
1. Combine the trout, cottage cheese, red onion, lemon juice, hot pepper sauce and Worcestershire sauce in a blender or food processor.
2. Process until smooth, stopping to scrape down the sides of the bowl as needed.
3. Fold in the diced celery.
4. Keep in an air-tight container in the refrigerator.

Nutrition:
Calories 57, Fat 4 g, Carbs 1 g, Protein 4 g

Creamy Sea Bass Mix

Prep time: 10 mins | Servings: 4 | Cooking: 10 mins
Ingredients:
- 1 tbsp chopped parsley
- 2 tbsp avocado oil
- 1 cup coconut cream
- 1 tbsp lime juice
- 1 chopped yellow onion
- ¼ tsp. black pepper
- 4 boneless sea bass fillets

Directions:
1. Heat up a pan with the oil over medium heat, add the onion, toss and sauté for 2 mins.
2. Add the fish and cook it for 4 mins on each side.
3. Add the rest of the Ingredients:, cook everything for 4 mins more, divide between plates and serve.

Nutrition:
Calories 283, Fat 12.3 g, Carbs 12.5 g, Protein 8 g

Tuna Melt

Prep time: 10 mins | Servings: 4
Ingredients:
- 3 oz. grated reduced-fat cheddar cheese
- 1/3 cup chopped celery
- Black pepper and salt
- ¼ cup chopped onion
- 2 whole-wheat English muffins
- 6 oz. drained white tuna
- ¼ cup low fat Russian

Directions:
1. Preheat broiler. Combine tuna, celery, onion and salad dressing.
2. Toast English muffin halves.

3. Place split-side-up on baking sheet and top each with 1/4 of tuna mixture.
4. Broil 2-3 mins or until heated through.
5. Top with cheese and return to broiler until cheese is melted, about 1 minute longer.

Nutrition:
Calories 320, Fat 16.7 g, Carbs 17.1 g, Protein 25.7 g

Crab Salad

Prep time: 10 mins | Servings: 4
Ingredients:
- 2 cup crab meat
- 1 cup halved cherry tomatoes
- 1 tbsp olive oil
- Black pepper
- 1 chopped shallot
- 1/3 cup chopped cilantro
- 1 tbsp lemon juice

Directions:
In a bowl, combine the crab with the tomatoes and the other Ingredients:, toss and serve.

Nutrition:
Calories 54, Fat 3.9 g, Carbs 2.6 g, Protein 2.3 g

Spicy Cod

Prep time: 29 mins | Servings: 4 | Cooking: 40 mins
Ingredients:
- 2 tbsp Fresh chopped parsley
- 2 lbs. cod fillets
- 2 cup low sodium salsa
- 1 tbsp flavorless oil

Directions:
1. Preheat the oven to 350 ° F.
2. In a large, deep baking dish drizzle the oil along the bottom. Place the cod fillets in the dish. Pour the salsa over the fish. Cover with foil for 20 mins. Remove the foil last 10 mins of cooking.
3. Bake in the oven for 20 – 30 mins, until the fish is flaky.
4. Serve with white or brown rice. Garnish with parsley.

Nutrition:
Calories 110, Fat 11 g, Carbs 83 g, Protein 16.5 g

Fish Tacos

Prep time: 5 mins | Servings: 4 | Cooking: 5 mins
Ingredients:
- 1 lb cod or white fish fillets, cut into 1-inch pieces
- 1 tbsp olive oil
- 2 tbsps lemon juice
- 1/2 package taco seasoning
- 12 (6-inch) warmed corn tortillas
- 1 cup shredded red cabbage
- 1 cup shredded green cabbage
- 2 cups chopped tomatoes
- 1/2 cup nonfat sour cream
- taco sauce to taste
- lime wedges for serving (optional)

Directions:
1. In a medium bowl, combine fish, olive oil, lemon juice, and seasoning mix; pour into a large skillet.
2. Cook, stirring constantly, over medium-high heat for 4 to 5 mins or until fish flakes easily when tested with a fork.
3. Fill tortillas with fish mixture.
4. Top with cabbage, tomato, sour cream, and taco sauce. Serve with lime wedge, if desired.

Nutrition:
Calories 239, Carbs 32 g, Fiber 4 g, Protein 19 g, Fat 5 g

Lemony Scallop

Prep time: 5 mins | Servings: 4 | Cooking: 15 mins
Ingredients:
- 3 medium green peppers, cut into 1-1/2-inch squares
- 1-1/2 lbs fresh bay scallops
- 1 pint cherry tomatoes
- 1/4 cup dry white wine
- 1/4 cup vegetable oil
- 3 tbsps lemon juice
- dash garlic powder
- black pepper to taste

Directions:
1. Parboil green peppers for 2 mins.
2. Alternately thread first three ingredients on skewers.
3. Combine next five ingredients.
4. Brush kabobs with wine/oil/lemon mixture, place on grill (or under broiler).
5. Grill 15 mins, turning and basting frequently.

Nutrition:
Calories 224, Fat 6 g, Carbs 83 g, Protein 16.5 g

Baked Trout

Prep time: 5 mins | Servings: 4 | Cooking: 20 mins

Ingredients:
- 2 lbs trout fillet, cut into 6 pieces (any kind of fish can be used)
- 3 tbsps lime juice (about 2 limes)
- 1 medium tomato, chopped
- 1/2 medium onion, chopped
- 3 tbsps cilantro, chopped
- 1/2 tsp olive oil
- 1/4 tsp black pepper
- 1/4 tsp red pepper (optional)

Directions:
1. Preheat oven to 350F.
2. Rinse fish and pat dry. Place into baking dish.
3. In a separate dish, mix remaining ingredients together and pour over fish.
4. Bake for 15-20 mins or until fork-tender.

Nutrition:
Calories 236, Fat 9 g, Protein 34 g, Carbs 2 g

Moustard Savoury Salmon

Prep time: 5 mins | Servings: 6 | Cooking: 20 mins
Ingredients:
- 1 cup sour cream, fat-free
- 2 tsps dried dill
- 3 tbsps scallions, finely chopped
- 2 tbsps Dijon mustard
- 2 tbsps lemon juice
- 1-1/2 lbs salmon fillet with skin, cut in center
- 1/2 tsp garlic powder
- 1/2 tsp black pepper
- nonstick cooking spray as needed

Directions:
1. Whisk sour cream, dill, onion, mustard, and lemon juice in small bowl to blend.
2. Preheat oven to 400° F. Lightly oil baking sheet with cooking spray.
3. Place salmon, skin side down, on prepared sheet. Sprinkle with garlic powder and pepper, then spread with the sauce.
4. Bake salmon until just opaque in center, about 20 mins.

Nutrition:
Calories 196, Fat 7 g, Protein 27 g, Carbs 5 g

Spinach Stuffed Sole

Prep time: 10 mins | Servings: 4 | Cooking: 25 mins
Ingredients:
- as needed nonstick cooking spray
- 1 tsp olive oil
- 1/2 lb fresh mushrooms, sliced
- 1/2 lb fresh spinach, chopped
- 1/4 tsp oregano leaves, crushed
- 1 clove garlic, minced
- 1-1/2 lbs sole fillets or other white fish
- 2 tbsps sherry
- 4 oz (1 cup) part-skim Mozzarella cheese, grated

Directions:
1. Preheat oven to 400ºF.
2. Spray a 10x6-inch baking dish with nonstick cooking spray.
3. Heat oil in skillet; Sauté mushrooms about 3 mins or until tender.
4. Add spinach and continue cooking about 1 minute or until spinach is barely wilted. Remove from heat; drain liquid into prepared baking dish.
5. Add oregano and garlic to drained Sautéed vegetables; stir to mix ingredients.
6. Divide vegetable mixture evenly among fillets, placing filling in center of each fillet.
7. Roll fillet around mixture and place seam-side down in prepared baking dish.
8. Sprinkle with sherry, then grated Mozzarella cheese. Bake 15-20 mins or until fish flakes easily. Lift out with a slotted spoon.

Nutrition:
Calories 262, Fat 11 g, Carbs 75 g, Protein 16.5 g

Lemon Salmon with Kaffir Lime

Prep time: 40 mins | Servings: 8 | Cooking: 30 mins
Ingredients:
- 1 quartered and bruised lemon grass stalk
- 2 kaffir torn lime leaves
- 1 thinly sliced lemon
- 1 ½ cup fresh coriander leaves
- 1 whole side salmon fillet

Directions:
1. Pre-heat the oven to 350 ◦ F.
2. Cover a baking pan with foil sheets, overlapping the sides
3. Place the Salmon on the foil, top with the lemon, lime leaves, the lemon grass and 1 cup of the coriander leaves. Option: season with salt and pepper.
4. Bring the long side of foil to the center before folding the seal. Roll the ends in order to close up the salmon.
5. Bake for 30 mins.

6. Transfer the cooked fish to a platter. Top with fresh coriander. Serve with white or brown rice.

Nutrition:
Calories 103, Fat 11.8 g, Carbs 43.5 g, Protein 18 g

Steamed Fish Balls

Prep time: 10 mins | Servings: 2 | Cooking: 10 mins
Ingredients:
- 2 whisked eggs
- 2 tbsp Rinsed and cooked rice
- 10 oz. minced white fish fillets

Directions:
1. Combine the minced fish with the rice.
2. Add eggs, season with salt and stir well.
3. Form the balls. Arrange in a steamer basket.
4. Place the basket in a pot with 1 inch of water.
5. Steam, covered, for 30 mins or until soft.

Nutrition:
Calories 169, Fat 4.3 g, Carbs 1.1 g, Protein 5.3 g

Shrimp Quesadillas

Prep time: 16 mins | Servings: 1 – 2 | Cooking: 3 mins
Ingredients:
- Two whole wheat tortillas
- ½ tsp. ground cumin
- 4 cilantro leaves
- 3 oz. diced cooked shrimp
- 1 de-seeded plump tomato
- ¾ cup grated non-fat mozzarella cheese
- ¼ cup diced red onion

Directions:
1. In medium bowl, combine the grated mozzarella cheese and the warm, cooked shrimp. Add the ground cumin, red onion, and tomato. Mix together. Spread the mixture evenly on the tortillas.
2. Heat a non-stick frying pan. Place the tortillas in the pan, then heat until they crisp.
3. Add the cilantro leaves. Fold over the tortillas.
4. Press down for 1 – 2 mins. Slice the tortillas into wedges.

Nutrition:
Calories 99, Fat 9 g, Carbs 7.2 g, Protein 59 g

Teriyaki Salmon

- Prep time: 10 mins | Servings: 2 tbsps light teriyaki sauce
- 1/4 cup mirin (or sweet rice wine)
- 2 tbsps rice vinegar
- 2 tbsps scallions (green onions), rinsed and minced
- 1-1/2 tbsps ginger, minced (or 1 tsp ground)
- 12 oz salmon fillets, cut into 4 portions (3 oz each)

4 | Cooking: 30 mins
Ingredients:
Directions:
1. Preheat oven to 350F.
2. Combine teriyaki sauce, mirin, rice vinegar, scallions, and ginger. Mix well. Pour over salmon, and marinate for 10–15 mins.
3. Remove salmon from the marinade, and discard unused portion.
4. Place salmon on a baking sheet, and bake for 10–15 mins or until fish flakes easily with a fork in the thickest part (minimum internal temperature of 145F).

Nutrition:
Calories 253, Fat 11 g, Protein 21 g, Carbs 16 g

Lemon-Parsley Baked Flounder

Prep Time: 10 mins |Servings: 2| Cooking:15 mins
Ingredients:
- 14 Brussels sprouts
- 2 tbsp olive oil, divided
- 3 tbsp freshly squeezed lemon juice
- 1 tbsp minced fresh garlic
- ¼ tsp dried dill
- 2 (6-ounce) flounder fillets

Directions:
1. Preheat the oven to 400°F. Rinse the Brussels sprouts and pat them dry. Cut their stem ends off, cut sprouts in half and place them on a foil-lined baking pan. Drizzle with 1 tbsp olive oil and toss to coat.
2. In a small bowl, stir together 1 tbsp olive oil, lemon juice, garlic, and dill.
3. Rinse flounder fillets and pat dry. Season lightly with salt and pepper. Place in baking dish and evenly drizzle oil-and-herb mixture over flounder fillets.
4. Bake for 10 to 11 mins or until the fish flakes easily when tested with a fork. The

Brussels sprouts should be lightly browned and also pierce easily with a fork.
5. Divide the flounder and Brussels sprouts between serving plates.

Nutrition:
Calories 319, Fat 17g, Carbs 13g, Fiber 5g, Protein 33g

Pan-Seared Scallops

Prep Time: 5 mins |Servings: 4| Cooking:6 mins
Ingredients:
- 2 cups chopped tomato
- ½ cup chopped fresh basil
- ¼ tsp freshly ground black pepper, divided
- 2 tbsp olive oil, divided
- 1½ lbs sea scallops
- 1 cup fresh corn kernels
- 1 cup zucchini, diced

Directions:
1. In a medium bowl, combine tomato, basil, and ⅛ tsp black pepper. Toss gently.
2. Heat a large skillet over high heat. Add 1 tbsp of olive oil to the pan, swirling to coat. Pat scallops dry with paper towels. Sprinkle with salt and remaining black pepper. Add scallops to the pan, cook for 2 mins or until browned. Turn scallops and cook for 2 mins more or until browned. Remove scallops from the pan and keep warm.
3. Heat the remaining olive oil in the pan. Add corn and zucchini to the pan. Sauté for 2 mins or until lightly browned. Add to tomato mixture and toss gently.
4. Serve scallops with a spinach salad, if desired.

Nutrition:
Calories 221, Fat 9g, Carbs 17g, Fiber 3g, Protein 20g

Baked Cod Packets with Broccoli and Squash

Prep Time: 10 mins |Servings: 4| Cooking: 20 mins
- 2 cups summer squash, sliced
- 2 cups small broccoli florets
- 4 garlic cloves, minced
- 2 tbsp olive oil
- Freshly ground black pepper
- 4 (4-ounce) cod fillets
- 4 tsps dried thyme
- Juice of 1 lemon

Directions:

1. Preheat the oven to 400°F. Cut aluminum foil into 4, 12-inch squares and arrange them on a work surface. Fold each piece in half to form a crease down the middle. Spray the foil with cooking spray.
2. Divide squash between the squares, arranging it just to the right of each crease. Top squash with broccoli and garlicup Drizzle with olive oil and sprinkle with salt and pepper.
3. Arrange 1 fillet on top of each pile of vegetables and then season fillets with salt and pepper. Top each fillet with 1 tsp of dried thyme.
4. Drizzle lemon juice over the fillets Wrap each square of foil to form a sealed pouch. Transfer pouches to a baking sheet and bake until the fish is cooked through (about 20 mins).

Set aside to rest for 3 to 4 mins. Then cut pouches open, being careful of the steam. Serve immediately.

Nutrition:
Calories 184, Fat 8g, Carbs 8g, Fiber 3g, Protein 22g

Lemony Ceviche

Prep Time: 5 mins |Servings: 4
Ingredients:
- 1/2 lb cooked small bay shrimp
- 1 cup diced cucumber
- 1/2 cup diced avocado
- 1/2 cup chopped tomatoes
- 1/4 cup finely chopped red onion
- 1/4 cup frozen corn, thawed
- 3 tbsps fresh lime juice
- 3 tbsps prepared taco sauce
- 1 serrano chili, seeds removed and finely chopped

Directions:

1. Combine all Ingredients: in a small bowl and stir well.
2. Spoon into 4 small dishes and garnish with cilantro. Serve.

Nutrition:
Calories 98, Carbs 9 g, Fiber 3 g, Protein 9 g, Fat 4 g

Mediterranean Baked Fish

Prep Time: 5 mins | Servings: 4| Cooking: 50 mins
Ingredients:
- 2 tsps olive oil

- 1 large onion, sliced
- 1 can (16 oz) whole tomatoes, drained (reserve juice) and coarsely chopped
- 1 bay leaf
- 1 clove garlic, minced
- 1 cup dry white wine
- 1/2 cup reserved tomato juice, from canned tomatoes
- 1/4 cup lemon juice
- 1/4 cup orange juice
- 1 tbsp fresh grated orange peel
- 1 tsp fennel seeds, crushed
- 1/2 tsp dried oregano, crushed
- 1/2 tsp dried thyme, crushed
- 1/2 tsp dried basil, crushed
- black pepper to taste
- 1 lb fish fillets (sole, flounder, or sea perch)

Directions:
1. Heat oil in large nonstick skillet. Add onion, and sauté over moderate heat 5 mins or until soft.
2. Add all remaining Ingredients: except fish.
3. Stir well and simmer 30 mins, uncovered.
4. Arrange fish in 10x6-inch baking dish; cover with sauce.
5. Bake, uncovered, at 375ºF about 15 mins or until fish flakes easily.

Nutrition:
Calories 177, Fat 4 g, Carbs 8g, Fiber 3g, Protein 22g

Garlic Salmon and Snap Peas

Prep Time: 5 mins |Servings: 2| Cooking: 15 mins
Ingredients:
- Cooking spray
- 2 (4-ounce) skinless salmon fillets
- 2 cups sugar snap peas, divided
- 2 garlic cloves, minced and divided
- Juice of 1 lemon, divided

Directions:
1. Preheat the oven to 450°F.
2. Cut 2 large squares of aluminum foil, each about 12-by-18 inches. Spray the center of each foil sheet with cooking spray.
3. Place 1 salmon fillet in the center of each sheet, top with 1 cup of sugar snap peas, 1 clove minced garlic, and drizzle with lemon juice. Sprinkle with salt and pepper if desired.
4. Bring up the sides of the foil and fold top over twice.
5. Seal ends, leaving room for air to circulate inside the packet.
6. Place packets on a baking sheet.
7. Cooking Time: bake for 15 to 18 mins, or until salmon is opaque.
8. Use caution when opening the packets as the steam will be very hot. Serve with lemon wedges on the side, if desired.

Nutrition:
Calories 211, Fat 5g, Carbs 14g, Fiber 3g, Protein 26g

Chapter 10: Vegan and Vegetarian

Pesto And Goat Cheese Terrine

Prep Time: 30 mins |Servings: 10 | Cooking: 25 mins
Ingredients:
- 1/4 cup toasted and chopped pine nuts
- ½ cup heavy cream
- 10 oz crumbled goat cheese
- 5 chopped sundried tomatoes
- 3 tbsp basil pesto
- 1 tbsp toasted and chopped pine nuts

Directions:
1. Mix the goat cheese with the heavy cream and stir using your mixer
2. Spoon half of this mix into a lined bowl and spread
3. Put the pesto on top and spread
4. Put another layer of cheese and then add sundried tomatoes and 1/4 cup pine nuts
5. Spread the final layer of cheese and top with 1 tbsp pine nuts
6. Refrigerate for about 20 mins
7. Flip upside down on a plate and serve cold.

Nutrition:
Calories 240, Fat 12g, Fiber 3g, Carbs 5g, Protein 12g

Green Crackers

Prep Time: 24 hours |Servings: 6 | Cooking: 24 hours
Ingredients:
- 2 cups flax seed, soaked overnight and drained
- 2 cups ground flax seed
- 1 bunch chopped basil
- 4 bunches chopped kale
- 1/3 cup olive oil
- ½ bunch chopped celery
- 4 minced garlic cloves

Directions:
1. Mix your ground flaxseed with celery, kale, basil and garlic in your food processor and blend well
2. Put oil and soaked flaxseed in the mix and blend again
3. Spread this nix on a tray and cut into medium crackers
4. Place in your dehydrator and dry the crackers for 24 hours at 115F, turning them halfway.

Place them on a platter and serve
Nutrition:
Calories 100g, Fat 1g, Carbs 1g, Fiber 2g, Protein 4g

Macaroni and Cheese

Prep Time: 30 mins |Servings: 8 | Cooking: 35 mins
Ingredients:
- 2 cups macaroni
- 2 cups onions, chopped
- 2 cups evaporated fat-free milk
- 1 medium egg, beaten
- 1/4 tsp black pepper
- 1-1/4 cups low-fat cheddar cheese, finely shredded
- nonstick cooking spray, as needed

Directions:
1. Preheat oven to 350 degrees F.
2. Lightly spray saucepan with nonstick cooking spray. Add onions to saucepan and sauté for about 3 mins.
3. In another bowl, combine macaroni, onions, and the rest of the Ingredients: and mix thoroughly.
4. Transfer mixture into casserole dish.
5. Bake for 20 mins or until bubbly. Let stand for 10 mins before serving.

Nutrition:
Calories 200, Fat 4 g, Fiber 1 g, Protein 11 g, Carbs 29 g

Springtime Pasta

Prep Time: 24 hours |Servings: 6 | Cooking: 15 mins
Ingredients:
- 2 cups dry whole-wheat pasta (8 oz)
- 1 tbsp olive oil
- 1 tsp garlic, minced (about 1 clove)
- 1 bag (16 oz) frozen peas and carrots
- 2 cups low-sodium chicken broth
- 2 tbsps cornstarch
- 1 tbsp fresh parsley, rinsed, dried, and chopped (or 1 tsp dried)
- 1 medium lemon, rinsed, for 1 tsp zest (use a grater to take a thin layer of skin off the lemon)

Directions:
1. In a 4-quart saucepan, bring 3 quarts of water to a boil over high heat.
2. Add pasta, and cook according to package. Drain.
3. Meanwhile, heat olive oil and garlic over medium heat in a large sauté pan. Cook until soft, but not browned.
4. Add peas and carrots. Cook gently until the vegetables are heated through.
5. In a bowl, combine chicken broth and cornstarch. Mix well. Add to pan with vegetables, and bring to a boil. Simmer gently for 1 minute.
6. Add parsley, pasta, lemon zest, and pepper. Toss gently, and cook until the pasta is hot.
7. Serve 2 cups of pasta and vegetables per portion.

Nutrition:.
Calories 329, Fat 6 g, Protein 13 g, Carbs 59 g

Shitake & Snow Peas Quinoa

Prep Time: 5 mins |Servings: 4 | Cooking: 10 mins
Ingredients:
- 3 cup fluffy quinoa
- 1 tbsp sesame oil
- 1 tbsp garlic cloves
- 4 oz shitake mushroom
- 4 oz snow peas
- 1 tbsp soy sauce
- 1 sliced green onion

Directions:
1. In a medium nonstick skillet heat your sesame oil on medium heat
2. Add your garlic and allow to cook for about a minute stirring frequently so that it doesn't burn
3. Add in your mushrooms and cook until tender (about 5 mins)
4. Add the snow peas, and ten continue stirring until peas become bright green in color (about 3 mins) then remove from the heat
5. Add in all the remaining Ingredients: and toss until fully combined

Nutrition:
Calories 210, Protein 8g, Carbs 32g, Fat 6g

Low-Carb Zucchini Lasagna Rolls

Prep Time: 15 mins |Servings: 24 | Cooking: 10 mins
Ingredients:
- 2 tbsp olive oil
- Tomato sauce for serving
- 3 thinly sliced zucchinis
- 2 tbsp chopped mint
- 1/4 cup chopped basil
- 24 basil leaves
- 1 ⅓ cup ricotta cheese

Directions:
1. Coat the zucchini slices with the olive oil, season with salt and pepper on both sides
2. Put them on the preheated grill of over medium heat and cook them for 2 mins, flip and cook for another 2 min
3. Arrange the zucchini slices on a plate and set aside to cool for now
4. Mix your ricotta with, pepper, mint, salt and chopped basil and stir well
5. Spread the mix over zucchini slices
6. Divide your whole basil leaves as well
7. Roll your zucchini slices and serve as an appetizer with some tomato sauce on the side

Nutrition:
Calories 40, Fiber 3g, Carbs 1g, Protein 2g, Fat 3

Baked Pumpkin Pasta

Prep Time: 10 mins |Servings: 4 | Cooking: 15 mins
Ingredients:
- 1 cup boneless chicken
- 1 cup pumpkin
- 1 package pasta
- ½ tsp garlic paste
- 1 chopped onion
- 1 tsp black pepper
- 2 tbsp olive oil
- 1 cup cheddar cheese

Directions:
1. Preheat oven at 355 F
2. Heat oil in pan and sauté onion with garlic for 1 minute
3. Add pumpkin and cook for 3-4 mins
4. Now add chicken pieces and stir for 1 minute

Nutrition:
Calories 307, Protein 17g, Carbs 55g, Fat 8g

Gruyere and Spinach Casserole

Prep Time: 10 mins |Servings: 5 | Cooking: 45 mins
Ingredients:
- 2 cup chopped spinach
- 2 eggs

- 1 tsp sugar
- 2 oz grated gruyere
- 1 cup grated parmesan cheese
- ½ cup chopped green onion
- 4 minced garlic cloves
- 2 eggs
- 1 tsp chili powder
- 1 cup heavy milk
- 2 tbsp olive oil

Directions:
1. Heat oil in saucepan and sauté garlic for 1 minute with onion
2. Add spinach and stir for 2-3 mins till its color is lightly changed
3. In separate bowl add eggs and whisks for 1-2 mins. Add in milk, gruyere and whisk again for 1 minute.
4. Transfer this mixture in spinach mixture and cook for 2 mins
5. Season with salt and chili powder
6. Preheat oven at 355 degrees. Add gruyere mixture in baking dish, top with parmesan cheese and bake for 40-45 mins

Nutrition:
Calories 270, Protein 18g, Carbs 8g, Fat 19g

Italian Cheese Sticks

Prep Time: 1 hour 30 mins |Servings: 16
Ingredients:
- 2 whisked eggs
- 8 mozzarella cheese strings, cut in halves
- ½ cup olive oil
- 1 minced garlic clove
- 1 cup grated Parmesan
- 1 tbsp Italian seasoning

Directions:
1. Toss parmesan with garlic and Italian seasoning in a suitable bowl
2. Beat eggs in another bowl
3. First, dip the mozzarella sticks in the egg mixture then dredge through the parmesan mixture
4. Repeat the layer twice then place them in a baking sheet
5. Freeze these sticks for 1 hour
6. Place a pan with oil on medium-high heat
7. Add cheese sticks and sear them until golden brown from all the sides evenly

Nutrition:
Calories 140, Fat 5g, Fiber 1g, Carbs 3g, Protein 4g

Broccoli Sticks

Prep Time: 30 mins |Servings: 20 | Cooking: 20 mins
Ingredients:
- 1/3 cup panko breadcrumbs
- 2 cups broccoli florets
- olive oil
- 1/3 cup Italian breadcrumbs
- 1 egg
- 2 tbsp chopped parsley
- 1/4 cup chopped yellow onion
- 1/3 cup grated cheddar cheese

Directions:
1. Heat a pot with water and put the broccoli and steam for 1 minute
2. Drain, chop and put the broccoli into a bowl
3. Add cheddar cheese, egg, panko and Italian bread crumbs, and parsley and combine properly
4. Carve out shapes of sticks out of this mix using your hands and place them on a baking sheet which you've greased with olive oil
5. Preheat your oven to a temperature 400F and bake for 20 mins
6. Place orderly on a platter and serve

Nutrition:
Calories 100, Fiber 2, Fat 4, Carbs 7g, Protein 7g

Halloumi Cheese Crunchy Fries

Prep Time: 15 mins |Servings: 4 | Cooking: 10 mins
Ingredients:
- 8 oz halloumi cheese, pat dried and sliced into fries
- 1 cup marinara sauce
- 2 oz tallow

Directions:
1. Heat a pan containing the tallow to over medium-high heat
2. Put halloumi pieces and cover, allowing cook for 2 mins on each side
3. Transfer halloumi pieces to paper towels
4. Drain excess grease
5. transfer them to a bowl and serve with marinara sauce on the side

Nutrition:
Calories 200, Fiber 1g, Carbs 1g, Protein 13g

Special Cucumber Cups

Prep Time: 10 mins |Servings: 24 | Cooking: 15 mins

Ingredients:
- ½ cup sour cream
- 2 peeled cucumbers
- cayenne pepper
- cut the cucumbers into ¾ inch slices, and some of the seeds scooped out
- 2 tsp lime juice
- 6 oz flaked smoked salmon
- 1/3 cup chopped cilantro
- 1 tbsp lime zest

Directions:
1. Get a bowl and mix the salmon with cayenne, sour cream, lime juice and zest and cilantro and stir properly
2. Fill each cucumber cup with this salmon mix
3. Place on a platter and serve as a appetizer.

Nutrition:
Calories 30, Fiber 1g, Carbs 1g, Protein 2g, Fat 11g

Black-Bean and Vegetable Burrito

Prep Time: 10 mins |Servings: 4| Cooking: 15 mins
Ingredients:
- ½ tbsp olive oil
- 2 red or green bell peppers, cored and chopped
- 1 zucchini or summer squash, diced
- ½ tsp chili powder
- 1 tsp cumin
- Freshly ground black pepper
- 2 (15-ounce) cans black beans, drained and rinsed
- 1 cup cherry tomatoes, halved
- 4 (8-inch) whole-wheat tortillas
- Optional: spinach, sliced avocado, chopped scallions or hot sauce

Directions:
1. Heat the oil in a large sauté pan over medium heat. Add the bell peppers and sauté until crisp tender (about 4 mins)
2. Add the zucchini, chili powder, cumin, and black pepper to taste and continue to sauté until the vegetables are tender (about 5 mins)
3. Add the black beans and cherry tomatoes
4. Cooking Time: until the tomatoes soften, the beans are heated through, and most of the moisture has evaporated (about 5 mins)
5. Divide between 4 burritos and serve topped with optional Ingredients: as desired

Nutrition:
Calories 311, Fat 6g, Carbs 52g, Fiber 21g, Protein 19g

Black Bean and Corn Pita

Prep Time: 10 mins |Servings: 4
Ingredients:
- 1 (15-ounce) can
- low-sodium black beans
- 1 cup frozen corn, thawed
- 1 cup fresh or no salt added canned tomatoes
- 1 avocado, chopped
- 1 clove garlic, finely chopped
- 1 tsp chopped fresh parsley
- 1/8 tsp cayenne pepper or more to taste
- 2 tsps lemon juice
- 1/2 tsp chili powder
- 2 medium whole wheat pita pockets
- 1/3 cup shredded part-skim Mozzarella cheese

Directions:
1. Drain and rinse beans. In a medium bowl, combine beans, corn, tomatoes, avocado, and garlicup Add parsley, cayenne pepper, lemon juice, and chili powder.
2. Cut pita bread in half to form 4 pockets, and spoon equal amounts of filling into each half. Top with cheese and serve.

Nutrition:
Calories 352, Carbs 54 g, Protein 16 g, Fat 10 g

Black Beans with Rice

Prep Time: 10 mins |Servings: 6 | Cooking: 1 hour
Ingredients:
- 1 lb dry black beans
- 7 cups water
- 1 medium green pepper, coarsely chopped
- 1-1/2 cups chopped onion
- 1 tbsp vegetable oil
- 2 bay leaves
- 1 clove garlic, minced
- 1 tbsp vinegar (or lemon juice)
- 6 cups rice, cooked in unsalted water
- 1 jar (4 oz) sliced pimento, drained
- 1 lemon cut into wedges

Directions:

1. Pick through beans to remove bad beans. Soak beans overnight in cold water. Drain and rinse.
2. In large soup pot or dutch oven stir together beans, water, green pepper, onion, oil, bay leaves, garlic, and salt. Cover and boil 1 hour.
3. Reduce heat and simmer, covered, 3-4 hours or until beans are very tender. Stir occasionally and add water if needed.
4. Remove about 1/3 of the beans, mash and return to pot. Stir and heat through.
5. Remove bay leaves and stir in vinegar or lemon juice when ready to serve.
6. Serve over rice. Garnish with sliced pimento and lemon wedges.

Nutrition:
Calories 561, Fat 4 g

Caribbean Pink Beans

Prep Time: 10 mins |Servings: 16 | Cooking: 15 mins
Ingredients:
- 1 lb pink beans
- 10 cups water
- 2 medium plantains, finely chopped
- 1 large tomato, finely chopped
- 1 small red pepper, finely chopped
- 1 medium white onion, finely chopped
- 3 cloves garlic, finely chopped

Directions:
1. Rinse and pick through the beans. Put the beans in a large pot and add 10 cups of water. Place the pot in the refrigerator and allow the beans to soak overnight.
2. Cook the beans until they are soft. Add more water as needed while the beans are cooking.
3. Add the plantains, tomato, pepper, onion, garlic, and salt. Continue cooking at low heat until the plantains are soft.

Nutrition:
Calories 133, Fat 1g

Lentils with Brown Rice

Prep Time: 10 mins |Servings: 4 | Cooking: 35 mins
Ingredients:
For lentils and kale
- 1 cup brown lentils, rinsed
- 1/8 tsp ground black pepper

For brown rice
- 1 cup instant brown rice, uncooked (for quinoa, follow cooking instructions on box)
- 1/2 tsp dried basil
- For onion
- 2 tbsps olive oil
- 2 cups onion, diced
- 1/8 tsp ground black pepper

Directions:
1. Rinse lentils thoroughly in a fine wire colander, and remove any stones or debris.
2. In a 4-quart saucepan, cover lentils with 2-1/2 cups of water. Add salt and pepper. Cover, and bring to a boil over high heat. Reduce heat. Simmer for 20 mins
3. In another saucepan, bring 2 cups of water to a boil. Add rice, salt, and basil. Cover, and cook for 10 mins. Set aside.
4. In a medium sauté pan, warm olive oil over medium heat and add onion, salt, and pepper. Cook and stir until the onion pieces become soft and dark brown (caramelized), but not burnt. If the onions start to stick to the pan, add a few drops of water and scrape the onions loose. Keep cooking until onions are completely caramelized (about 10–15 mins total). Remove from pan and set aside.
5. When the lentils are tender, but not mushy, mix the lentils, and caramelized onions in the sauté pan and stir.
6. To serve, put 1 cup of the lentil mixture, in the form of a ring, on each of four dinner plates. Fill the center of each ring with one-fourth of the brown rice. Serve immediately.

Nutrition:
Calories 456, Fat 9 g, Protein 21 g, Carbs 77 g

Tortilla Pizzas

Prep Time: 5 mins |Servings: 6 | Cooking: 8 mins
Ingredients:
- 12 small corn or flour tortillas vegetable oil or margarine
- 1 (16-ounce) can refried beans 1/4 cup chopped onion
- 2 oz fresh or canned green chili peppers, diced
- 6 tbsps red taco sauce
- 3 cups chopped vegetables, such as broccoli, mushrooms, spinach, and red bell pepper

- 1/2 cup (2 oz) shredded part-skim Mozzarella cheese
- 1/2 cup chopped fresh cilantro (optional)

Directions:
1. Brush one side of each of two tortillas with water. Press the wet sides of the tortillas together to form a thick crust for the pizza.
2. Brush the outside of the tortillas with a small amount of oil or margarine. Evenly brown both sides in a heated frying pan.
3. Heat refried beans, onion, and half of the chili peppers together in a medium saucepan over medium heat, stirring occasionally. Remove from heat.
4. Spread about 1/3 cup of the bean mixture on each tortilla pizza. Sprinkle with 1 tbsp taco sauce, then top with 1/2 cup of the chopped vegetables, 1 tsp chili peppers, and 1 tbsp cheese for each pizza.
5. Return to frying pan and heat until cheese melts. Top with cilantro, if desired. Serve immediately.

Nutrition: Information
Calories 235, Carbs 39 g, Protein 11 g, Fat 5 g

Beans from Tuscany - Italy

Prep Time: 5 mins |Servings: 4
Ingredients:
- 1 can (15-1/2 oz) low-sodium chickpeas (or garbanzo beans), drained and rinsed
- 2 cups cherry tomatoes, rinsed and halved
- 1 tbsp olive oil
- 1 tsp balsamic vinegar
- 2 tbsps fresh oregano, minced (or 1 tsp dried)
- 1/8 tsp ground black pepper
- 1/2 tsp salt-free seasoning blend
- 4 whole inner leaves of romaine lettuce, rinsed and dried

Directions:
1. In a large salad bowl, combine beans and tomatoes.
2. In a small bowl, combine olive oil, vinegar, oregano, pepper, and salt-free seasoning blend. Using a wire whisk, beat the Ingredients: until they blend into one thick sauce at the point where the oil and vinegar no longer separate.
3. Pour the dressing over the beans and tomatoes, and mix gently to coat.
4. Line four salad bowls with one romaine lettuce leaf each.
5. Top each leaf with one-fourth of the bean mixture, and serve.

Nutrition:
Calories 265, Fat 10 g, Protein 12 g, Carbs 35 g

Veggie Tortilla Roll-Ups

Prep Time: 5 mins |Servings: 4
Ingredients:
- 4 (7-inch) whole wheat tortillas
- 8 tbsps (1/2 cup) nonfat cream cheese
- 2 cups shredded romaine lettuce or fresh chopped spinach
- 1 cup chopped tomato
- 1/2 cup chopped bell pepper (red, green, orange, yellow, or a mixture)
- 1/2 cup chopped cucumber
- 1/4 cup diced canned green chiles
- 1/4 cup sliced ripe olives, drained

Directions:
1. Spread each tortilla with 2 tbsps of cream cheese.
2. Top with equal amounts of vegetables.
3. Roll up tightly to enclose filling and serve.

Nutrition:
Calories 128, Carbs 20 g, Protein 8 g, Fat 2 g

Baked Eggs In Avocado

Prep Time: 10 mins |Servings: 4| Cooking: 15 mins
Ingredients:
- 2 avocados
- Juice of 2 limes
- Freshly ground black pepper
- 4 eggs
- 2 (8-inch) whole-wheat or corn tortillas, warmed
- Optional for Servings: halved cherry tomatoes and chopped cilantro

Directions:
3. Adjust oven rack to the middle position and preheat the oven to 450°F.
4. Bake until whites are set and yolk is runny (10 to 15 mins).
5. Remove from oven and garnish with optional cilantro and cherry tomatoes and serve with warm tortillas.

Nutrition:
Calories 534, Fat 39g, Carbs 30g, Fiber 20g, Protein 23g

White Beans with Spinach and Tomatoes

Prep Time: 15 mins |Servings: 2| Cooking: 10 mins
Ingredients:
- 1 tbsp olive oil
- 4 small plum tomatoes, halved lengthwise
- 10 oz frozen spinach, defrosted and squeezed of excess water
- 2 garlic cloves, thinly sliced
- 2 tbsp water
- ¼ tsp freshly ground black pepper
- 1 (15 oz) can white beans, drained and rinsed
- Juice of 1 lemon

Directions:
1. Heat the oil in a large skillet over medium high heat. Add the tomatoes, cut-side down.
2. Cooking Time: shaking the pan occasionally, until browned and starting to soften (about 3 to 5 mins). Turn and cook for 1 minute more. Transfer to a plate.
3. Reduce heat to medium and add the spinach, garlic, water, and pepper to the skillet.
4. Toss while cooking until the spinach is heated through (2 to 3 mins).
5. Return the tomatoes to the skillet. Add the white beans and lemon juice, and toss until heated through (about 1 to 2 mins).

Nutrition:
Calories 293, Fat 9g, Carbs 43g, Fiber 16g, Protein 15g

Black-Eyed Peas and Greens Power Salad

Prep Time: 5 mins |Servings: 2| Cooking: 6 mins
Ingredients:
- 1 tbsp olive oil
- 3 cups purple cabbage, chopped
- 5 cups baby spinach
- 1 cup shredded carrots
- 1 (15-ounce) can black-eyed peas, drained and rinsed
- Juice of ½ lemon

Directions:
1. In a medium pan, add the oil and cabbage and sauté for 1 to 2 mins on medium heat.
2. Add in your spinach. Cover and cook for 3 to 4 mins on medium heat until greens are wilted.
3. Remove from the heat and add to a large bowl.
4. Add in the carrots, black-eyed peas, and a splash of lemon juice.

Nutrition:
Calories 320, Fat 9g, Carbs 49g, Fiber 18g, Protein 16g

Butternut-Squash Macaroni and Cheese

Prep Time: 10 mins |Servings: 2| Cooking: 20 mins
Ingredients:
- 1 cup whole-wheat ziti macaroni
- 2 cups peeled and cu bed butternut squash
- 1 cup nonfat or low-fat milk, divided
- Freshly ground black pepper
- 1 tsp Dijon mustard
- 1 tbsp olive oil
- ¼ cup shredded low-fat cheddar cheese

Directions:
1. Cook the pasta al dente.
2. In a medium saucepan, add the butternut squash and ½ cup milk and place cook at medium-high heat. Season with black pepper. Bring to a simmer. Reduce heat to low and cover. Cook until fork tender (8 to 10 mins).
3. Place a large sauté pan over medium heat and add olive oil. Add the squash purée and remaining ½ cup of milk. Bring to a simmer.
4. Cook until thickened (about 5 mins). Add the cheese and stir to combine.
5. Add the pasta to the sauté pan and stir to combine.

Nutrition:
Calories 373, Fat 10g, Carbs 59g, Fiber 10g, Protein 14g

Pasta with Tomatoes and Peas

Prep Time: 10 mins |Servings: 2| Cooking: 15 mins
Ingredients:
- ½ cup whole-grain pasta of choice
- 8 cups water, plus ¼ for finishing
- 1 cup frozen peas
- 1 tbsp olive oil
- 1 cup cherry tomatoes, halved
- ¼ tsp freshly ground black pepper
- 1 tsp dried basil
- ¼ cup grated Parmesan cheese (low-sodium)

Directions:

1. Cook the pasta al dente.
2. Add the water to the same pot you used to cook the pasta. Bring the water to a boil and add the peas. Cook until tender, but still firm (about 5 mins). Drain and set aside.
3. Heat the oil in a large skillet over medium heat. Add the cherry tomatoes. Put a lid on the skillet and let the tomatoes soften for about 5 mins, stirring a few times.
4. Season with black pepper and basil.
5. Toss in the pasta, peas, and ¼ cup of water. Stir and remove from the heat.
6. Serve topped with Parmesan cheese.

Nutrition:
Calories 266, Fat 12g, Carbs 30g, Fiber 6g, Protein 13g

Healthy Vegetable Fried Rice

Prep Time: 5 mins | Servings: 4| Cooking: 10 mins
Ingredients:
For The Sauce:
- ⅓ cup garlic vinegar
- 1½ tbsp dark molasses
- 1 tsp onion powder

For The Fried Rice:
- 1 tsp olive oil
- 2 whole eggs plus 4 egg whites, lightly beaten
- 1 cup frozen mixed vegetables
- 1 cup frozen edamame
- 2 cups cooked brown rice

Directions:
To make the sauce
1. Prepare the sauce by combining the garlic vinegar, molasses, and onion powder in a glass jar. Shake well.

To make the fried rice
1. Heat oil in a large wok or skillet over medium-high heat. Add eggs and egg whites and let cook until the eggs are set (about 1 minute). Break eggs into small pieces with a spatula or. Add frozen mixed vegetables and frozen edamame. Cook for 4 mins, stirring frequently.
2. Add the brown rice and sauce to the vegetable-and-egg mixture. Cook for 5 mins or until heated through.

Nutrition:
Calories 210, Fat 6g, Carbs 28g, Fiber 3g, Protein 13g

Portobello-Mushroom Cheeseburgers

Prep Time: 5 mins |Servings: 4| Cooking: 10 mins
Ingredients:
- 4 Portobello mushrooms, caps removed and brushed clean
- 1 tbsp olive oil
- ½ tsp freshly ground black pepper
- 1 tbsp red wine vinegar
- 4 slices reduced-fat Swiss cheese, sliced thin
- 4 whole-wheat 100-calorie sandwich thins
- ½ avocado, sliced thin

Directions:
1. Heat a skillet or grill pan over medium-high heat. Clean the mushrooms and remove the stems. Brush each cap with olive oil and sprinkle with black pepper. Place in skillet, cap-side up and cook for about 4 mins. Flip and cook for another 4 mins.
2. Sprinkle with the red wine vinegar and turn over. Add the cheese and cook for 2 more mins. For optimal melting, place a lid loosely over the pan.
3. Toast the sandwich thins. Create your burgers by topping each with sliced avocado.

Nutrition:
Calories 245, Fat 12g, Carbs 28g, Fiber 8g, Protein 14g

Baked Chickpea-and-Rosemary Omelet

Prep Time: 10 mins |Servings: 2| Cooking: 15 mins
Ingredients:
- ½ tbsp olive oil
- 4 eggs
- ¼ cup grated Parmesan cheese
- 1 (15-ounce) can chickpeas, drained and rinsed
- 2 cups packed baby spinach
- 1 cup button mushrooms, chopped
- 2 sprigs rosemary, leaves picked (or 2 tsps dried rosemary)

Directions:
1. Preheat the oven to 400°F and place a baking tray on the middle shelf.
2. Line an 8-inch springform pan with baking paper and grease generously with olive oil. If you don't have a springform pan, grease

an oven-safe skillet (or cast-iron skillet) with olive oil.
3. Lightly whisk together the eggs and Parmesan.
4. Place chickpeas in the pan. Layer the spinach and mushrooms on top of the beans. Pour the egg mixture on top and scatter the rosemary. Season to taste with salt and pepper.
5. Place the pan on the preheated tray and bake until golden and puffy and the center feels firm and springy (about 15 mins).

Nutrition:
Calories 418, Fat 19g, Carbs 33g, Fiber 12g, Protein 30g

Black-Bean Soup

Prep Time: 5 mins |Servings: 4| Cooking: 20 mins
Ingredients:
- 1 yellow onion
- 1 tbsp olive oil
- 2 (15-ounce) cans black beans, drained and rinsed
- 1 cup diced fresh tomatoes
- 5 cups low-sodium vegetable broth
- ¼ tsp freshly ground black pepper
- ¼ cup chopped fresh cilantro

Directions:
1. In a large saucepan, cook the onion in the olive oil over medium heat until softened (about 4 to 5 mins)
2. Add the black beans, tomatoes, vegetable broth, and black pepper. Bring to a boil. Reduce heat and simmer for about 15 mins
3. Remove from the heat and working in batches ladle the soup into a blender and process until somewhat smooth. Return the soup to the pot, add the cilantro and heat until warmed through.

Nutrition:
Calories 234, Fat 5g, Carbs 37g, Fiber 13g, Sugars 3g, Protein 11g

Loaded Baked Sweet Potatoes

Prep Time: 10 mins |Servings: 4| Cooking: 20 mins
Ingredients:
- 4 sweet potatoes
- ½ cup nonfat or low-fat plain Greek yogurt
- Freshly ground black pepper
- 1 tsp olive oil
- 1 red bell pepper, cored and diced
- ½ red onion, diced
- 1 tsp ground cumin
- 1 (15-ounce) can chickpeas, drained and rinsed

Directions:
1. Poke holes in the potatoes with a fork.
2. Cook on your microwave's potato setting until potatoes are soft and cooked through (about 8 to 10 mins for 4 potatoes)
3. Combine the yogurt and black pepper in a small bowl and mix well
4. Heat the oil in a medium pot over medium heat. Add bell pepper, onion, cumin, and additional black pepper to taste.
5. Add the chickpeas, stir to combine, and heat through (about 5 mins)
6. Slice the potatoes lengthwise down the middle and top each half with a portion of the bean mixture followed by 1 to 2 tbsp of the yogurt.

Nutrition:
Calories 264, Fat 2g, Carbs 51g, Fiber 10g, Protein 11g

Lemon Roasted Artichokes

Prep time: 10 mins | Servings: 2
Ingredients:
- 2 peeled and sliced garlic cloves
- 3 lemon pieces
- 2 artichoke pieces
- 3 tbsp olive oil
- Sea flavored vinegar

Directions:
1. Wash your artichokes well and dip them in water and cut the stem to about ½ inch long
2. Trim the thorny tips and outer leaves and rub the chokes with lemon
3. Poke garlic slivers between the choke leaves and place a trivet basket in the Instant Pot ten add artichokes
4. Lock up the lid and cook on high pressure for 7 mins
5. Release the pressure naturally over 10 mins
6. Transfer the artichokes to cutting board and allow them to cool then cut half lengthwise and cut the purple white center
7. Pre-heat your oven to 400 degree Fahrenheit
8. Take a bowl and mix 1 and ½ lemon and olive oil
9. Pour over the choke halves and sprinkle flavored vinegar and pepper

10. Place an iron skillet in your oven and heat it up for 5 mins
11. Add a few tsp of oil and place the marinated artichoke halves in the skillet
12. Brush with lemon and olive oil mixture
13. Cut third lemon in quarter and nestle them between the halves
14. Roast for 20-25 mins until the chokes are browned

Nutrition:
Calories 263, Fat 16 g, Carbs 8 g, Protein 23 g

Chocolate Aquafaba Mousse

Prep time: 20 mins | Servings: 4-6
Ingredients:
- 1 tsp. pure vanilla extract
- 15 oz. unsalted chickpeas
- Fresh raspberries
- ¼ tsp. tartar cream
- 6 oz. dairy-free dark chocolate
- 2 tbsp coconut sugar

Directions:
1. Chop dark chocolate into coarse bits and place the chocolate into a glass bowl over boiling water on the stovetop or in a double boiler.
2. Melt the chocolate gently, stirring until completely melted.
3. Remove the melted chocolate from the heat and pour the chocolate into a large bowl.
4. Drain the chickpeas, reserving the brine (aquafaba), and store the chickpeas for another recipe like hummus.
5. Add in the aquafaba along with cream of tartar.
6. Mix on high speed using an electric hand mixer for 7-10 mins, or until soft peaks begin to form.
7. Add in the salt, vanilla extract, and coconut sugar and beat the mixture until well mixed.
8. Add half of the melted chocolate to the whipped aquafaba and fold it in until incorporated.
9. Fold in the remaining aquafaba until smooth and well combined to form the mousse.
10. Gently spoon the chocolate mousse into glasses, ramekins or small mason jars.
11. Cover with cling film and chill for at least 3 hours.
12. Sprinkle he mousse with raspberries and serve.

Nutrition:
Calories 280, Fat 13.8 g, Carbs 34.7 g, Protein 3.9

Peas Feta Rice

Prep time: 15 mins | Servings: 2 | Cooking: 10 mins
Ingredients:
- 1 ¼ cup vegetable broth
- ¾ cup brown rice
- ¼ cup finely crumbled feta cheese
- ¾ cup sliced scallions
- 1 ½ cup frozen peas
- Freshly ground pepper
- ¼ cup sliced fresh mint

Directions:
1. Boil broth in a saucepan over medium heat.
2. Add rice and bring it to a simmer. Cook for 4 mins.
3. Stir in peas and cook for 6 mins.
4. Turn off the heat then add feta, mint, scallions, and pepper.
5. Serve warm.

Nutrition:
Calories 28.1, Fat 18.2 g, Carbs 10.3 g, Protein 8.8 g

Rhubarb and Strawberry Compote

Prep time: 10 mins | Servings: 4
Ingredients:
- 3 tbsp Date paste
- ½ cup water
- Fresh mint
- 2 lbs. rhubarb
- 1 lb. strawberries

Directions:
1. Peel the rhubarb using a paring knife and chop it up ½ inch pieces
2. Add the chopped up rhubarb to your pot alongside water
3. Lock up the lid and cook on HIGH pressure for 10 mins
4. Stem and quarter your strawberries and keep them on the side
5. Add the strawberries and date paste, give it a nice stir
6. Lock up the lid and cook on HIGH pressure for 20 mins
7. Release the pressure naturally and enjoy the compote!

Nutrition:

Calories 41.1, Fat 2.1 g, Carbs 5.5 g, Protein 1.4 g

Zucchini Cakes

Prep time: 10 mins | Servings: 4
Ingredients:
- Freshly ground black pepper
- 1 finely diced red onion
- 1 egg white
- Homemade horseradish sauce
- 1 shredded medium zucchini
- ¾ cup salt-free bread crumbs

Directions:
1. Preheat oven to 400°F. Spray a baking sheet lightly with oil and set aside.
2. Press shredded zucchini gently between paper towels to remove excess liquid.
3. In a large bowl, combine zucchini, onion, egg white, bread crumbs, seasoning, and black pepper. Mix well.
4. Shape mixture into patties and place on the prepared baking sheet.
5. Place baking sheet on middle rack in oven and bake for 10 mins. Gently flip patties and return to oven to bake for another 10 mins.
6. Remove from oven and serve immediately.

Nutrition:
Calories: 94, Fat:1 g, Carbs:19 g, Protein:4 g

Vegan Rice Pudding

Prep time: 5 mins | Servings: 8
Ingredients:
- ½ tsp. ground cinnamon
- 1 cup rinsed basmati
- 1/8 tsp. ground cardamom
- ¼ cup sugar
- 1/8 tsp. pure almond extract
- 1 quart vanilla nondairy milk
- 1 tsp. pure vanilla extract

Directions:
1. Measure all of the Ingredients: into a saucepan and stir well to combine. Bring to a boil over medium-high heat.
2. Once boiling, reduce heat to low and simmer, stirring very frequently, about 15–20 mins.
3. Remove from heat and cool. Serve sprinkled with additional ground cinnamon if desired.

Nutrition:
Calories 148, Fat 2 g, Carbs 26 g, Protein 4 g

Couscous from Middle-East

Prep Time: 10 mins |Servings: 4 | Cooking: 10 mins
Ingredients:
- 1 cup couscous (try whole-wheat couscous)
- 1 tsp olive oil
- 2 tbsps walnuts, coarsely chopped
- 1/2 tsp pumpkin pie spice or cinnamon
- 1-1/3 cups water
- 2 tbsps raisins
- 1/2 cup carrots, rinsed, peeled, and shredded or thinly sliced; cut in half

Directions:
1. In a 4-quart saucepan over medium heat, cook and stir couscous, olive oil, walnuts, salt, pepper, and spice just until couscous begins to brown.
2. Slowly add water, then raisins and carrots. Cover. Bring to a boil over high heat.
3. Remove from the heat, and let stand for 10 mins.
4. Fluff with a fork. Serve immediately.

Nutrition:
Calories 218, Fat 4 g, Protein 6 g, Carbs 39 g

Kasha with Bell Pepper

Prep Time: 10 mins |Servings: 4| Cooking: 20 mins
Ingredients:
- 2 tsps olive oil
- 1/2 cup onion, diced
- 1/4 cup red/yellow/green bell pepper, rinsed and diced
- 1 can (14-1/2 oz) low-sodium chicken broth
- 3/4 cup kasha
- 1/4 tsp dried oregano

Directions:
1. Heat oil in a 4-quart saucepan over medium heat. Add onion. Cook for 5 mins, stirring occasionally.
2. Add bell peppers to saucepan. Cook and stir for 2 mins. Remove vegetables from pan and set aside.
3. Add chicken broth to saucepan. Cover. Bring to a boil over high heat.
4. Stir in kasha. Reduce heat to medium-low. Cover. Simmer for about 10 mins, until kasha is cooked and liquid is absorbed.
5. Stir in peppers and onion mixture, oregano, salt, and pepper. Heat for 1 minute. Serve immediately.

Nutrition:
Calories 144, Fat 3 g, Protein 4 g, Carbs 27 g

Easy Chickpea Veggie Burgers

Prep Time: 10 mins |Servings: 4| Cooking: 20 mins
Ingredients:
- 1 15-ounce can chickpeas, drained and rinsed
- ½ cup frozen spinach, thawed
- ⅓ cup rolled oats
- 1 tsp garlic powder
- 1 tsp onion powder

Directions:
1. Preheat oven to 400°F. Grease a sheet or line one with parchment paper and set aside.
2. In a mixing bowl, add half of the beans and mash with a fork until fairly smooth. Set aside.
3. Add the remaining half of the beans, spinach, oats, and spices to a food processor or blender and blend until puréed. Add the mixture to the bowl of mashed beans and stir until well combined.
4. Divide mixture into 4 equal portions and shape into patties. Bake for 7 to 10 mins. Carefully turn over and bake for another 7 to 10 mins or until crusty on the outside.
5. Place on a whole grain bun with your favorite toppings.

Nutrition:
Calories 118, Fat 1g, Carbs 21g, Fiber 7g, Protein 7g

Cinnamon-Scented Quinoa

Prep time: 5 mins | Servings: 4
Ingredients:
- Chopped walnuts
- 1 ½ cup water
- Maple syrup
- 2 cinnamon sticks
- 1 cup quinoa

Directions:
1. Add the quinoa to a bowl and wash it in several changes of water until the water is clear. When washing quinoa, rub grains and allow them to settle before you pour off the water.
2. Use a large fine-mesh sieve to drain the quinoa. Prepare your pressure cooker with a trivet and steaming basket. Place the quinoa and the cinnamon sticks in the basket and pour the water.
3. Close and lock the lid. Cook at high pressure for 6 mins. When the cooking time is up, release the pressure using the quick release method.
4. Fluff the quinoa with a fork and remove the cinnamon sticks. Divide the cooked quinoa among serving bowls and top with maple syrup and chopped walnuts.

Nutrition:
Calories 160, Fat 3 g, Carbs 28 g, Protein 6 g

Thyme Mushrooms

Prep time: 10 mins | Servings: 4
Ingredients:
- 1 tbsp chopped thyme
- 2 tbsp olive oil
- 2 tbsp chopped parsley
- 4 minced garlic cloves
- Black pepper
- 2 lbs. halved white mushrooms

Directions:
1. In a baking pan, combine the mushrooms with the garlic and the other Ingredients:, toss, introduce in the oven and cook at 400 °F for 30 mins.
2. Divide between plates and serve.

Nutrition:
Calories 251, Fat 9.3 g, Carbs 13.2 g, Protein 6 g

Rosemary Endives

Prep time: 10 mins | Servings: 4
Ingredients:
- 2 tbsp olive oil
- 1 tsp. dried rosemary
- 2 halved endives
- ¼ tsp. black pepper
- ½ tsp. turmeric powder

Directions:
1. In a baking pan, combine the endives with the oil and the other Ingredients:, toss gently, introduce in the oven and bake at 400 °F for 20 mins.
2. Divide between plates and serve.

Nutrition:
Calories 66, Fat 7.1 g, Carbs 1.2 g, Protein 0.3 g

Roasted Beets

Prep time: 10 mins | Servings: 4
Ingredients:

- 2 minced garlic cloves
- ¼ tsp. black pepper
- 4 peeled and sliced beets
- ¼ cup chopped walnuts
- 2 tbsp olive oil
- ¼ cup chopped parsley

Directions:
1. In a baking dish, combine the beets with the oil and the other Ingredients:, toss to coat, introduce in the oven at 420 °F, and bake for 30 mins.
2. Divide between plates and serve.

Nutrition:
Calories 156, Fat 11.8 g, Carbs 11.5 g, Protein 3.8 g

- 1 tbsp chopped sage
- 2 tbsp olive oil
- 1 lb. peeled and roughly cubed carrots
- ¼ tsp. black pepper
- 1 chopped red onion

Directions:
1. In a baking pan, combine the carrots with the oil and the other Ingredients:, toss and bake at 380 °F for 30 mins.
2. Divide between plates and serve.

Nutrition:
Calories 200, Fat 8.7 g, Carbs 7.9 g, Protein 4 g

Dates and Cabbage Sauté

Prep time: 5 mins | Servings: 4
Ingredients:
- 2 tbsp olive oil
- 2 tbsp lemon juice
- 1 lb. shredded red cabbage
- Black pepper
- 8 pitted and sliced dates
- 2 tbsp chopped chives
- ¼ cup low-sodium veggie stock

Directions:
- Heat up a pan with the oil over medium heat, add the cabbage and the dates, toss and cook for 4 mins.
- Add the stock and the other Ingredients:, toss, cook over medium heat for 11 mins more, divide between plates and serve.

Nutrition:
Calories 280, Fat 8.1 g, Carbs 8.7 g, Protein 6.3 g

Baked Squash Mix

Prep time: 10 mins | Servings: 4
Ingredients:
- 2 tsps. chopped cilantro
- 2 lbs. peeled and sliced butternut squash
- ¼ tsp. black pepper
- 1 tsp. garlic powder
- 2 tbsp olive oil
- 1 tsp. chili powder
- 1 tbsp lemon juice

Directions:
In a roasting pan, combine the squash with the oil and the other Ingredients:, toss gently, bake in the oven at 400 °F for 45 mins, divide between plates and serve.

Nutrition:
Calories 167, Fat 7.4 g, Carbs 27.5 g, Protein 2.5 g

Garlic Mushrooms and Corn

Prep time: 10 mins | Servings: 4
Ingredients:
- 2 cup corn
- 1 lb. halved white mushrooms
- ¼ tsp. black pepper
- ½ tsp. chili powder
- 2 tbsp olive oil
- 1 cup no-salt-added, chopped and canned tomatoes
- 4 minced garlic cloves

Directions:
1. Heat up a pan with the oil over medium heat, add the mushrooms, garlic and the corn, stir and sauté for 10 mins.
2. Add the rest of the Ingredients:, toss, cook over medium heat for 10 mins more, divide between plates and serve.

Nutrition:
Calories 285, Fat 13 g, Carbs 14.6 g, Protein 6.7 g

Cilantro Broccoli

Prep time: 10 mins | Servings: 4
Ingredients:
- 2 tbsp chili sauce
- 2 tbsp olive oil
- 2 minced garlic cloves
- ¼ tsp. black pepper
- 1 lb. broccoli florets
- 2 tbsp chopped cilantro
- 1 tbsp lemon juice

Directions:
1. In a baking pan, combine the broccoli with the oil, garlic and the other Ingredients:, toss a bit, introduce in the oven and bake at 400 °F for 30 mins.
2. Divide the mix between plates and serve.

Nutrition:
Calories 103, Fat 7.4 g, Carbs 8.3 g, Protein 3.4 g

Paprika Carrots

Prep time: 10 mins | Servings: 4
Ingredients:
- 1 tbsp sweet paprika
- 1 tsp. lime juice
- 1 lb. trimmed baby carrots
- ¼ tsp. black pepper
- 3 tbsp olive oil
- 1 tsp. sesame seeds

Directions:
- Arrange the carrots on a lined baking sheet, add the paprika and the other Ingredients: except the sesame seeds, toss, introduce in the oven and bake at 400 ⁰F for 30 mins.
- Divide the carrots between plates, sprinkle sesame seeds on top and serve.

Nutrition:
Calories 142, Fat 11.3 g, Carbs 11.4 g, Protein 1.2 g

Mashed Cauliflower

Prep time: 10 mins | Servings: 4
Ingredients:
- ½ cup coconut milk
- 1 tbsp chopped chives
- 2 lbs. cauliflower florets
- ¼ tsp. black pepper
- 1 tbsp chopped cilantro
- ½ cup low-fat sour cream

Directions:
1. Put the cauliflower in a pot, add water to cover, bring to a boil over medium heat, and cook for 25 mins and drain.
2. Mash the cauliflower, add the milk, black pepper and the cream, whisk well, divide between plates, sprinkle the rest of the Ingredients: on top and serve.

Nutrition:
Calories 188, Fat 13.4 g, Carbs 15 g, Protein 6.1 g

Spinach Spread

Prep time: 10 mins | Servings: 4
Ingredients:
- 1 cup coconut cream
- 1 tbsp chopped dill
- 1 lb. chopped spinach
- ¼ tsp. black pepper
- 1 cup shredded low-fat mozzarella

Directions:
1. In a baking pan, combine the spinach with the cream and the other Ingredients:, stir well, introduce in the oven and bake at 400 ⁰F for 20 mins.
2. Divide into bowls and serve.

Nutrition:
Calories 340, Fat 33 g, Carbs 4 g, Protein 5 g

Mustard Greens Sauté

Prep time: 10 mins | Servings: 4
Ingredients:
- 2 tbsp olive oil
- 2 chopped spring onions
- 6 cup mustard greens
- 2 tbsp sweet paprika
- Black pepper
- ½ cup coconut cream

Directions:
1. Heat up a pan with the oil over medium-high heat, add the onions, paprika and black pepper, stir and sauté for 3 mins.
2. Add the mustard greens and the other Ingredients:, toss, cook for 9 mins more, divide between plates and serve.

Nutrition:
Calories: 163, Fat:14.8 g, Carbs:8.3 g, Protein:3.6 g

Cauliflower with Breadcrumbs

Prep time: 10 mins | Servings: 4
Ingredients:
- Prep time: 10 mins | Servings: 4
- Ingredients:rgarine
- 1/8 tsp ground black pepper

Directions:
1. Place the bread in a toaster oven on very low heat. Toast as long as possible without burning (about 5 mins).
2. While bread toasts, trim leaves and stalks from cauliflower. Cut into individual florets.
3. Place 1 inch of water in a 4-quart pot with lid. Insert steamer basket, and place cauliflower in basket. Sprinkle with salt. Cover. Bring to a boil over high heat. Reduce heat to medium. Steam for 5–8 mins, until easily pierced with a sharp knife. Do not overcook.
4. While cauliflower steams, break toast into small pieces. Pulse toast in food processor until medium-sized crumbs form. Tip: If you don't have a food processor, break or crush the toasted bread into finer pieces or

buy whole-wheat breadcrumbs and use 2 tbsp
5. When cauliflower is done, remove from heat. Melt margarine in another pan over medium heat. Add breadcrumbs and pepper. Cook and stir, about 5 mins. Add cauliflower to pan with breadcrumbs. Toss until well coated. Serve immediately.

Nutrition:
Calories 45, Fat 4 g, Protein 2 g, Carbs 5 g

Chayotes Stuffed with Cheese

Prep time: 10 mins | Servings: 4
Ingredients:
- 6 small chayotes, cut in half, lengthwise
- 2 quarts water
- 1 cup low fat cheddar cheese, shredded
- 1/4 tsp salt
- 1 tbsp margarine
- 1/2 cup plain bread crumbs

Directions:
1. Wash chayotes and bring to a boil in water. Cover and boil at moderate heat for about 1 hour or until fork-tender.
2. Preheat oven to 350° F.
3. Drain chayotes, remove cores and fibrous part under cores. Scoop out pulp, being careful not to break shells. Place shells on cookie sheet.
4. Immediately mash pulp and mix with cheese, salt, and margarine.
5. Stuff shells with the mixture. Sprinkle with bread crumbs.
6. Bake for 30 mins.

Nutrition:
Calories 129, Fat 33 g, Carbs 4 g, Protein 5 g

Rotelle Pasta with Sun-Dried Tomato

Prep Time: 10 mins |Servings: 4| Cooking: 20 mins
Ingredients:
- 2 tbsp olive oil
- 4 garlic cloves, mashed

Directions:
1. Preheat olive oil in a skillet over medium heat.
2. Sauté garlic for 30 seconds. Then add tomatoes and broth.
3. Cover the mixture and then simmer for 10 mins.
4. Fill a pot with water and boil pasta in it for 10 mins until al dente.
5. Drain the pasta and keep it aside.
6. Add parsley and olives to the tomato mixture and mix well.
7. Serve the plate with tomato sauce and add 1 tsp parmesan cheese.

Nutrition:
Calories 335, Fat 4.4 g, Carbs 31.2 g, Fiber 2.7 g, Protein 7.3 g

Chapter 11: Side Dishes and Appetizers

Garlic Steamed Squash

Prep time: 5 mins | Servings: 4
Ingredients:
- 2 small zucchini
- Freshly ground black pepper
- All-purpose salt-free seasoning
- 2 medium yellow squash
- 6 peeled garlic cloves

Directions:
1. Trim the squash and zucchini and cut into 1-inch rounds.
2. Fill a steamer pot about 1 inch deep with water. Place pot over high heat and bring to a boil.
3. Place the veggies and garlic into the steamer basket. Place the steamer basket into the pot and cover tightly with lid. Steam for 10 mins.
4. Remove pot from heat and carefully remove lid. Pluck garlic cloves from pot and gently mash with a fork.
5. Transfer the steamed veggies to a serving bowl, add the mashed garlic and toss gently to coat. Season to taste with all-purpose salt-free seasoning and freshly ground black pepper. Serve immediately.

Nutrition:
Calories 38, Fat 0 g, Carbs 8 g, Protein 2 g

Grilled Asparagus

Prep time: 5 mins | Servings: 6
Ingredients:
- ¼ tsp. garlic powder
- 1 tbsp olive oil
- 2 bunches trimmed asparagus
- 1 tsp. lemon zest

Directions:
1. Preheat the grill to 375 – 400F.
2. Add the trimmed asparagus spears to a baking sheet.
3. Drizzle the asparagus with olive oil, garlic powder and salt, and using clean hands toss the asparagus well to coat with the seasoning.
4. Place the asparagus directly onto the grill grates and grill for 3-4 mins, until slightly caramelized.
5. Remove from the grill and season with the, fresh lemon zest, and serve.

Nutrition:
Calories 45, Fat 2 g, Carbs 6 g, Protein 3 g

Apple Glazed Sweet Potatoes

Prep Time: 10 mins |Servings: 4| Cooking: 25 mins
Ingredients:
- 2-1/2 cups unsweetened 100% apple juice
- 1/2 tsp ground cinnamon
- 2 lbs sweet potatoes (about 4 small potatoes), peeled and thinly sliced

Directions:
1. Combine apple juice, cinnamon, and salt in a large skillet. Add sliced sweet potatoes and bring to a boil over high heat.
2. Reduce heat slightly and simmer potatoes, stirring occasionally, for 20 to 25 mins or until potatoes are tender and juice has been reduced to a glaze. Serve while hot.

Nutrition:
Calories 208, Carbs 50 g, Fiber 5 g, Protein 3 g

Cauliflower and Potato Mash

Prep time: 5 mins | Servings: 4
Ingredients:
- ½ tsp. flavored vinegar
- 1 minced garlic clove
- 2 lbs. Sliced potatoes
- 1 ½ cup water
- 8 oz. cauliflower florets

Directions:
3. Add water to your Instant Pot
4. Add potatoes and sprinkle cauliflower florets on top
5. Lock up the lid and cook on HIGH pressure for 5 mins
6. Release the pressure naturally over 10 mins
7. Sprinkle a bit of flavored vinegar and garlic
8. Mash and serve!

Nutrition:
Calories 249, Fat 0.6 g, Carbs 55 g, Protein 7.5 g

Mexican Cauliflower Rice

Prep time: 5 mins | Servings: 4
Ingredients:
- 4 tbsp Tomato paste
- 1 ½ cup water
- 1 can fire roasted tomatoes
- 3 cup chopped onion
- 6 cup cooked brown rice
- 2 cup salsa
- 6 garlic cloves

Directions:
1. Add the listed Ingredients: to your Instant Pot
2. Lock up the lid and cook on HIGH pressure for 5 mins
3. Release the pressure naturally
4. Stir in chopped cilantro and top up with your desired toppings

Nutrition:
Calories 562, Fat 25 g, Carbs 63 g, Protein 23 g

Asparagus with Lemon Sauce

Prep time: 5 mins | Servings: 4 | Cooking: 15 mins
Ingredients:
- 20 medium asparagus spears, rinsed and trimmed
- 1 fresh lemon, rinsed (for peel and juice)
- 2 tbsps reduced-fat mayonnaise
- 1 tbsp dried parsley
- 1/8 tsp ground black pepper

Directions:
1. Place 1 inch of water in a 4-quart pot with a lid. Place a steamer basket inside the pot, and add asparagus.
2. Cover and bring to a boil over high heat. Reduce heat to medium. Cook for 5–10 mins, until asparagus is easily pierced with a sharp knife. Do not overcook.
3. While the asparagus cooks, grate the lemon zest into a small bowl. Cut the lemon in half and squeeze the juice into the bowl. Use the back of a spoon to press out extra juice and remove pits. Add mayonnaise, parsley, pepper, and salt. Stir well. Set aside.
4. When the asparagus is tender, remove the pot from the heat. Place asparagus spears in a serving bowl. Drizzle the lemon sauce evenly over the asparagus (about 1-1/2 tsps per portion) and serve.

Nutrition:
Calories 39, Fat 0 g

Autumn Salad

Prep time: 5 mins | Servings: 6
Ingredients:
- 1 medium Granny Smith apple, sliced thinly (with skin)
- 2 tbsps lemon juice
- 1 bag (about 5 cups) mixed lettuce greens (or your favorite lettuce)
- 1/2 cup dried cranberries n 1/4 cup walnuts, chopped
- 1/4 cup unsalted sunflower seeds
- 1/3 cup low-fat raspberry vinaigrette dressing

Directions:
1. Sprinkle lemon juice on the apple slices.
2. Mix the lettuce, cranberries, apple, walnuts, and sunflower seeds in a bowl.
3. Toss with 1/3 cup of raspberry vinaigrette dressing, to lightly cover the salad.

Nutrition:
Calories 138, Fat 7 g, Protein 3 g, Carbs 19 g

Broccoli and Cheese

Prep time: 5 mins | Servings: 4 | Cooking: 15 mins
Ingredients:
- 6 cups fresh broccoli, rinsed and cut into bite-sized florets (or substitute 6 cups frozen broccoli, thawed and warmed, and skip step 1)

For sauce
- 1 cup fat-free evaporated milk
- 1 tbsp cornstarch
- 1/2 cup shredded cheddar cheese
- 1/4 tsp Worcestershire sauce
- 1/4 tsp hot sauce
- 1 slice whole-wheat bread, diced and toasted (for croutons)

Directions:
1. Bring a large pot of water to boil over high heat. Add fresh broccoli, and cook until easily pierced by a fork, about 7–10 mins. Drain and set aside.
2. In a separate saucepan, combine evaporated milk and cornstarch. Slowly bring to a boil while stirring often.
3. When the milk comes to a boil, remove it from the heat and add the cheese. Continue to stir until the cheese is melted and evenly mixed.
4. Add the Worcestershire and hot sauces, and stir.

5. Pour cheese over hot broccoli.
6. Sprinkle whole-wheat croutons over broccoli and cheese mixture, and serve.

Nutrition:
Calories 162, Fat 5 g, Fiber 4 g, Protein 11 g, Carbs 19 g

Caribbean Casserole

Prep time: 5 mins | Servings: 10 | Cooking: 10 mins
Ingredients:
- 1 medium onion, chopped
- 1/2 green pepper, diced
- 1 tbsp canola oil
- 1 14-1/2-ounce can stewed tomatoes
- 1 16-ounce can black beans (or beans of your choice)
- 1 tsp oregano leaves
- 1/2 tsp garlic powder
- 1-1/2 cups instant brown rice, uncooked

Directions:
1. Sauté onion and green pepper in canola oil, in a large pan, until tender. Do not brown.
2. Add tomatoes, beans (include liquid from both), oregano, and garlic powder. Bring to a boil. Stir in rice and cover. Reduce heat to simmer for 5 mins. Remove from heat and let stand for 5 mins.

Nutrition:
Calories 185, Fat 1 g, Protein 7 g, Carbs 37 g

Avocado Garden Salad

Prep time: 5 mins | Servings: 6| Cooking: 10 mins
Ingredients:
- 6 cups torn or cut mixed salad greens
- 3 medium tomatoes, chopped
- 5 green onions, chopped
- 1 small cucumber, peeled and chopped
- 2 tbsps lemon juice
- 1/3 tsp garlic powder
- 1/2 tsp ground black pepper
- 1/2 tsp salt
- 1 large avocado, peeled

Directions:
Combine all the ingredients and serve.

Nutrition:
Calories 78, Carbs 9 g, Fiber 4 g, Protein 2 g, Fat 5 g

Oven-Fried Yucca

Prep time: 5 mins | Servings: 6 | Cooking: 35 mins
Ingredients:
- 1 lb fresh yucca (cassava), cut into 3-inch sections and peeled (or 1 lb peeled frozen yucca)
- nonstick cooking oil spray

Directions:
1. In a kettle, combine the yucca with enough cold water to cover it by 1 inch. Bring the water to a boil, and slowly simmer the yucca for 20 to 30 mins, or until it is tender.
2. Preheat oven to 350° F.
3. Transfer the yucca with a slotted spoon to a cutting board, let it cool, and cut it lengthwise into 3/4-inch-wide wedges, discarding the thin woody core.
4. Spray cookie sheet with the nonstick cooking oil spray. Spread yucca wedges on cookie sheet, and spray wedges with cooking oil spray. Cover with foil paper and bake for 8 mins. Uncover and return to oven to bake for an additional 7 mins.

Nutrition:
Calories 91, Fat 1 g, Fiber 4 g, Protein 11 g, Carbs 19 g

Celery with Cheese Mousse

Prep time: 5 mins | Servings: 4
Ingredients:
- 1/4 cup low-fat whipped cream cheese
- 1/4 cup fat-free plain yogurt
- 2 tbsps scallions (green onions), rinsed and chopped
- 1 tbsp lemon juice
- 1/2 tsp ground black pepper
- 6 celery sticks, rinsed, with ends cut off
- 1 tbsp chopped walnuts

Directions:
1. Combine cream cheese, yogurt, scallions, lemon juice, and pepper. Mix well with a wooden spoon.
2. Spread mixture evenly down the middle of each celery stick.
3. Cut each stick into 5 pieces. Top with chopped walnuts, and serve.

Nutrition:
Calories 35, Fiber 1 g, Protein 2 g, Carbs 3 g, Fat 2 g

Chicken Tomatillo Salad

Prep time: 5 mins | Servings: 6 | Cooking: 20 mins
Ingredients:
Dressing
- 1 cup husked and quartered tomatillos

- 3 tbsps light Italian dressing
- 1 fresh Anaheim chili, seeded and chopped
- 1/4 tsp ground black pepper

Salad
- 2 cups chopped, cooked chicken or turkey
- 1 cup chopped red bell pepper
- 1 cup frozen corn, thawed
- 1 cup chopped carrots
- 4 green onions, sliced
- 1/4 cup chopped fresh cilantro

Directions:
1. In a blender or food processor container, purée tomatillos with dressing, Anaheim chili, and ground black pepper; set aside.
2. Combine all salad Ingredients: in a large bowl and toss.
3. Drizzle dressing over salad and toss well to coat.
4. Cover and chill for 20 mins or make a day ahead to allow flavors to blend.
5. Serve on lettuce-lined plates or bowls.

Nutrition:
Calories 141, Carbs 12 g, Protein 16 g, Fat 4 g

Green Beans Sauté

Prep time: 5 mins | Servings: 6 | Cooking: 20 mins
Ingredients:
- 1 lb fresh or frozen green beans, cut in 1-inch pieces
- 1 tbsp vegetable oil
- 1 large yellow onion, halved lengthwise and thinly sliced
- 1 tbsp fresh parsley, minced

Directions:
1. If using fresh green beans, cook green beans in boiling water for 10-12 mins or steam for 2-3 mins until barely fork tender. Drain well. If using frozen green beans, thaw first.
2. Heat oil in a large skillet. Sauté onion until golden.
3. Stir in green beans, salt and pepper. Heat through.
4. Toss with parsley before serving.

Nutrition:
Calories 64, Fiber 1 g, Protein 2 g, Carbs 3 g, Fat 2 g

Romaine Lettuce With Dressing

Prep time: 5 mins | Servings: 4
Ingredients:
- 1 slice whole wheat-bread
- 2 heads romaine lettuce, rinsed and halved lengthwise
- 4 tsps olive oil
- 4 tsps light Caesar dressing
- 4 tbsps shredded parmesan cheese
- 16 cherry tomatoes, rinsed and halved

Directions:
1. Preheat grill pan on high temperature.
2. Cube the bread. Spread in a single layer on a foil-covered tray for a toaster oven or conventional oven. Toast to a medium-brown color and crunchy texture. Remove. Allow to cool.
3. Brush the cut side of each half of romaine lettuce with 1 tsp of olive oil.
4. Place cut side down on a grill pan on the stovetop. Cook just until grill marks appear and romaine is heated through, about 2–5 mins.
5. Place each romaine half on a large salad plate. Top each with one-fourth of the bread cubes. Drizzle each with 1 tsp of light Caesar dressing. Sprinkle each with 1 tbsp of shredded parmesan cheese. Garnish with eight tomato halves around each plate.

Nutrition:
Calories 162, Carbohydrate 17 g, Dietary Fiber 2 g, Protein 1 g, Total Fat 1

Corn and Green Chili Salad

Prep time: 5 mins | Servings: 4
Ingredients:
- 2 cups frozen corn, thawed
- 1 (10-ounce) can diced tomatoes with green chilies, drained
- 1/2 tbsp vegetable oil
- 1 tbsp lime juice
- 1/3 cup sliced green onions
- 2 tbsps chopped fresh cilantro

Directions::s
Combine all Ingredients: in a medium bowl; mix well and serve.

Nutrition: Information
Calories 94, Carbs 19 g, Protein 3 g, Fat 2 g

Avocado appetizer

Prep time: 7 mins | Servings: 4
Ingredients:
- 1 tbsp vinegar
- 2 tbsp moustard
- 2 tbsps lemon juice

- 1/3 tsp garlic powder
- 1/2 tsp ground black pepper
- 2 large avocado, divided in two parts

Directions:
Combine all the ingredients and put the vinaigrette on top of each half avocado and serve.
Nutrition:
Calories 78, Carbs 8 g, Fiber 5 g, Protein 4 g, Fat 5 g

Cabbage and Tomato Salad

Prep time: 5 mins | Servings: 8
Ingredients:
- 1 small head cabbage, sliced thinly
- 2 medium tomatoes, cut in cubes
- 1 cup sliced radishes
- 2 tsps olive oil
- 2 tbsps rice vinegar (or lemon juice)
- 2 tbsps fresh cilantro, chopped

Directions:
1. In a large bowl, mix together the cabbage, tomatoes, and radishes.
2. In another bowl, mix together the rest of the ingredients and pour over the vegetables.

Nutrition:
Calories 41, Carbohydrate 7 g, Dietary Fiber 2 g, Protein 1 g, Total Fat 1

Creole Green Beans

Prep time: 5 mins | Servings: 8 | Cooking: 7 mins
Ingredients:
- 2 tsps vegetable oil
- 2 small cloves garlic, chopped
- 1 (16-ounce) package frozen cut green beans
- 1 cup chopped red bell pepper
- 1 cup chopped fresh tomatoes
- 1/2 cup chopped celery
- 1/4 tsp cayenne pepper

Directions:
1. Heat oil in a large skillet over low heat.
2. Sauté garlic in oil for 1 minute.
3. Add green beans and bell peppers; increase heat to medium and cook for 7 mins.
4. Stir in tomatoes, celery, and seasonings; cook for 7 mins more. Serve while hot.
5. Nutrition:

Calories 35, Carbohydrate 6 g, Fiber 2 g, Protein 1 g, Total Fat 1 g

Mango and Blackeye Pea Salsa

Prep time: 5 mins | Servings: 10
Ingredients:
- 1 (15-1/2-ounce) can black-eyed peas, drained and rinsed
- 1-1/2 tomatoes, finely chopped
- 1 mango, peeled and finely chopped
- 2 green onions, chopped
- 1 tbsp vegetable oil
- 1 tbsp white vinegar
- juice of half a lime
- 1 tsp ground cumin
- 1/2 tsp garlic powder

Directions:
1. In a large bowl, combine all ingredients and mix well.
2. Serve immediately or cover and refrigerate for up to 4 hours to allow the flavors to blend.
3. Serve with baked pita or corn chips.

Nutrition:
Calories 83, Carbohydrate 14 g, Fiber 2 g, Protein 1 g, Total Fat 1

Garden Potato Salad

Prep time: 10 mins | Servings: 10
Ingredients:
- 3 lbs (about 6 large) potatoes, boiled in jackets, peeled and cut into 1/2-inch cubes
- 1 cup chopped celery
- 1/2 cup sliced green onion
- 2 tbsps chopped parsley
- 1 cup low-fat cottage cheese
- 3/4 cup skim milk
- 3 tbsps lemon juice
- 2 tbsps cider vinegar
- 1/2 tsp celery seed
- 1/2 tsp dill weed
- 1/2 tsp dry mustard

Directions:
1. In a large bowl, place potatoes, celery, green onion, and parsley.
2. Meanwhile, in a blender or food processor, blend cottage cheese, milk, lemon juice, vinegar, celery seed, dill weed, dry mustard, and white pepper until smooth. Chill for 1 hour.
3. Pour chilled cottage cheese mixture over vegetables; mix well. Chill at least 30 mins before serving.

Nutrition:
Calories 151, Carbs 11 g, Fiber 6 g, Protein 3 g, Total Fat 1 g

Oven Fries

Prep time: 10 mins | Servings: 4 | Cooking: 14 mins
Ingredients:
- nonstick cooking spray
- 2 large russet potatoes, cut into wedges

Seasoning Mix
- 2 cloves garlic, finely chopped
- 1 tsp Italian herb seasoning mix
- 1 tsp chili powder and/or paprika

Directions:
1. Preheat oven to 400°F.
2. Spray a cookie sheet with nonstick cooking spray. Place potato wedges on the cookie sheet.
3. In a small bowl, combine garlic with seasonings and sprinkle 1/2 of the mixture over the top of the potato wedges.
4. Bake wedges for about 7 mins or until they start to brown. Flip wedges over. Sprinkle with the remaining mixture, and bake for another 7 mins or until the wedges are browned and cooked through. Serve while hot.

Nutrition:
Calories 146, Carbs 33 g, Fiber 6 g, Protein 3 g, Fat 8 g

Parmesan Rice and Pasta

Prep time: 10 mins | Servings: 4 | Cooking: 25 mins
Ingredients:
- 2 tbsps olive oil
- 1/2 cup finely broken vermicelli, uncooked
- 2 tbsps diced onion
- 1 cup long-grain white rice, uncooked
- 1-1/4 cups hot chicken stock
- 1-1/4 cups hot water
- 1 bay leaf
- 2 tbsps grated parmesan cheese

Directions:
1. In a large skillet, heat oil. Sauté vermicelli and onion until golden brown, about 2 to 4 mins over medium-high heat. Drain off oil.
2. Add rice, stock, water, pepper, and bay leaf. Cover and simmer 15-20 mins. Fluff with fork. Cover and let stand 5-20 mins. Remove bay leaf.
3. Sprinkle with cheese and serve immediately.

Nutrition:
Calories 172, Carbs 11 g, Fiber 6 g, Protein 3 g, Total Fat 1 g

Potato Sauté with Onions

Prep time: 10 mins | Servings: 4 | Cooking: 15 mins
Ingredients:
- 2 cups water
- 2 large russet potatoes, cleaned and cut in half
- 1 tbsp vegetable oil
- 1/2 cup chopped onion
- 1/2 cup no salt added canned corn or frozen corn, thawed
- 1/2 cup chopped tomato
- 1/2 tsp oregano
- 1/4 cup crumbled reduced fat Monterey Jack cheese

Directions:
6. Bring water to a boil in a large pan. Add potatoes and cook until crisp-tender, about 15 mins. Drain well and cut into bite-size pieces.
7. Heat oil in a large skillet. Sauté onion until golden brown and soft. Add potatoes and cook over medium-high heat, stirring frequently, until golden brown.
8. Stir in corn, tomato, oregano, salt, and ground black pepper. Top with cheese and serve.

Nutrition:
Calories 217, Carbs 39 g, Fiber 6 g, Protein 6 g, Fat 5 g

Garlic Mashed Potatoes

Prep time: 10 mins | Servings: 4 | Cooking: 45 mins
Ingredients:
- 1 lb (about 2 large) potatoes, peeled and quartered
- 2 cups skim milk
- 2 large cloves garlic, chopped
- 1/2 tsp white pepper

Directions:
1. Cook potatoes, covered, in a small amount of boiling water for 20-25 mins or until tender. Remove from heat. Drain and recover.

2. Meanwhile, in a small saucepan over low heat, cook garlic in milk until garlic is soft, about 30 mins.
3. Add milk-garlic mixture and white pepper to potatoes. Beat with an electric mixer on low speed or mash with a potato masher until smooth.

Microwave Directions

Scrub potatoes, pat dry, and prick with a fork. On a plate, cook potatoes, uncovered, on 100% power (high) until tender, about 12 mins, turning potatoes over once. Let stand 5 mins. Peel and quarter. Meanwhile, in a 4-cup glass measuring cup, combine milk and garlicup Cook, uncovered, on 50% power (medium) until garlic is soft, about 4 mins. Continue as directed above.

Nutrition:
Calories 141, Carbohydrate 18 g, Fiber 2 g, Protein 1 g, Total Fat 1 g

Red Hot Fusilli

Prep time: 10 mins | Servings: 4 | Cooking: 15 mins
Ingredients:
- 1 tbsp olive oil
- 2 cloves garlic, minced
- 1/4 cup freshly minced parsley
- 4 cups ripe tomatoes, chopped
- 1 tbsp fresh basil, chopped or 1 tsp dried basil
- 1 tbsp oregano leaves, crushed or 1 tsp dried oregano
- ground red pepper or cayenne to taste
- 8 oz uncooked fusilli pasta (4 cups cooked)

Directions:
- Heat oil in a medium saucepan. Sauté garlic and parsley until golden.
- Add tomatoes and spices. Cook uncovered over low heat 15 mins or until thickened, stirring frequently.
- Cook pasta firm in unsalted water.
- To serve, spoon sauce over pasta and sprinkle with coarsely chopped parsley

Nutrition:
Calories 304, Carbs 39 g, Fiber 6 g, Protein 6 g, Fat 5 g

Egg and Beans

Prep time: 5 mins | Servings: 3
Ingredients:
- 5 beaten eggs
- 1 tsp. chili powder
- 2 chopped garlic cloves
- ½ cup milk
- ½ cup tomato sauce
- 1 cup cooked white beans

Directions:
1. Add milk and eggs to a bowl and mix well
2. Add the rest of the Ingredients: and mix well
3. Add a cup of water to the pot
4. Transfer the bowl to your pot and lock up the lid
5. Cook on HIGH pressure for 18 mins
6. Release the pressure naturally over 10 mins
7. Serve with warm bread

Nutrition:
Calories 206, Fat 9 g, Carbs 23 g, Protein 9 g

Glazed Carrots

Prep time: 5 mins | Servings: 4 | Cooking: 10 mins
Ingredients:
- 4 cups baby carrots, rinsed and split lengthwise if very thick (or frozen pre-sliced carrots)
- 2 tbsps soft tub margarine
- 2 tbsps brown sugar
- 1/2 tsp ground cinnamon

Directions:
1. Place the carrots in a small saucepan. Add just enough water to barely cover the carrots. Cover. Bring to a boil. Cook for 7–8 mins
2. Combine margarine, brown sugar, cinnamon, and salt in a small saucepan, and melt together over low heat (or put in a microwave-safe bowl and microwave for a few seconds on high power, until margarine is mostly melted). Stir well to combine ingredients.
3. Drain carrots, leaving them in the saucepan. Pour cinnamon mixture over carrots. Cook and stir over medium heat for 2–3 mins, just until carrots are thoroughly coated and the glaze thickens slightly

Nutrition:
Calories 67, Fat 3 g, Fiber 2 g, Protein 1 g, Carbs 10 g

Fresh Cabbage and Tomato Salad

Prep time: 5 mins | Servings: 8
Ingredients:
- 1 small head cabbage, sliced thinly

- 2 medium tomatoes, cut in cubes
- 1 cup sliced radishes
- 2 tsps olive oil
- 2 tbsps rice vinegar (or lemon juice)
- 1/2 tsp red pepper
- 2 tbsps fresh cilantro, chopped

Directions:
1. In a large bowl, mix together the cabbage, tomatoes, and radishes.
2. In another bowl, mix together the rest of the Ingredients: and pour over the vegetables.

Nutrition:
Calories 41, Fat 1 g

Garlic Mashed Potatoes

Prep time: 5 mins | Servings: 4 | Cooking: 35 mins
Ingredients:
- 1 lb (about 2 large) potatoes, peeled and quartered
- 2 cups skim milk
- 2 large cloves garlic, chopped

Directions:
1. Cook potatoes, covered, in a small amount of boiling water for 20-25 mins or until tender. Remove from heat. Drain and recover.
2. Meanwhile, in a small saucepan over low heat, cook garlic in milk until garlic is soft, about 30 mins.
3. Add milk-garlic mixture and white pepper to potatoes. Beat with an electric mixer on low speed or mash with a potato masher until smooth.

Microwave Directions:
Scrub potatoes, pat dry, and prick with a fork. On a plate, cook potatoes, uncovered, on 100% power (high) until tender, about 12 mins, turning potatoes over once. Let stand 5 mins. Peel and quarter. Meanwhile, in a 4-cup glass measuring cup, combine milk and garlicup Cook, uncovered, on 50% power (medium) until garlic is soft, about 4 mins. Continue as directed above.

Nutrition:
Calories 141, Fat less than 1 g

Corn and Green Chili Salad

Prep time: 5 mins | Servings: 4
Ingredients:
- 2 cups frozen corn, thawed
- 1 (10-ounce) can diced tomatoes with green chilies, drained
- 1/2 tbsp vegetable oil
- 1 tbsp lime juice
- 1/3 cup sliced green onions
- 2 tbsps chopped fresh cilantro

Directions:
Combine all ingredients in a medium bowl; mix well and serve.

Nutrition:
Calories 94, Carbs 19 g, Protein 3 g, Fat 2 g

Cheddar and Apple Sandwich

Prep time: 5 mins | Servings: 2
Ingredients:
- Cooking spray
- ½ cup arugula
- 4 whole-wheat bread slices
- 4 low-fat cheddar cheese slices
- 2 tbsp low-fat honey mustard
- 1 thinly sliced apple

Directions:
1. Set Panini press on medium heat.
2. Spread the mustard on each slice of the bread. Lay the apple on two of the bread slices, top with cheese and then the arugula. Top with the other two slices of bread.
3. Coat the Panini press with cooking spray and grill each sandwich for 4-5 mins.
4. Allow to cool before serving.

Nutrition:
Calories 22, Fat 4 g, Carbs 23 g, Protein 11 g

Herbed Potato Salad

Prep time: 5 mins | Servings: 6 | Cooking: 10 mins
Ingredients:
- 1-1/2 lbs red potatoes (about 8 potatoes), cut into cubes
- 1/2 cup light Italian dressing
- 1/2 tbsp spicy brown mustard
- 1 tbsp chopped fresh parsley
- 1 tsp garlic salt
- 1/4 tsp ground black pepper
- 1/2 cup chopped red bell pepper
- 1/2 cup chopped green bell pepper
- 1/2 cup chopped green onions

Directions:
1. In a large pot, cook potatoes in boiling water until tender, about 10 mins (do not overcook).
2. Drain well and let cool.

3. Cut potatoes into bite-size pieces and place in a medium bowl.
4. In a small bowl, combine dressing, mustard, parsley, and seasonings; pour over potatoes and toss well.
5. Carefully stir in bell peppers and green onions. Cover and chill until ready to serve.

Nutrition:
Calories 132, Carbs 24 g, Fiber 4 g, Protein 2 g, Fat 4 g

Herbed Vegetable Mix

Prep time: 5 mins | Servings: 7 | Cooking: 13 mins
Ingredients:
- 2 tbsps water
- 1 cup thinly sliced zucchini
- 1-1/4 cups thinly sliced yellow squash
- 1/2 cup green bell pepper, cut into 2-inch strips
- 1/4 cup celery, cut into 2-inch strips
- 1/4 cup chopped onion
- 1/2 tsp caraway seeds
- 1/8 tsp garlic powder
- 1 medium tomato, cut into 8 wedges

Directions:
1. Heat water in a medium pan. Add zucchini, squash, bell pepper, celery, and onion.
2. Cover and cook over medium heat until vegetables are crisp-tender, about 4 mins.
3. Sprinkle seasonings over vegetables. Top with tomato wedges.
4. Cover again and cook over low heat until tomato wedges are warm, about 2 mins. Serve warm.

Nutrition:
Calories 24, Carbs 5 g, Fiber 4 g, Protein 2 g, Fat 4 g

Limas and Spinach

Prep time: 5 mins | Servings: 7 | Cooking: 13 mins
Ingredients:
- 2 cups frozen lima beans
- 1 tbsp vegetable oil
- 1 cup fennel, cut in 4-inch strips
- 1/2 cup onion, chopped
- 1/4 cup low-sodium chicken broth
- 4 cups leaf spinach, washed thoroughly
- 1 tbsp distilled vinegar
- 1/8 tsp black pepper
- 1 tbsp raw chives

Directions:
1. Steam or boil lima beans in unsalted water for about 10 mins. Drain.
2. In skillet, sauté onions and fennel in oil.
3. Add beans and broth to onions and cover. Cook for 2 mins.
4. Stir in spinach. Cover and cook until spinach has wilted, about 2 mins.
5. Stir in vinegar and pepper. Cover and let stand for 30 seconds.
6. Sprinkle with chives and serve.

Nutrition:
Calories 93, Fat 2 g, Protein 5 g, Carbs 15 g

Oriental Rice

Prep time: 5 mins | Servings: 6 | Cooking: 13 mins
Ingredients:
- 1-1/2 cups water
- 1 cup chicken stock or broth, skim fat from top
- 1-1/3 cups uncooked long-grain white rice
- 2 tsps vegetable oil
- 2 tbsps finely chopped onion
- 2 T finely chopped green pepper
- 1/2 cup chopped pecans
- 1/4 tsp ground sage
- 1 cup finely chopped celery
- 1/2 cup sliced water chestnuts
- 1/4 tsp nutmeg

Directions:
1. Bring water and stock to a boil in medium-size saucepan.
2. Add rice and stir. Cover and simmer 20 mins.
3. Remove pan from heat. Let stand, covered, 5 mins or until all liquid is absorbed. Reserve.
4. Heat oil in large nonstick skillet.
5. Sauté onion and celery over moderate heat 3 mins. Stir in remaining Ingredients: including reserved cooked rice. Fluff with fork before serving.

Nutrition:
Calories 139, Total Fat 5 g, Saturated Fat less

Parmesan Rice and Pasta Pilaf

Prep time: 5 mins | Servings: 6 | Cooking: 13 mins
Ingredients:
- 2 tbsps olive oil
- 1/2 cup finely broken vermicelli, uncooked
- 2 tbsps diced onion
- 1 cup long-grain white rice, uncooked
- 1-1/4 cups hot chicken stock

- 1-1/4 cups hot water
- 1/4 tsp ground white pepper
- 1 bay leaf
- 2 tbsps grated parmesan cheese

Directions:
4. In a large skillet, heat oil. Sauté vermicelli and onion until golden brown, about 2 to 4 mins over medium-high heat. Drain off oil.
5. Add rice, stock, water, pepper, and bay leaf. Cover and simmer 15-20 mins. Fluff with fork. Cover and let stand 5-20 mins. Remove bay leaf.
6. Sprinkle with cheese and serve immediately.

Nutrition:
Calories 172, Fat 6 g

Roasted Carrots

Prep time: 15 mins | Servings: 4 | Cooking: 30 mins
Ingredients:
- 2 lbs. peeled and halved carrots
- 2 tbsp olive oil
- Flat leaf parsley
- 1 tbsp raw honey

Directions:
1. Preheat the oven to 400F.
2. Peel the carrots, cutting off the stems, and then cut the carrots in half creating a piece with a wide and narrow half.
3. Halve each carrot in half again lengthwise.
4. Place all the cut carrots into a bowl and add the olive oil, salt, pepper, and raw honey. Toss the carrots well to coat.
5. Spread the carrots evenly onto a baking sheet lined with aluminum foil, making sure they are all in a single layer.
6. Bake the carrots for 30 mins, and then remove from oven to cool.
7. Garnish with fresh flat leaf parsley, if desired.

Nutrition:
Calories 109, Fat 5.8 g, Carbs 14 g, Protein 1.4 g

Turkey and Cheese Sandwich

Prep time: 10 mins | Servings: 2 | Cooking: 5 mins
Ingredients:
- 2 tsps. Dijon mustard
- ½ cup thinly sliced cucumber
- 2 whole-grain bread slices
- 2 low-sodium smoked turkey slices
- Pepper.

- ¼ cup shredded low-fat mozzarella

Directions:
1. Spread the mustard on each of the slices.
2. Lay the smoked turkey slice and then the cucumber slices on top of the bread. Sprinkle with the mozzarella and season with pepper.
3. Toaster to melt the cheese for about 3 mins.
4. Serve while warm.

Nutrition:
Calories 380, Fat 13.5 g, Carbs 40 g, Protein 25 g

Crunchy Mashed Sweet Potatoes

Prep time: 5 mins | Servings: 4 | Cooking: 10 mins
Ingredients:
- ¼ tsp. nutmeg
- 1 cup water
- 2 lbs. Sliced garnet sweet potatoes
- Sea flavored vinegar
- 2 tbsp Maple syrup
- 3 tbsp Vegan butter

Directions:
1. Peel the sweet potatoes and cut up into 1 inch chunks
2. Pour 1 cup of water to the pot and add steamer basket
3. Add sweet potato chunks in the basket
4. Lock up the lid and cook on HIGH pressure for 8 mins
5. Quick release the pressure
6. Open the lid and place the cooked sweet potatoes to the bowl
7. Use a masher to mash the potatoes
8. Add ¼ tsp of nutmeg, 2-3 tbsp of unflavored vinegar butter, 2 tbsp of maple syrup
9. Mash and mix
10. Season with flavored vinegar

Nutrition:
Calories 249, Fat 8 g, Carbs 37 g, Protein 7 g

Special Roast Potatoes

Prep time: 5 mins | Servings: 4 | Cooking: 17 mins
Ingredients:
- Pepper
- 2 lbs. baby potatoes
- 3 skinned out garlic clove
- ½ cup stock
- 5 tbsp Olive oil
- 1 rosemary sprig

Directions:
1. Set your pot to Sauté mode and add oil

2. Once it is heated up, add in the garlic, rosemary and potatoes
3. Sauté the potatoes for 10 mins and brown them
4. Take a sharp knife and cut a small piece in the middle of your potatoes and pour the stock
5. Lock up the lid and cook on HIGH pressure for 7 mins
6. Once done, wait for 10 mins and release the pressure naturally
7. Add garlic cloves and peel the potatoes skin
8. Sprinkle a bit of pepper and enjoy!

Nutrition:
Calories 42, Fat 1.3 g, Carbs 7.3 g, Protein 0.8 g

Crazy Eggs

Prep time: 5 mins | Servings: 6 | Cooking: 10 mins
Ingredients:
- Guacamole
- Furikake
- Mayonnaise
- 8 large eggs
- 1 cup water
- Sliced radishes

Directions:
1. Add 1 cup of water to your Instant Pot
2. Place the steamer insert in your pot
3. Arrange the eggs on top of the insert
4. Lock up the lid and cook for about 6 mins at HIGH pressure
5. Allow the pressure to release naturally
6. Transfer the eggs to an ice bath and peel the skin
7. Cut the eggs in half and garnish them with dressings of Guacamole, sliced up radishes, Mayonnaise, Furikake, Sliced up Parmesan etcup!

Nutrition:
Calories 137, Fat 10 g, Carbs 1 g, Protein 11 g

Potato, Onions and Bell Peppers

Prep time: 20 mins | Servings: 4 | Cooking: 20 mins
Ingredients:
- 2 cups water
- 2 large russet potatoes, cleaned and cut in half
- 1 tbsp vegetable oil
- 1/2 cup chopped onion
- 1/2 cup chopped green and red bell pepper
- 1/2 cup no salt added canned corn or frozen corn, thawed
- 1/2 cup chopped tomato
- 1/2 tsp oregano
- 1/4 cup crumbled reduced fat Monterey Jack cheese

Directions:
1. Bring water to a boil in a large pan. Add potatoes and cook until crisp-tender, about 15 mins. Drain well and cut into bite-size pieces.
2. Heat oil in a large skillet. Sauté onion until golden brown and soft. Add potatoes and bell pepper to skillet and cook over medium-high heat, stirring frequently, until golden brown.
3. Stir in corn, tomato, oregano, salt, and ground black pepper. Top with cheese and serve.

Nutrition:
Calories 217, Carbs 39 g, Protein 6 g, Fat 5 g

Green Pea Purée

Prep time: 20 mins | Servings: 2
Ingredients:
- 2 boiled sliced carrots
- ¼ cup 20% fat sour cream
- Pepper.
- 2 cup green peas

Directions:
1. Boil the carrots and the peas.
2. Using a blender purée the vegetables. Season with salt and pepper. Top with sour cream.

Nutrition:
Calories 101, Fat 2.1 g, Carbs 14 g, Protein 7 g

Green Beans with Nuts

Prep time: 20 mins | Servings: 2 | Cooking: 8 mins
Ingredients:
- 3 minced garlic cloves
- 1 tbsp olive oil
- ½ cup chopped walnuts
- 2 cup sliced green beans

Directions:
1. Boil the beans in salted water until tender.
2. Place the beans, garlic and walnuts in a preheated pan and cook for about 5-7 mins on the stove.

Nutrition:

Calories 285, Fat 24.1 g, Carbs 7.1 g, Protein 10 g

Beets Stewed with Apples

Prep time: 1 hour | Servings: 2 | Cooking: 30 mins
Ingredients:
- 2 tbsp Tomato paste
- 1 tbsp Olive oil
- 1 cup water
- 2 peeled, cored and sliced apples
- 3 peeled, boiled and grated beets
- 2 tbsp Sour cream

Directions:

1. Boil the beets until half-done
2. In a deep pan preheated with olive oil cook the grated beets for 15 mins.
3. Add the sliced apples, tomato paste, sour cream and 1 cup water. Stew for 30 mins covered.

Nutrition:
Calories 346, Fat 7.7 g, Carbs 26.8 g, Protein 2 g

Cabbage Quiche

Prep time: 30 mins | Servings: 4
Ingredients:
- 2 beaten eggs
- 2 tbsp Sour cream
- 2 tsps. Semolina
- Fresh parsley
- ½ shredded white cabbage head
- 2 tbsp milk

Directions:
1. In a saucepan stew the shredded cabbage with milk until soft and done.
2. Sprinkle the semolina over the cabbage, constantly stirring, and cook for 10 mins more.
3. Remove from the heat, let cool and stir in the beaten eggs. Season with salt.
4. Arrange the cabbage mixture in a baking dish, coat with sour cream and bake at 400F for 20 mins.
5. Serve with sour cream and fresh parsley leaves.

Nutrition:
Calories 93, Fat 0.5 g, Carbs 27.8 g, Protein 19.4 g

Baked Tomatoes

Prep time: 5 mins | Servings: 2 | Cooking: 10 mins
Ingredients:
- 2 minced garlic cloves
- 2 tbsp Olive oil
- 2 sliced large tomatoes
- 2 tbsp Minced basil
- 1 minced rosemary sprig

Directions:
1. Brush a baking sheet with olive oil.
2. Arrange the tomato slices on the baking sheet. Sprinkle with garlic, basil and rosemary. Brush with olive oil.
3. Bake in a preheated 350°F oven for 5-10 mins.

Nutrition:
Calories 161, Fat 14.5 g, Carbs 2 g, Protein 0.4 g

Cabbage Rolls with Dried Apricots

Prep time: 30 mins | Servings: 4 | Cooking: 40 mins
Ingredients:
- 4 tbsp Rinsed and chopped dried apricots,
- 2 peeled, cored and grated apples
- 1/3 tsp. cinnamon
- 1 boiled cabbage head
- 2 tbsp Rinsed raisins
- 1 tbsp sugar

Directions:
1. Combine the grated apples, raisins, dried apricots, sugar and cinnamon.
2. Prepare the cabbage leaves: place the head of cabbage into water and bring to a boil. As the cabbage softens take it out, remove the outer leaves and carefully peel the leaves off one by one.
3. Spread the leaves out on paper towels and fill with apricot stuffing. Roll them up.
4. Place the rolls into preheated to 400F oven for 40 mins.

Nutrition:
Calories 175, Fat 0.4 g, Carbs 16.6 g, Protein 10.8 g

Herbed Green Beans

Prep time: 5 mins | Servings: 4 | Cooking: 8 mins
Ingredients:
- ½ cup chopped fresh mint
- 2 minced garlic cloves
- 1 tsp. lemon zest
- 4 cup trimmed green beans
- 1 tbsp olive oil
- 1 tsp. coarse ground black pepper
- ½ cup chopped fresh parsley

Directions:

1. Heat the olive oil in a large sauté pan over medium heat. Add the green beans and garlicup
2. Sauté until the green beans are crisp tender, approximately 5-6 mins.
3. Add the mint, parsley, lemon zest, and black pepper. Toss to coat.

Nutrition:
Calories 66.2, Fat 3.5 g, Carbs 8.3 g, Protein 2.1 g

Chickpea Meatballs

Prep time: 5 mins | Servings: 4 | Cooking: 8 mins
Ingredients:
- 400g canned chickpeas
- 4 sprigs of flat parsley
- 4 cup breadcrumbs
- 4 cup olive oil
- 2 cloves garlic
- 2 shallots
- 1 egg

Directions:
1. Peel and chop the shallots and garlic cloves.
2. Rinse and chop the parsley.
3. Rinse and drain the chickpeas.
4. Heat 1 tbsp oil in a nonstick skillet, and fry the garlic and shallots 2 min over medium heat, stirring.
5. Then mix with the chickpeas and parsley and add the egg.
6. Form dumplings with your wet hands, and roll them into the bread crumbs.
7. Heat the remaining oil in a pan and brown the meatballs.
8. Serve with a tomato sauce.

Nutrition:
Calories 161, Fat 14.5 g, Carbs 2 g, Protein 0.4 g

Lemon Roasted Radishes

Prep time: 5 mins | Servings: 2
Ingredients:
- 2 bunches rinsed and quartered radishes
- 2 tsps. Lemon juice
- 1½ tsp. roughly fresh chopped rosemary
- 1 tbsp melted coconut oil

Directions:
1. Heat the oven to 350°F. Line a baking sheet with parchment paper.
2. Add pepper, salt, coconut oil, and radishes to a bowl and mix until combined.

3. Place the mixture on a baking sheet and bake for about 35 mins, stirring occasionally.
4. When it is done, toss with rosemary and lemon juice.

Nutrition:
Calories 37, Fat 2 g, Carbs 4 g, Protein 1 g

Green Beans with Nuts

Prep time: 20 mins | Servings: 2
Ingredients:
- 3 minced garlic cloves
- 1 tbsp olive oil
- ½ cup chopped walnuts
- 2 cup sliced green beans

Directions:
3. Boil the beans in salted water until tender.
4. Place the beans, garlic and walnuts in a preheated pan and cook for about 5-7 mins on the stove.

Nutrition:
Calories 285, Fat 24.1 g, Carbs 7.1 g, Protein 10 g

Beets Stewed with Apples

Prep time: 1 hour | Servings: 2
Ingredients:
- 2 tbsp Tomato paste
- 1 tbsp Olive oil
- 1 cup water
- 2 peeled, cored and sliced apples
- 3 peeled, boiled and grated beets
- 2 tbsp Sour cream

Directions:
4. Boil the beets until half-done
5. In a deep pan preheated with olive oil cook the grated beets for 15 mins.
6. Add the sliced apples, tomato paste, sour cream and 1 cup water. Stew for 30 mins covered.

Nutrition:

Calories 346, Fat 7.7 g, Carbs 26.8 g, Protein 2 g

Cabbage Quiche

Prep time: 30 mins | Servings: 4 | Cooking: 20 mins
Ingredients:
- 2 beaten eggs
- 2 tbsp Sour cream
- 2 tsps. Semolina
- Fresh parsley
- ½ shredded white cabbage head

- 2 tbsp milk

Directions:
1. In a saucepan stew the shredded cabbage with milk until soft and done.
2. Sprinkle the semolina over the cabbage, constantly stirring, and cook for 10 mins more.
3. Remove from the heat, let cool and stir in the beaten eggs. Season with salt.
4. Arrange the cabbage mixture in a baking dish, coat with sour cream and bake at 400F for 20 mins.
5. Serve with sour cream and fresh parsley leaves.

Nutrition:
Calories 93, Fat 0.5 g, Carbs 27.8 g, Protein 19.4 g

Rice and Chicken Stuffed Tomatoes

Prep time: 10 mins | Servings: 4 | Cooking: 25 mins
Ingredients:
- 1 pack grilled and sliced chicken breast
- 2 tbsp Chopped basil leaf
- 2 cup cooked brown rice
- 1 tbsp olive oil
- 4 large tomatoes
- ½ cup grated parmesan cheese
- 2 minced garlic cloves

Directions:
1. Set the oven at 350F.
2. Take the top of the tomatoes off and then carefully scoop the seeds using a spoon.
3. In a large bowl, mix together the cooked brown rice, chicken, basil, garlic, and parmesan (leave about 1 tsp. of parmesan). Use this mixture to stuff the tomatoes.
4. Sprinkle the stuffed tomatoes with the remaining parmesan. Place them in an oven-safe dish and brush with the olive oil.
5. Place in the oven to cook for 25 mins.
6. Let it cool down before serving.

Nutrition:
Calories 230, Fat 4.1 g, Carbs 27.3 g, Protein 21.5 g

Berry Soufflé

Prep time: 15 mins | Servings: 2 | Cooking: 15 mins
Ingredients:
- 2 tbsp sugar
- ½ cup water
- 3 oz. rinsed berries
- 3 egg whites

Directions:
1. Combine the berries sugar and water in a saucepan and boil until thick.
2. Using an electric beater beat the egg whites until foamy.
3. Constantly stirring, combine the berry mixture with egg whites.
4. Pour the soufflé mixture into a mold.
5. Bake at 390°F for 15 mins.
6. Serve immediately, sprinkled with confectioners' sugar if desired.

Nutrition:
Calories 79, Fat 0.4 g, Carbs 28.6 g, Protein 8.3 g

Stuffed Turnips

Prep time: 5 mins | Servings: 4 | Cooking: 1 hour
Ingredients:
- 2 peeled and grated carrots
- 2 tbsp Olive oil
- 2 tbsp Honey
- 4 rinsed turnips.
- 2 peeled and grated apples

Directions:
1. Preheat the oven to 400°F.
2. Mix grated carrots with grated apples in honey.
3. Boil the turnips until half-done.
4. When the turnips are cool enough to handle, cut off the tops and scoop out some of the flesh.
5. Rub the turnips inside with olive oil and fill with vegetable stuffing.
6. Bake for 1 hr.

Nutrition:
Calories 197, Fat 7.3 g, Carbs 8 g, Protein 4 g

Roasted Asparagus

Prep time: 1 hour | Servings: 2
Ingredients:
- Black pepper
- 1 tsp. olive oil
- 2 cup quartered mushrooms
- Zest of 1 lemon
- 1 lb. sliced asparagus
- 2 tbsp Balsamic vinegar

Directions:
1. In a bowl combine all Ingredients: until well coated.
2. Place into the fridge for 1 hour to marinate.
3. Broil the asparagus mixture under high heat until lightly browned.

Nutrition:
Calories 143, Fat 7.6 g, Carbs 3.9 g, Protein 22 g

Brussels Sprouts with Walnuts

Prep time: 10 mins | Servings: 4
Ingredients:
- ½ cup fresh shaved parmesan
- 1 tsp. thyme
- 2 tbsp olive oil
- 1 tsp. black pepper
- ½ cup chopped walnuts
- ½ cup diced red onion
- 4 cup shaved Brussels sprouts

Directions:
1. Heat the olive oil in a skillet over medium heat. Add the onions and sauté until tender, approximately 2-3 mins.
2. Add the Brussels sprouts and cook for 5 mins. Season with thyme and black pepper.
3. Remove from heat and stir in the walnuts.
4. Garnish with fresh Parmesan for serving.

Nutrition:
Calories 173.0, Fat 12.8 g, Carbs 10.0 g, Protein 5.7 g

Grilled Pesto Shrimps

Prep time: 10 mins | Servings: 2| Cooking: 3/4 mins
Ingredients:
- 1 garlic clove
- ¼ kg. peeled and deveined large shrimp
- ½ cup chopped basil
- Skewers
- 2 tbsp olive oil
- 2 tbsp parmesan cheese

Directions:
1. Place the fresh basil, garlic, cheese, salt and pepper in a food processor and pulse. Gradually add the oil to the mixture until you create a pesto sauce.
2. Place the shrimps in a bowl and pour over the pesto sauce. Toss gently and let it marinate in t fridge for at least an hour.
3. When you're ready to cook, pre-heat your grill to medium-low heat.
4. Thread the shrimps into the skewers and cook on the grill for about 3-4 mins on each side.
5. Serve warm with a bowl of yogurt and fresh fruits.

Nutrition:
Calories 219.7, Fat 7.8 g, Carbs 22.2 g, Protein 15.1 g

Rosemary Potato Shells

Prep time: 5 mins | Servings: 2 | Cooking: 1 hour
Ingredients:
- Butter-flavored cooking spray
- 2 medium russet potatoes
- 1/8 tsp. freshly ground black pepper
- 1 tbsp minced fresh rosemary

Directions:
1. Switch on the oven and set it to 375 °F to preheat.
2. Pierce the mashed potatoes with a fork and place them in a baking sheet.
3. Bake for 1 hour until crispy.
4. Allow the potatoes to cool for handling then cut them in half.
5. Scoop out the pulp leaving the 1/8-inch-thick shell.
6. Brush the shells with melted butter and season with pepper and rosemary.
7. Bake for another 5 mins.
8. Serve.

Nutrition:
Calories 167, Fat 0 g, Carbs 27 g, Protein 7.6 g

Basil Tomato Crostini

Prep time: 10 mins | Servings: 4 | Cooking: 30 mins
Ingredients:
- ¼ cup minced fresh basil
- ¼ lb. sliced and toasted bread
- 4 chopped plum tomatoes
- 2 tsps. olive oil
- Freshly ground pepper
- 1 minced garlic clove

Directions:
1. Toss tomatoes with oil, garlic, pepper, and basil in a bowl.
2. Cover and allow them sit for 30 mins.
3. Top the toasts with this mixture.
4. Serve.

Nutrition:
Calories 104, Fat 3.5 g, Carbs 15 g, Protein 3 g

Cranberry Spritzer

Prep time: 10 mins | Servings: 4
Ingredients:
- 1 cup raspberry sherbet
- 1-quart sugar-free cranberry juice

- ¼ cup sugar
- 10 lemon wedges
- ½ cup fresh lemon juice
- 1-quart carbonated water

Directions:
1. Refrigerate carbonated water, lemon juice, and cranberry juice until cold.
2. Mix cranberry juice with sugar, sherbet, lemon juice, and carbonated water.
3. Garnish with a lemon wedge.
4. Serve.

Nutrition:
Calories 50, Fat 0 g, Carbs 15.1 g, Protein 1.2 g

Penne with Broccoli

Prep time: 5 mins | Servings: 2 | Cooking: 10 mins
Ingredients:
- 3 minced garlic cloves
- 2 tbsp grated parmesan cheese
- Pepper.
- 1/3 lb. Penne pasta
- 2 cup broccoli florets
- 2 tsps. olive oil

Directions:
1. Fill a large saucepan with water and bring to a boil. Following the instructions on the package add the pasta and cook until al dente.
2. In a separate pot add 1 inch water and bring to boil. Put the broccoli florets into a steamer basket and steam for 10 mins.
3. In a large bowl combine the cooked pasta with broccoli. Toss with garlic, olive oil, Parmesan cheese, and black pepper.

Nutrition:
Calories 46.2, Fat 14.9 g, Carbs 25 g, Protein 14 g

White Sponge Cake

Prep time: 15 mins | Servings: 4 | Cooking: 20 mins
Ingredients:
- 1 tbsp sugar
- 1 tbsp flour
- 2 egg whites

Directions:
1. Using an electric mixer beat the egg whites until foamy.
2. Slowly add sugar, continuing to whisk.
3. Slowly add the flour, constantly stirring.
4. Pour the mixture into a silicone mold.
5. Bake at 400F for 20 min. Check for doneness with a toothpick.

Nutrition:
Calories 23, Fat 0.1 g, Carbs 36.4 g, Protein 4.6 g

Pan Seared Acorn Squash and Pecans

Prep time: 5 mins | Servings: 6 | Cooking: 13 mins
Ingredients:
- 1 tsp. chopped rosemary
- 1 cup sliced sweet yellow onion
- 2 tbsp vegetable oil
- 4 cup cubed acorn squash
- 1 tbsp honey
- 1 cup chopped pecans

Directions:
1. Add the vegetable oil to a sauté pan over medium high heat.
2. Add the onion and sauté until tender, 2-3 mins.
3. Add the acorn squash, tossing gently for 5-7 mins.
4. Add the honey, pecans, and rosemary. Stir to coat and cook an additional 3 mins.
5. Serve warm.

Nutrition:
Calories 222.3, Fat 17.6 g, Carbs 17.4 g, Protein 2.7 g

Squash Pancakes

Prep time: 10 mins | Servings: 4 | Cooking: 20-30 mins
Ingredients:
- 2 beaten eggs
- Sour cream
- 2 peeled, deseeded and grated medium summer squashes
- 1 tbsp flour

Directions:
1. Drain the liquid from the grated squashes.
2. Add eggs, flour and season with salt. Mix well. Form this mixture into pancakes.
3. Line a baking sheet with parchment paper and scoop the pancakes onto it.
4. Bake in the oven at 400F for 20-30 mins.
5. Serve with sour cream.

Nutrition:
Calories 31, Fat 0.4 g, Carbs 12.7 g, Protein 5.8 g

Apples Stuffed with Quark

Prep time: 5 mins | Servings: 4 | Cooking: 20 mins
Ingredients:
- 8 oz. cottage cheese
- 1 tsp. confectioners' sugar

- 2 tbsp Sugar
- 4 cored apples
- 1 whisked egg
- 1 tbsp raisins

Directions:
4. Combine the quark with egg, sugar and raisins. Mix well.
5. Scrape out the some of the apples' flesh and fill with quark mixture.
6. Place on a baking sheet and bake at 400F for 20 mins.

Nutrition:
Calories 189, Fat 0.6 g, Carbs 9 g, Protein 12 g

Meringue Cookies

Prep time: 5 mins | Servings: 4| Cooking: 15 mins
Ingredients:
- 2 tbsp Sugar
- 3 beaten egg whites

Directions:
6. Using a blender beat the cooled egg whites on high.
7. Constantly blending add sugar little by little.
8. Line a baking sheet with parchment paper. Using an icing bag, squeeze our portions of the egg mixture unto the parchment paper.
9. Place into a preheated to 155°F oven for 15 min.

Nutrition:
Calories 35, Fat 0 g, Carbs 6 g, Protein 0.4 g

Rose Hip Jelly

Prep time: 7 hours | Servings: 2
Ingredients:
- 2 cup water
- 1 tsp. gelatin
- 2 tbsp Sugar
- 2 tbsp Rinsed and crushed rose-hip berries
- 2 lemon slices

Directions:
1. Bring the 2 cups water to a boil, add the crushed rose hips and boil for 5 mins
2. Leave the hips in the liquid to infuse for 6 hours. Then strain the infusion through a sieve, retaining the liquid.
3. Dissolve sugar in ½ cup of rose-hip water and bring to boil. Add the remaining rose-hip water and lemon slices.
4. Soak the gelatin in cool water for 25-30 mins.
5. Add the gelatin to the rose-hip extract and bring to a boil. Take it from the heat immediately and pour into molds or jars
6. Place in the fridge to cool and thicken.

Nutrition:
Calories 45, Fat 0 g, Carbs 11 g, Protein 0 g

Easy Broccoli and Pasta

Prep time: 10 mins | Servings: 3
Ingredients:
- 3 chopped garlic cloves
- 6 oz. uncooked whole-wheat pasta
- Ground pepper
- 3 cup roughly chopped broccoli florets
- 1 tbsp olive oil
- 2 tbsp Grated Romano cheese

Directions:
1. Cook the penne in a pot according to the package instructions. Add the florets to cook with the pasta.
2. Before draining, take ¼ cup of the pasta water and set aside.
3. Place the pot back to the stove and heat the olive oil over high heat. Sauté the garlic for about a minute.
4. Reduce the heat and then add the pasta and broccoli to the pot. Stir well.
5. Add the Romano and ¼ cup of the pasta water. Mix well. Season with pepper.

Nutrition:
Calories 419.8, Fat 12.9 g, Carbs 52 g, Protein 32.2 g

Chapter 12: Snacks and Desserts

Hearty Chia And Blackberry Pudding

Prep Time: 45 mins |Servings: 2
Ingredients:
- ¼ cup chia seeds
- ½ cup blackberries, fresh
- 1 tsp liquid sweetener
- 1 cup coconut almond milk, full fat and unsweetened
- 1 tsp vanilla extract

Directions::s
1. Take the vanilla ,liquid sweetener and coconut almond milk and add to blender
2. Process until thick
3. Add in blackberries and process until smooth
4. Divide the mixture between cups and chill for 30 mins

Nutrition:
Calories 314.8, Fat 25.0 g, Carbs 22.1 g, Protein 4.5 g

Special Cocoa Brownies

Prep Time: 15 mins |Servings: 12 |Cooking time: 25 mins
Ingredients:
- 2 tbsps grass-fed almond butter
- 1 whole egg
- 2 tsps vanilla extract
- ¼ tsp baking powder
- 1/3 cup heavy cream
- 3/4 cup almond butter
- ¼ cocoa powder
- A pinch of sunflower seeds

Directions:
1. Break the eggs and whisk until smooth
2. Add in all the wet Ingredients: and mix well
3. Make the batter by mixing all the dry Ingredients: and sifting them into the wet Ingredients:
4. Pour into a greased baking pan Bake for 25 mins at 350 degrees F or until a toothpick inserted in the middle comes out clean

Nutrition:
Calories 355.8, Fat 25.0 g, Carbs 22.1 g, Protein 4.5 g

Gentle Blackberry Crumble

Prep Time: 10 mins |Servings: 4 |Cooking time: 45 mins
Ingredients:
- ½ a cup of coconut flour
- ½ a cup of banana, peeled and mashed
- 6 tbsp of water
- 3 cups of fresh blackberries
- ½ a cup of arrowroot flour
- 1 and a ½ tsp of baking soda
- 4 tbsp of almond butter, melted
- 1 tbsp of fresh lemon juice

Directions:
1. Pre-heat your oven to 300 degrees F
2. Take a baking dish and grease it lightly
3. Take a bowl and mix all of the Ingredients: except blackberries, mix well
4. Place blackberries in the bottom of your baking dish and top with flour
5. Bake for 40 mins

Nutrition:
Calories 325.8, Fat 20.0 g, Carbs 22.1 g, Protein 5.5 g

Nutmeg Nougats

Prep Time: 10 mins |Servings: 12 |Cooking time: 5 mins +30mins
Freeze Time: 30 mins
Ingredients:
- 1 cup coconut, shredded
- 1 cup low-fat cream
- 1 cup cashew almond butter
- ½ tsp ground nutmeg

Directions:
1. Melt the cashew almond butter over a double boiler
2. Stir in nutmeg and dairy cream
3. Remove from the heat
4. Allow to cool down a little
5. Keep in the refrigerator for at least 30 mins
6. Take out from the fridge and make small balls
7. Coat with shredded coconut
8. Let it cool for 2 hours and then serve

Nutrition:
Calories 334, Fat 28.0 g, Carbs 20.1 g, Protein 4.5 g

Apple And Almond Muffins

Prep Time: 10 mins |Servings: 6 |Cooking time: 20 mins
Ingredients:
- 6 oz ground almonds
- 1 tsp cinnamon
- ½ tsp baking powder
- 1 pinch sunflower seeds
- 1 whole egg
- 1 tsp apple cider vinegar
- 2 tbsps Erythritol
- 1/3 cup apple sauce

Directions:
1. Pre-heat your oven to 350 degree F
2. Line muffin tin with paper muffin cups, keep them on the side
3. Mix in almonds, cinnamon, baking powder, sunflower seeds and keep it on the side
4. Take another bowl and beat in eggs, apple cider vinegar, apple sauce, Erythritol
5. Add the mix to dry Ingredients: and mix well until you have a smooth batter
6. Pour batter into tin and bake for 20 mins
7. Once done, let them cool

Nutrition:
Calories 314, Fat 21.0 g, Carbs 18.1 g, Protein 6.5 g

Sweet Potatoes and Apples Mix

Prep time: 10 mins | Servings: 1
Ingredients:
- 1 tbsp low-fat butter
- ½ lb. cored and chopped apples
- 2 tbsp water
- 2 lbs. sweet potatoes

Directions:
1. Arrange the potatoes around the lined baking sheet, bake inside oven at 400 ⁰F for an hour, peel them and mash them in the meat processor.
2. Put apples in the very pot, add the river, bring using a boil over medium heat, reduce temperature, and cook for ten mins.
3. Transfer to your bowl, add mashed potatoes, stir well and serve every day.
4. Enjoy!

Nutrition:
Calories 140, Fat 1 g, Carbs 8 g, Protein 6 g

Sautéed Bananas with Orange Sauce

Prep time: 5 mins | Servings: 4

Ingredients:
- ¼ cup frozen pure orange juice concentrate
- 2 tbsp margarine
- ¼ cup sliced almonds
- 1 tsp. orange zest
- 1 tsp. fresh grated ginger
- 4 firm, sliced ripe bananas
- 1 tsp. cinnamon

Directions:
1. Melt the margarine over medium heat in a large skillet, until it bubbles but before it begins to brown.
2. Add the cinnamon, ginger, and orange zest. Cook, while stirring, for 1 minute before adding the orange juice concentrate. Cook, while stirring until an even sauce has formed.
3. Add the bananas and cook, stirring carefully for 1-2 mins, or until warmed and evenly coated with the sauce.
4. Serve warm with sliced almonds.

Nutrition:
Calories 164.3, Fat 9.0 g, Carbs 21.4 g, Protein 2.3 g

Caramelized Apricot

Prep time: 10 mins | Servings: 6
Ingredients:
- ¼ cup white sugar
- 2 tsps. lemon juice
- ½ tsp. thyme
- 3 cup sliced apricots
- 1 tbsp brown sugar
- 1 cup part skim ricotta cheese
- 1 tsp. lemon zest

Directions:
1. Preheat the broiler of your oven.
2. Place the apricots in a bowl and toss with the lemon juice.
3. In another bowl, combine the ricotta cheese, thyme, and lemon zest. Mix well.
4. Spread a layer of the ricotta mixture into the bottoms of 6 large baking ramekins.
5. Spoon the apricots over the top of the ricotta cheese in each.
6. Combine the white sugar and brown sugar. Sprinkle evenly over the apricots, avoiding large clumps of sugar as much as possible.
7. Place the ramekins under the broiler for approximately 5 mins, or until caramelized.
8. Serve warm.

Nutrition:
Calories 133.6, Fat 3.6 g, Carbs 21.6 g, Protein 5.8 g

Rhubarb Pie

Prep time: 10 mins | Servings: 12
Ingredients:
- 4 cup chopped rhubarb
- 8 oz. low-fat cream cheese
- 1 cup melted low-fat butter
- 1 ¼ cup coconut sugar
- 2 cup whole wheat flour
- 1 cup chopped pecans
- 1 cup sliced strawberries

Directions:
1. In a bowl, combine the flour while using the butter, pecans and ¼ cup sugar and stir well.
2. Transfer this for some pie pan, press well in for the pan, introduce inside the oven and bake at 350 ºF for 20 mins.
3. In a pan, combine the strawberries with all the current rhubarb, cream cheese and 1 cup sugar, stir well and cook over medium heat for 4 mins.
4. Spread this inside the pie crust whilst inside fridge for the couple hours before slicing and serving.

Nutrition:
Calories 162, Fat 5 g, Carbs 15 g, Protein 6 g

Berry Bars

Prep time: 10 mins | Servings: 18
Ingredients:
- 1 cup natural peanut butter
- ¼ cup chopped dried blueberries
- 3 cup oatmeal
- ¼ cup chopped dried cranberries
- 3 tbsp honey

Directions:
1. Line a baking pan with wax paper or parchment paper.
2. Microwave the peanut butter for 10-15 seconds, just until it softens and begins to liquefy.
3. Combine the oatmeal, peanut butter, honey, cranberries, and blueberries together in a bowl and mix until blended.
4. Spread the mixture out evenly into the pan.
5. Place in the refrigerator and let set for 2 hours before cutting into squares.

Nutrition:
Calories 145.0, Fat 6.4 g, Carbs 17.9 g, Protein 4.4 g

Chocolate Avocado Pudding

Prep Time: 30 mins |Servings: 2
Ingredients:
- 1 avocado, chunked
- 1 tbsp natural sweetener such as stevia
- 2 oz cream cheese, at room temp
- ¼ tsp vanilla extract
- 4 tbsps cocoa powder, unsweetened

Directions:
1. Blend listed Ingredients: in blender until smooth
2. Divide the mix between dessert bowls, chill for 30 mins

Nutrition:
Calories 284, Fat 18.0 g, Carbs 20.1 g, Protein 5.5 g

Ginger Peach Pie

Prep time: 10 mins | Servings: 10
Ingredients:
- 5 cup diced peaches
- ½ cup sugar
- 2 refrigerated whole wheat pie crust doughs
- 1 tsp. cinnamon
- ½ cup orange juice
- ¼ cup chopped candied ginger
- ½ cup cornstarch

Directions:
1. Preheat the oven to 425°F.
2. Place one of the pie crusts in a standard size pie dish. Spread some coffee beans or dried beans in the bottom of the pie crust to use as a weight. Place the dish in the oven and bake for 10-15 mins, or until lightly golden. Remove from the oven and let cool.
3. Combine the peaches, candied ginger, and cinnamon in a bowl. Toss to mix.
4. Combine the sugar, cornstarch, and orange juice in a saucepan and heat over medium until syrup begins to thicken.
5. Pour the syrup over the peaches and toss to coat.
6. Spread the peaches in the pie crust and top with the remaining crust. Crimp along the edges and cut several small slits in the top.
7. Place in the oven and bake for 25-30 mins, or until golden brown.
8. Let set before slicing.

Nutrition:

Calories 289.0, Fat 13.1 g, Carbs 41.6 g, Protein 3.9 g

Pomegranate Mix

Prep time: 10 mins | Servings: 2
Ingredients:
- Single pomegranate seeds
- 2 cup pomegranate juice
- 1 cup steel cut oats

Directions:
In a bit pot, combine the pomegranate juice with pomegranate seeds and oats, toss, cook over medium heat for 5 mins, divide into bowls and serve cold.
Nutrition:
Calories 172, Fat 4 g, Carbs 10 g, Protein 5 g

Blueberry Cream

Prep time: 5 mins | Servings: 1
Ingredients:
- 1 tbsp low-fat peanut butter
- 2 dates
- ¾ cup blueberries
- 1 peeled banana
- ¾ cup almond milk

Directions:
1. In a blender, combine the blueberries with peanut butter, milk, banana and dates, pulse well, divide into small cups and serve cold.

Nutrition:
Calories 120, Fat 3 g, Carbs 6 g, Protein 7 g

Mocha Ricotta Cream

Prep time: 10 mins | Servings: 4
Ingredients:
- 2 cup part skin ricotta cheese
- 1 tbsp espresso powder
- Almond cookie crumbs
- ½ cup powdered sugar
- 1 tbsp dark cocoa powder
- 1 tsp. pure vanilla extract

Directions:
1. Combine the ricotta cheese, powdered sugar, espresso powder, cocoa powder, and vanilla extract in a bowl.
2. Using an electric mixer, blend until creamy.
3. Cover and refrigerate for at least 4 hours.
4. Serve in individual dishes, garnished with cookie crumbs, if desired.

Nutrition:
Calories 230.6, Fat 9.9g, Carbs 22.0g, Protein 14.3g

Mango Sweet Mix

Prep time: 10 mins | Servings: 8
Ingredients:
- 1 tsp. cinnamon powder
- 1 ½ lbs. peeled and cubed mango
- 3 tbsp coconut sugar
- ½ cup apple cider vinegar treatment
- 1 tsp. nigella seeds

Directions:
1. In a tiny pot, combine the mango while using nigella seeds, sugar, vinegar and cinnamon, toss, bring using a simmer over medium heat, cook for 10 mins, divide into bowls and serve.

Nutrition:
Calories 160, Fat 3 g, Carbs 8 g, Protein 3 g

Ginger Peach Pie

Prep time: 10 mins | Servings: 10
Ingredients:
- 5 cup diced peaches
- ½ cup sugar
- 2 refrigerated whole wheat pie crust doughs
- 1 tsp. cinnamon
- ½ cup orange juice
- ¼ cup chopped candied ginger
- ½ cup cornstarch

Directions:
1. Preheat the oven to 425°F.
2. Place one of the pie crusts in a standard size pie dish. Spread some coffee beans or dried beans in the bottom of the pie crust to use as a weight. Place the dish in the oven and bake for 10-15 mins, or until lightly golden. Remove from the oven and let cool.
3. Combine the peaches, candied ginger, and cinnamon in a bowl. Toss to mix.
4. Combine the sugar, cornstarch, and orange juice in a saucepan and heat over medium until syrup begins to thicken.
5. Pour the syrup over the peaches and toss to coat.
6. Spread the peaches in the pie crust and top with the remaining crust. Crimp along the edges and cut several small slits in the top.
7. Place in the oven and bake for 25-30 mins, or until golden brown.
8. Let set before slicing.

Nutrition:
Calories 289.0, Fat 13.1 g, Carbs 41.6 g, Protein 3.9 g

Berries Mix

Prep time: 10 mins | Servings: 6
Ingredients:
- 4 tbsp coconut sugar
- 2 tsps. freshly squeezed fresh lemon juice
- 1 lb. strawberries
- 1 lb. blackberries

Directions:
1. In a pan, combine the strawberries with blackberries and sugar, stir, provide your simmer over medium heat and cook for ten mins.
2. Divide into cups and serve cold.

Nutrition:
Calories 120, Fat 2 g, Carbs 4 g, Protein 4 g

Coconut Cream

Prep time: 1 hour | Servings: 4
Ingredients:
- 1 tsp. cinnamon powder
- 5 tbsp coconut sugar
- 2 cup coconut cream
- Zest of one grated lemon
- 3 whisked eggs

Directions:
1. In just a little pan, combine the cream with cinnamon, eggs, sugar and lemon zest. Whisk well
2. Simmer over medium heat for 10 mins.
3. Divide into ramekins and inside fridge for an hour before serving

Nutrition:
Calories 130, Fat 5 g, Carbs 8 g, Protein 6 g

Coconut Figs

Prep time: 6 mins | Servings: 4
Ingredients:
- 12 halved figs
- 1 cup toasted and chopped almonds
- 2 tbsp coconut butter
- ¼ cup coconut sugar

Directions:
1. Put butter inside the pot, get hot over medium heat, add sugar, whisk well, include almonds and figs, toss, cook for 5 mins, divide into small cups and serve cold.

Nutrition:
Calories 150, Fat 4 g, Carbs 7 g, Protein 4 g

Cinnamon Apples

Prep time: 10 mins | Servings: 4
Ingredients:
- 1 tbsp cinnamon powder
- 4 tbsp raisins
- 4 cored big apples

Directions:
1. Stuff the apples while using the raisins, sprinkle the cinnamon, stick them inside a baking dish, introduce inside oven at 375 ºF, bake for 20 mins and serve cold.

Nutrition:
Calories: 205, Fat: 1 g, Carbs:8 g, Protein:4 g

Green Apple Bowls

Prep time: 10 mins | Servings: 3
Ingredients:
- 1 tbsp coconut sugar
- ½ tsp. vanilla flavoring
- 1 cup halved strawberries
- 3 cored and cubed big green apples
- ½ tsp. cinnamon powder

Directions:
In a bowl, combine the apples with strawberries, sugar, cinnamon and vanilla, toss and serve.

Nutrition:
Calories 205, Fat 1 g, Carbs 8 g, Protein 4 g

Pecan Granola

Prep time: 5 mins | Servings: 10
Ingredients:
- 50 g maple syrup
- ½ g nutmeg
- 1400 g raw pecans
- 2 ½ g cayenne pepper
- 5 g ground cinnamon

Directions:
1. Preheat oven to about 400 ºF.
2. In a large bowl, mix the pecans maple syrup, and spices, and toss till perfectly coated.
3. Spread out nuts on a baking sheet and roast for about 10 mins.
4. Cool for another 10 mins, then store or serve.

Nutrition:
Calories 174, Fat 100.8 g, Carbs 23 g, Protein 13 g

Banana Sashimi

Prep time: 5 mins| Servings: 1
Ingredients:
- ¼ tsp. chia seeds
- 15 g almond butter
- 1 medium banana

Directions:
1. Peel banana and cover one side in the nut butter, while placing it face up.
2. Slice banana evenly into even 1-centimeter thick pieces.
3. Sprinkle on toppings and serve!

Nutrition:
Calories 194, Fat 8 g, Carbs 30 g, Protein 5 g

Creamy Peanuts with Apples

Prep time: 10 mins | Servings: 2
Ingredients:
- 4 oz. fat-free cream cheese
- 1 tbsp diced peanuts
- ¼ cup orange juice
- 2 cored and sliced medium apples
- 1 tbsp brown sugar
- ¾ tsp. vanilla

Directions:
- Set your cream cheese on the counter for about five mins to soften it.
- Make the dip by mixing the cream cheese, vanilla, and brown sugar in a bowl. Add peanuts and mix until combined.
- Add the sliced apples in a separate bowl and drizzle with orange juice to stop the apples from turning brown.
- Serve the apples with the dip and enjoy!

Nutrition:
Calories 110, Fat 2 g, Carbs 18 g, Protein 5 g

Maple Malt

Prep time: 10 mins | Servings: 2
Ingredients:
- 2 ½ g vanilla essence
- 45 g maple syrup
- 5 g cinnamon
- 30 g chocolate
- 45 g cocoa powder
- 340 g almond milk

Directions:
1. Literally just pour it all into a saucepan and boil till it thickens.

Nutrition:
Calories 1180, Fat 85.8 g, Carbs 80 g, Protein 40 g

Walnut Green Beans

Prep time: 15-20 mins | Servings: 2-3
Ingredients:
- 2 cup roughly cut green beans
- 1 tbsp olive oil
- 3 minced garlic cloves
- ½ cup chopped walnuts

Directions:
1. In a cooking pot, add and boil the beans in salted water until tender.
2. In a saucepan, add the beans, garlic, oil, and walnuts; cook for about 5-7 mins stirring constantly.
3. Serve warm.

Nutrition:
Calories 130, Fat 7 g, Carbs 15 g, Protein 5 g

Cheese Stuffed Apples

Prep Time: 20-25 min. | Servings: 4
Ingredients:
- 1 tbsp raisins
- 1 whisked egg
- 8 oz. cottage cheese
- 1 tsp. confectioners' sugar
- 2 tbsp honey
- 4 cored apples

Directions:
- Preheat the oven to 400 °F.
- In a mixing bowl, thoroughly mix the egg, cheese, honey, and raisins.
- Spoon some flesh from the core part of the apples and fill with the cheese mix.
- Bake for 18-20 mins; top with confectioner's sugar and serve.

Nutrition:
Calories 194, Fat 5.2 g, Carbs 23.8 g, Protein 3.6 g

Green Tea Cream

Prep time: 1 hour |Servings: 6
Ingredients:
- 2 tbsp green tea extract powder
- 3 tbsp coconut sugar
- 14 oz. coconut milk
- 14 oz. coconut cream

Directions:
1. Put the milk in the very pan, add sugar and green tea herb powder, stir, give your simmer, cook for two mins, remove heat, cool down, add coconut cream, whisk well,

divide into small bowls whilst from the fridge for just two hours before serving.
Nutrition:
Calories 160, Fat 3 g, Carbs 7 g, Protein 6 g

Fresh Figs With Walnuts And Ricotta

Prep Time: 5 mins |Servings: 4 | Cooking time: 2-3 mins
Ingredients:
- 8 dried figs, halved
- ¼ cup ricotta cheese
- 16 walnuts, halved
- 1 tbsp honey

Directions:
1. Take a skillet and place it over medium heat, add walnuts and toast for 2 mins
2. Top figs with cheese and walnuts
3. Drizzle honey on top

Nutrition:
Calories 204, Fat 10.0 g, Carbs 12.1 g, Protein 4.5 g

Coconut Mousse

Prep time: 10 mins | Servings: 12
Ingredients:
- 1 tsp. vanilla flavoring
- 1 tsp. coconut extract
- 1 cup toasted coconut
- 2 ¾ cup coconut milk
- 4 tsps. coconut sugar

Directions:
1. In a bowl, combine the coconut milk with the coconut extract, vanilla flavor, coconut and sugar, whisk well, divide into small cups and serve cold.

Nutrition:
Calories 152, Fat 5 g, Carbs 11 g, Protein 3 g

Rice Pudding with Oranges

Prep time: 15 mins | Servings: 3-4
Ingredients:
- 3 large navel oranges
- ¼ cup low-fat sweetened condensed milk
- 4 tbsp sugar
- ¾ cup Basmati rice white rice
- ½ halved vanilla bean
- 4 cup fat-free evaporated milk

Directions:
1. Take a 2 quart pan and boil 2 cups of water, add rice and cover it with lowering the heat.
2. Cook it for 20 mins till it is soft and the water is taken up by the rice. Take a clean orange, extract 1 tsp of zest from it.
3. Cut it in half and juice it, save it. Remove the rind from rest of the oranges, extract the white pith. Clear the bifurcations.
4. When the rice is soft, add half cup of the orange juice, the zest, evaporated milk, condensed milk, vanilla bean and sugar.
5. Cook the mix over medium flame for 20 to 25 mins, without the cover, stirring regularly till it creams up.
6. Clear off the vanilla bean and pour the rice mixture among bowls to serve hot.

Nutrition:
Calories 230.5, Fat 6.7 g, Carbs 39 g, Protein 4.2 g

Chickpeas and Pepper Hummus

Prep time: 10 mins | Servings: 4
Ingredients:
- Juice of ½ lemon
- 4 chopped walnuts
- 1 tbsp sesame paste
- 14 oz. no-salt-added, drained and rinsed canned chickpeas
- 2 chopped roasted red peppers

Directions:
1. In your blender, combine the chickpeas with all the sesame paste, red peppers, lemon juice and walnuts, pulse well, divide into bowls and serve as being a snack.
2. Enjoy!

Nutrition:
Calories 231, Fat 12 g, Carbs 15 g, Protein 14 g

Tortilla Chips

Prep time: 10 mins | Servings: 6
Ingredients:
- ¼ tsp. cayenne
- 2 tbsp organic extra virgin olive oil
- 12 whole wheat grain tortillas
- 1 tbsp chili powder

Directions:
1. Spread the tortillas for the lined baking sheet, add the oil, chili powder and cayenne, toss, introduce inside oven and bake at 350 ⁰F for 25 mins.
2. Divide into bowls and serve as a side dish.

Nutrition:
Calories 199, Fat 3 g, Carbs 12 g, Protein 5 g

Kale Popcorn

Prep time: 10 mins | Servings: 4
Ingredients:
- 2 tsps. grape seed oil
- 2 tsps. lemon zest
- 10 cup popped popcorn
- ½ bunch chopped kale

Directions:
1. Calories 131, Fat 4 g, Carbs 22 g, Protein 5 g Preheat the oven to 325F.
2. Pat the kale completely dry with kitchen paper and then coat with olive oil and salt.
3. Place onto the baking sheet and bake for 11 mins until crispy.
4. Stir once or twice halfway through cooking and be careful that the kale does not burn.
5. Remove the kale and let cool.
6. Place the cooled kale into a food processor together with the lemon zest and process into a fine powder.
7. Add this seasoning to the prepared popcorn and serve.

Nutrition:

Peas and Parsley Hummus

Prep time: 10 mins | Servings: 4
Ingredients:
- Juice of ½ lemon
- 2 cup drained chickpeas
- 2 tbsp oil
- 1 clove garlic
- 4 tbsp chopped parsley
- 12 black olives

Directions:
Pour the chickpeas and juice in a blender together with garlic and oil.
Serve with olives and parsley.
Nutrition:
Calories 107, Fat 9g, Carbs 15g, Protein 11g

White Beans Hummus

Prep time: 10 mins | Servings: 4
Ingredients:
- Juice of ½ lemon
- 1 box of natural white beans
- 1 tbsp tahini
- 1 tsp garlic powder
- sesame seeds

Directions:

1. Pour the tbsp of tahini in a blender together with natural white beans (previously drained), and garlic powder.
2. Pour the lemon juice and tase.

Nutrition:
Calories 151, Fat 14 g, Carbs 12 g, Protein 11 g

Peanuts Snack Bar

Prep Time: 15 mins | Servings: 10
Ingredients:
- 420 g roasted peanuts
- 30 pitted dates

Directions:
1. Go ahead and throw your dates all into the food processor and add the salt and blend until it forms a smooth paste.
2. Add in the roasted peanuts and pulse until the nuts are coarsely chopped and grab a spoon and make a big ball of date-nut dough.
3. Roll your dough into a 1 inch thick mat and cut into sticks or bars and serve.

Nutrition:
Calories 307, Fat 21g, Carbs 25g, Protein 11g

Chickpeas Dip

Prep time: 10 mins | Servings: 4
Ingredients:
- ½ cup chopped coriander
- Zest one grated lemon
- 1 tbsp olive oil
- 4 tbsp pine nuts
- Juice of one lemon
- 14 oz. no-salt-added drained and rinsed canned chickpeas

Directions:
1. In a blender, combine the chickpeas with lemon zest, freshly squeezed lemon juice, coriander and oil, pulse well, divide into small bowls, sprinkle pine nuts at the pinnacle and serve as a conference dip.

Nutrition:
Calories 200, Fat 12 g, Carbs 9 g, Protein 7 g

Special Raspberry Chocolate Bombs

Prep Time: 10 mins |Servings: 6 |Freeze time: 1 hours
Ingredients:
- ½ cacao almond butter
- ½ coconut manna
- 4 tbsps powdered coconut almond milk

- 3 tbsps granulated stevia
- ¼ cup dried and crushed raspberries, frozen

Directions:
1. Prepare your double boiler to medium heat and melt cacao almond butter and coconut manna
2. Stir in vanilla extract
3. Take another dish and add coconut powder and sugar substitute
4. Stir the coconut mix into the cacao almond butter, 1 tbsp at a time, making sure to keep mixing after each addition
5. Add the crushed dried raspberries
6. Mix well and portion it out into muffin tins
7. Chill for 60 mins and enjoy!

Nutrition:
Calories 264, Fat 25.0 g, Carbs 20.1 g, Protein 6.5 g

Cranberry Muffins

Prep Time: 10 mins |Servings: 24 |Cooking time: 20mins
Ingredients:
- 2 cups almond flour
- 2 tsps baking soda
- ¼ cup avocado oil
- 1 whole egg
- ¾ cup almond milk
- ½ cup Erythritol
- ½ cup apple sauce
- Zest of 1 orange
- 2 tsps ground cinnamon
- 2 cup fresh cranberries

Directions:
1. Pre-heat your oven to 350 degree F
2. Line muffin tin with paper muffin cups and keep them on the side
3. Add flour, baking soda and keep it on the side
4. Take another bowl and whisk in remaining Ingredients: and add flour, mix well
5. Pour batter into prepared muffin tin and bake for 20 mins
6. Once done, let it cool for 10 mins

Nutrition:
Calories 232, Fat 25.0 g, Carbs 24.1 g, Protein 4.5 g

Broad Bean Hummus

Prep Time: 5 mins |Servings: 4
Ingredients:
- 2 cup cooked chickpeas
- 1 cup fresh beans
- 2 tbsp olive oil
- 1 lime
- 2 tsp of tahini
- 1 tsp of oregano
- 1 tsp ground cumin
- 1 tsp garlic

Directions:
1. Shovel the beans and cook for 8 minutes in boiling water. Rinse the chickpeas and drain.
2. In the blender mix all the ingredients
3. blend until smooth and serve

Nutrition:
Calories 151, Fat 14 g, Carbs 12 g, Protein 11 g

Carrot Cake

Prep Time: 5 mins |Servings: 10 |Cooking time: 35 mins
Ingredients:
- 2 cups of flour
- 1 cup grated carrots on a fine grater
- 4 eggs
- 1 cup of sugar
- 1.25 cup of vegetable oil
- 0.5 cup of chopped walnuts and raisins
- 2 tsp baking powder
- 1.5 tsp ground cinnamon
- 1 tsp vanilla sugar

Directions:
1. Beat eggs with regular and vanilla sugar in a blender.
2. Add vegetable oil, carrots, sifted flour with baking powder, cinnamon, and a pinch of salt.
3. Stir until a thick dough.
4. Add raisins and walnuts to the dough.
5. Pour the dough into a heat-resistant round mold with a diameter of 22-24 cm, greased with oil and covered with parchment, and bake at 350ºF for 35 minutes.

6. Before serving, sprinkle with powdered sugar.

Nutrition:
Calories 188, Total Fat 5 g, Carbs 24.1 g, Protein 4.5 g

Hearty Almond Bread

Prep Time: 15 mins |Servings: 8 |Cooking time: 60 mins

Ingredients:
- 3 cups almond flour
- 1 tsp baking soda
- 2 tsps baking powder
- ¼ tsp sunflower seeds
- ¼ cup almond milk
- ½ cup + 2 tbsps olive oil
- 3 whole eggs

Directions:
4. Pre-heat your oven to 300 degree F
5. Take an 9x5 inch loaf pan and grease, keep it on the side
6. Add listed Ingredients: to a bowl and pour the batter into the loaf pan
7. Bake for 60 mins
8. Once baked, remove from oven and let it cool

Nutrition:
Calories 256, Fat 20.0 g, Carbs 28.1 g, Protein 4.5 g

Apple Coffee Cake

Prep Time: 5 mins |Servings: 20 |Cooking time: 40 mins

Ingredients:
- 5 cups tart apples, cored, peeled, chopped
- 1 cup sugar
- 1 cup dark raisins
- 1/2 cup pecans, chopped
- 1/4 cup vegetable oil
- 2 tsps vanilla
- 1 egg, beaten
- 2-1/2 cups sifted all-purpose flour
- 1-1/2 tsps baking soda
- 2 tsps ground cinnamon

Directions:
1. Preheat oven to 350ºF.
2. Lightly oil a 13x9x2-inch pan.
3. In a large mixing bowl, combine apples with sugar, raisins, and pecans; mix well. Let stand 30 mins.
4. Stir in oil, vanilla, and egg. Sift together flour, soda, and cinnamon; stir into apple mixture about 1/3 at a time just enough to moisten dry Ingredients:.
5. Turn batter into pan. Bake 35 to 40 mins. Cool cake slightly before serving.

Nutrition:
Calories 188, Total Fat 5 g, Carbs 24.1 g, Protein 4.5 g

Baked Apple Slices

Prep Time: 5 mins |Servings: 4 |Cooking time: 30 mins

Ingredients:
- 2 oranges
- 2 tbsps honey
- 1/4 tsp ground cinnamon
- 1/4 tsp ground cloves
- 3 Granny Smith apples, peeled, cored, and cut into 1/2-inch slices
- 5 tbsps raisins
- 1/4 cup chopped walnuts, divided
- 1/4 cup vanilla yogurt, low-fat

Directions:
1. Preheat the oven to 500°F.
2. Grate the zest of one of the oranges and set aside.
3. Squeeze the juice from both oranges into a small bowl. Stir the honey, cinnamon, cloves, and half the zest into the juice.
4. Lay half the apple slices in a glass baking dish. Scatter the raisins and 2 tbsps of the walnuts on top. Pour on half the juice mixture and top with the remaining apples and juice. Combine the remaining 2 tbsps of walnuts with the orange zest and scatter over the top.
5. Cover lightly with foil, and bake 30 mins or until the apples are soft and the juices, bubbly. Serve warm or cold with a dollop of low-fat vanilla yogurt.

Nutrition:
Calories 206, Fat 6 g, Carbs 41 g, Protein 5.8 g

Frosted Cake

Prep Time: 5 mins |Servings: 10 |Cooking time: 50 mins

Ingredients:
Cake
- 2-1/4 cups cake flour
- 2-1/4 tsp baking powder

- 4 tbsps margarine
- 1-1/4 cups sugar
- 4 eggs
- 1 tsp vanilla
- 1 tbsp orange peel
- 3/4 cup skim milk

Icing
- 3 oz low fat cream cheese
- 2 tbsps skim milk
- 6 tbsps cocoa
- 2 cups sifted confectioners sugar
- 1/2 tsp vanilla extract

Directions:
1. Preheat the oven to 325° F.
2. Grease with small amount of cooking oil or use nonstick cooking oil spray on a 10-inch round pan (at least 2-1/2 inches high). Powder pan with flour. Tap out excess flour.
3. Sift together flour and baking powder.
4. In a separate bowl, beat together margarine and sugar until soft and creamy.
5. Beat in eggs, vanilla, and orange peel.
6. Gradually add the flour mixture alternating with the milk, beginning and ending with flour.
7. Pour the mixture into the pan. Bake for 40 to 45 mins or until done. Let cake cool for 5 to 10 mins before removing from the pan. Let cool completely before icing.

Icing
- Cream together cream cheese and milk until smooth. Add cocoa. Blend well.
- Slowly add sugar until icing is smooth. Mix in vanilla.
- Smooth icing over top and sides of cooled cake.

Nutrition:
Calories 241, Fat 5 g, Carbs 48 g, Protein 4.8 g

Fruit Skewers with Yogurt Dip

Prep Time: 5 mins |Servings: 4 | Cooking time: 10 mins
Ingredients:
- 1 cup strawberries, rinsed, stems removed, and cut in half
- 1 cup fresh pineapple, diced (or canned pineapple chunks in juice, drained)
- 1/2 cup blackberries
- 1 tangerine or Clementine, peeled and cut into 8 segments
- 8 6-inch wooden skewers

For dip
- 1 cup strawberries, rinsed, stems removed, and cut in half
- 1/4 cup fat-free plain yogurt
- 1/8 tsp vanilla extract
- 1 tbsp honey

Directions:
1. Thread two strawberry halves, two pineapple chunks, two blackberries, and one tangerine segment on each skewer.
2. To prepare the dip, puree strawberries in a blender or food processor. Add yogurt, vanilla, and honey, and mix well.
3. Serve two skewers with yogurt dip on the side.

Nutrition:
Calories 71, Fat 0 g, Protein 1 g, Carbs 18 g

Fudgy Fruit

Prep Time: 5 mins |Servings: 4 | Cooking time: 10 mins
Ingredients:
- 2 tbsps semi-sweet chocolate chips
- 2 large bananas, peeled and cut into quarters
- 8 large strawberries
- 1/4 cup chopped unsalted peanuts

Directions:
1. Place chocolate chips in a small microwave safe bowl. Heat on high for 10 seconds and stir. Repeat until chocolate is melted, about 30 seconds.
2. Place fruit on a small tray covered with a piece of waxed paper. Use a spoon to drizzle the melted chocolate on top of the fruit.
3. Sprinkle the fruit with chopped nuts.
4. Cover the fruit and place in the refrigerator for 10 mins or until the chocolate hardens. Serve chilled.

Nutrition:
Calories 151, Carbs 24 g, Protein 3 g, Fat 6 g

Mousse Vanilla Banana

Prep Time: 5 mins |Servings: 4
Ingredients:
- 2 tbsps low fat (1%) milk

- 4 tsps sugar
- 1 tsp vanilla
- 1 medium banana, cut in quarters
- 1 cup plain low fat yogurt
- 8 1/4-inch banana slices

Directions:
1. Place milk, sugar, vanilla, and banana in blender. Process 15 seconds at high speed until smooth.
2. Pour mixture into a small bowl; fold in yogurt. Chill. Spoon into 4 dessert dishes; garnish each with 2 banana slices just before serving.

Nutrition: Information
Calories 94, Fat 1 g, Carbs 24 g, Protein 3 g

Oatmeal Cookies

Prep Time: 5 mins |Servings: 8 | Cooking time: 18 mins
Ingredients:
- 3/4 cup sugar
- 2 tbsps margarine
- 1 egg
- 1/4 cup canned applesauce
- 2 tbsps milk, low-fat
- 1 cup flour
- 1/4 tsp baking soda
- 1/2 tsp ground cinnamon
- 1 cup + 2 tbsps quick rolled oats

Directions:
1. Preheat oven to 350° F and lightly grease cookie sheets.
2. In a large bowl, use an electric mixer on medium speed to mix sugar and margarine. Mix until well blended, about 3 mins.
3. Slowly add egg; mix on medium speed 1 minute. Gradually add applesauce and milk; mix on medium speed 1 minute. Scrape sides of bowl.
4. In another bowl, combine flour, baking soda, and cinnamon. Slowly add to applesauce mixture; mix on low speed until blended, about 2 mins. Add oats and blend 30 seconds on low speed. Scrape sides of bowl.
5. Drop by tspfuls onto cookie sheet, about 2 inches apart.
6. Bake until lightly browned, about 13-15 mins. Remove from baking sheet while still warm. Cool on wire rack.

Nutrition:
Calories 215, Fat 4 g, Carbs 24 g, Protein 3 g

Oven Fried Plantains

Prep Time: 5 mins |Servings: 8 | Cooking time: 45 mins
Ingredients:
- nonstick cooking spray
- 4 very ripe medium plantains
- 1/8 tsp ground nutmeg
- 4 tbsps brown sugar

Directions:
1. Place an oven rack in the middle of the oven. Preheat oven to 425°F.
2. Spray cookie sheet well with nonstick cooking spray.
3. Peel and slice each plantain into 16 thin diagonal slices.
4. Sprinkle plantains with nutmeg and brown sugar.
5. Bake until crisp, about 45 mins. Serve while warm.

Nutrition:
Calories 158, Carbs 42 g, Protein 1 g, Fat 0 g

Mixed Fruits Freeze

Prep Time: 5 mins |Servings: 4
Ingredients:
- 1 large banana
- 2 cups strawberries
- 2 ripe mangos, chopped
- 1/2 cup of ice cubes

Directions:
1. Combine all Ingredients: in a blender or food processor container. Blend until mixture is smooth.
2. Pour into glasses and serve.

Nutrition:
Calories 121, Carbs 31 g, Fiber 4 g, Protein 1 g, Fat 1 g

Peach Apple Crisp

Prep Time: 5 mins |Servings: 8 | Cooking time: 20 mins
Ingredients:

- 20 oz canned peaches, light-syrup pack, drained
- 2 medium apples, tart, peeled and sliced
- 1/2 tsp vanilla
- 1/4 tsp ground cinnamon
- 3/4 cup + 3 tbsps flour
- 1/4 cup brown sugar, packed
- 3 tbsps soft (tub) margarine

Directions:
1. Preheat oven to 350° F. Lightly grease 9- by 9- by 2-inch casserole dish.
2. Combine peaches, apples, vanilla, and cinnamon in a bowl. Toss well and spread evenly in greased casserole dish.
3. Combine flour and sugar in small bowl. Cut in margarine with two knives until the mixture resembles coarse meal.
4. Sprinkle flour mixture evenly over fruit.
5. Bake until lightly browned and bubbly, about 20 mins.

Nutrition:
Calories 175, Fat 5 g, Carbs 24 g, Protein 3 g

Peach Crumble

Prep Time: 5 mins | Servings: 12 | Cooking time: 25 mins
Ingredients:
- nonstick cooking spray
- 4 (15-ounce) cans juice packed peach slices, drained*
- 2 tbsps cornstarch
- 1 tsp vanilla
- 1-1/4 tsp ground cinnamon
- 2/3 cup old fashioned oats
- 1/4 cup brown sugar
- 1/3 cup flour
- 2-1/2 tbsps butter

Directions:
1. Preheat oven to 400°F.
2. Spray a 9-inch deep dish pie pan with nonstick cooking spray and pour peaches in the pan.
3. In a small bowl, stir in cornstarch, vanilla, and 1 tsp cinnamon; pour the mixture over peaches.
4. In a large bowl, mix the remaining cinnamon, oats, brown sugar, flour, and butter with a fork until crumbly; sprinkle over peaches.
5. Bake for 20 to 25 mins or until juices are thickened and bubbly, and topping is lightly browned. Serve while hot.

Nutrition:
Calories 139, Carbs 28 g, Protein 2 g, Fat 3 g

Peachy Pita

Prep Time: 5 mins | Servings: 4 | Cooking time: 1 mins
Ingredients:
- 2 medium whole wheat pita pockets
- 1/4 cup reduced fat chunky peanut butter
- 1/2 apple, cored and thinly sliced
- 1/2 banana, thinly sliced
- 1/2 fresh peach, thinly sliced

Directions:
1. Cut pitas in half to make 4 pockets and warm in the microwave for about 10 seconds to make them more flexible.
2. Carefully open each pocket and spread a thin layer of peanut butter on the inside walls.
3. Fill with a combination of apple, banana, and peach slices. Serve at room temperature.

Nutrition:
Calories 180, Carbs 26 g, Protein 7 g, Fat 3 g

Peanut Butter Hummus

Prep Time: 5 mins | Servings: 8 | Cooking time: 10 mins
Ingredients:
For dip
- 2 cups low-sodium garbanzo beans (chick peas), rinsed
- 1/4 cup low-sodium chicken broth
- 1/4 cup lemon juice
- 2–3 tbsps garlic, diced (about 4–6 garlic cloves, depending on taste)
- 1/4 cup creamy peanut butter (or substitute other nut or seed butter)
- 1/4 tsp cayenne pepper (or substitute paprika for less spice)
- 1 tbsp olive oil

For pita chips
- 4 (6-1/2-inch) whole-wheat pitas, each cut into 10 triangles

- 1 tbsp olive oil
- 1 tsp garlic, minced (about 1 clove) (or 1/2 tsp garlic powder)
- 1/4 tsp ground black pepper

Directions:
1. Preheat oven to 400ºF.
2. To prepare the hummus, combine all Ingredients: for the dip and mix them in a food processor or blender. Puree until smooth.
3. Prepare the chips, toss the pita triangles with the olive oil, garlic, and pepper.
4. Bake chips on a baking sheet in a 400ºF oven for 10 mins, or until crispy.
5. Arrange pita chips on a platter, and serve with the hummus.

Nutrition:
Calories 235, Fat 9 g, Protein 9 g, Carbs 32 g

Rainbow Salad

Prep Time: 5 mins |Servings: 8
Ingredients:
Fruit salad
- 1 large mango, peeled and diced
- 2 cups fresh blueberries
- 2 bananas, sliced
- 2 cups fresh strawberries, halved
- 2 cups seedless grapes
- 2 nectarines, unpeeled and sliced
- 1 kiwi fruit, peeled and sliced

Honey orange sauce
- 1/3 cups unsweetened orange juice
- 2 tbsps lemon juice
- 1-1/2 tbsps honey
- 1/4 tsp ground ginger
- dash nutmeg

Directions:
1. Prepare the fruit.
2. Combine all the Ingredients: for the sauce and mix.
3. Just before serving, pour honey orange sauce over the fruit.

Nutrition:
Calories 96, Fat 1 g, Carbs 32 g

Savory Grilled Fruit

Prep Time: 5 mins |Servings: 8
Ingredients:
- 4 peaches, plums, or nectarines, halved and pitted

Directions:
Cook 4 halved peaches, plums, and/or nectarines over medium, indirect heat for 8 mins in a covered barbecue grill. Turn after 4 mins. Serve while hot.

Nutrition:
Calories 19, Carbs 5 g, Protein 0 g, Total Fat 0 g

Southern Banana Pudding

Prep Time: 5 mins |Servings: 10
Ingredients:
- 3-3/4 cups cold, fat-free milk
- 2 small packages (4 serving size) of fat-free, sugar-free instant vanilla pudding and pie-filling mix
- 32 reduced-fat vanilla wafers
- 2 medium bananas, sliced
- 2 cups fat-free, frozen whipped topping, thawed

Directions:
1. Mix 3-1/2 cups of the milk with the pudding mixes. Beat the pudding mixture with a wire whisk for 2 mins until it is well blended. Let stand for 5 mins.
2. Fold 1 cup of the whipped topping into the pudding mix.
3. Arrange a layer of wafers on the bottom and sides of a 2-quart serving bowl. Drizzle 2 tbsps of the remaining milk over the wafers. Add a layer of banana slices and top with one-third of the pudding.
4. Repeat layers, drizzling wafer layer with remaining milk and ending with pudding. Spread the remaining whipped topping over the pudding.
5. Refrigerate for at least 3 hours before serving.

Nutrition:
Calories 143, Fat 2 g, Protein 4 g, Carbs 29 g

Tropical Fruit and Nut Snack Mix

Prep Time: 5 mins |Servings: 10
Ingredients:
- 1 tbsp butter
- 1/4 cup honey*
- 1 tsp almond or coconut extract
- 1 tsp ground cinnamon

- 2 cups old fashioned oats
- nonstick cooking spray
- 1/2 cup sliced almonds
- 3/4 cup dried tropical fruit bits
- 1/2 cup banana chips
- 1/4 cup raisins

Directions:
1. Preheat oven to 350°F.
2. Melt butter in a medium saucepan. Add honey, almond or coconut extract, and cinnamon; mix well.
3. Stir in oats and transfer to a baking sheet coated with nonstick cooking spray. Spread into a 1-inch thick layer.
4. Bake for 10 mins, stirring once. Stir in almonds and bake for 5 to 10 mins more.
5. Remove from oven and toss with dried fruit. Let cool completely and serve.

Nutrition:
Calories 384, Carbs 62 g, Protein 9 g, Fat 13 g

Fruit Compote

Prep Time: 5 mins |Servings: 8
Ingredients:
- 3/4 cup water
- 1/2 cup sugar
- 2 tsps fresh lemon juice
- 1 piece lemon peel
- 1/2 tsp rum or vanilla extract (optional)
- 1 pineapple cored and peeled, cut into 8 slices
- 2 mangos peeled and pitted, cut into 8 pieces
- 3 bananas peeled, cut into 8 diagonal pieces

Directions:
1. In a saucepan combine 3/4 cup of water with the sugar, lemon juice, and lemon peel (and rum or vanilla extract if desired). Bring to a boil, then reduce the heat and add the fruit. Cook at a very low heat for 5 mins.
2. Pour the syrup in a cup. Remove the lemon rind and cool the cooked fruit for 2 hours.
3. To serve the compote, arrange the fruit in a serving dish and pour a few tsps of syrup over the fruit. Garnish with mint leaves.
4. Serve with Homemade Sour Cream

Nutrition:
Calories 148, Fat 1 g, Protein 4 g, Carbs 29 g

Winter/Summer Crisp

Prep Time: 5 mins |Servings: 6
Ingredients:
Filling
- 1/2 cup sugar
- 3 tbsps all-purpose flour
- 1 tsp lemon peel, grated
- 3/4 tsps lemon juice
- 5 cups apples, unpeeled, sliced
- 1 cup cranberries

Topping
- 2/3 cups rolled oats
- 1/3 cups brown sugar, packed
- 1/4 cup whole wheat flour
- 2 tsps ground cinnamon
- 1 tbsp soft margarine, melted

Directions:
1. To prepare filling, in a medium bowl combine sugar, flour, and lemon peel; mix well. Add lemon juice, apples, and cranberries; stir to mix. Spoon into a 6-cup baking dish.
2. To prepare topping, in a small bowl, combine oats, brown sugar, flour, and cinnamon. Add melted margarine; stir to mix.
3. Sprinkle topping over filling. Bake in a 375°F oven for approximately 40-50 mins or until filling is bubbly and top is brown. Serve warm or at room temperature.

Variation

Summer Crisp: Prepare as directed, substituting 4 cups fresh or unsweetened frozen (thawed) peaches and 3 cups fresh or unsweetened frozen (unthawed) blueberries for apples and cranberries. If frozen, thaw peaches completely (do not drain). Do not thaw blueberries before mixing or they will be crushed.

Nutrition:
Calories 28, Fat 2 g, Protein 4 g, Carbs 29 g

Chapter 13: Breads

Apricot Breads

Prep Time: 15 mins |Servings: 2 | Cooking: 45 mins
Ingredients:
- 1 (6 oz) package of dried apricots cut into small pieces
- 2 cups water
- 2 tbsps margarine
- 1 cup sugar
- 1 egg, slightly beaten
- 1 tbsp freshly grated orange peel
- 3-1/2 cups sifted all-purpose flour
- 1/2 cup nonfat dry milk powder
- 2 tsps baking powder
- 1 tsp baking soda
- 1/2 cup orange juice
- 1/2 cup chopped pecans

Directions:
1. Preheat oven to 350ºF. Lightly oil two 9x5-inch loaf pan.
2. Cook apricots in water in a covered medium-size saucepan for 10-15 mins or until tender but not mushy. Drain; reserve 3/4 cup liquid. Set apricots aside to cool.
3. Cream together margarine and sugar. By hand, beat in egg and orange peel.
4. Sift together flour, dry milk, baking powder, soda, and salt. Add to creamed mixture alternately with reserved apricot liquid and orange juice.
5. Stir apricot pieces and pecans into batter.
6. Turn batter into prepared pans.
7. Bake for 40-45 mins or until bread springs back when lightly touched in center.
8. Cool 5 mins in pan. Remove from pan and completely cool on wire rack before slicing.

Nutrition:
Calories 97, Fat 2 g, Carbs 20.1 g, Protein 4.5 g

Banana & Pecans Breads

Prep Time: 5 mins |Servings: 2 | Cooking: 55 mins
Ingredients:
- 1 cup mashed ripe bananas
- 1/3 cups low-fat buttermilk
- 1/2 cup packed brown sugar
- 1/4 cup margarine
- 1 egg
- 2 cups sifted all-purpose flour
- 1 tsp baking powder
- 1/2 tsp baking soda
- 1/2 cup chopped pecans

Directions:
1. Preheat oven to 350ºF. Lightly oil two 9x5-inch loaf pan.
2. Stir together mashed bananas and buttermilk; set aside.
3. Cream brown sugar and margarine together until light. Beat in egg. Add banana mixture; beat well.
4. Sift together flour, baking powder, baking soda, and salt; add all at once to liquid Ingredients:. Stir until well blended.
5. Stir in nuts and turn into prepared pan.
6. Bake for 50-55 mins or until toothpick inserted in center comes out clean. Cool 5 mins in pan.
7. Remove from pan and complete cooling on a wire rack before slicing.

Nutrition:
Calories 133, Total Fat 5 g, Carbs 20.1 g, Protein 4.5 g

Carrots Bread

Prep Time: 10 mins |Servings: 2 | Cooking: 55 mins
Ingredients:
- 1-1/2 cups sifted all-purpose flour
- 1/2 cup sugar
- 1 tsp baking powder
- 1/4 tsp baking soda
- 1-1/2 tsps ground cinnamon
- 1/4 tsp ground allspice
- 1 egg, beaten
- 1/2 cup water
- 2 tbsps vegetable oil
- 1/2 tsp vanilla
- 1-1/2 cups finely shredded carrots
- 1/4 cup chopped pecans
- 1/4 cup golden raisins

Directions:
1. Preheat oven to 350ºF. Lightly oil a 9x5x3 inch loaf pan.
2. Stir together dry Ingredients: in large mixing bowl. Make a well in center of dry mixture.

3. In separate bowl, mix together remaining Ingredients:; add this mixture all at once to dry Ingredients:. Stir just enough to moisten and evenly distribute carrots.
4. Turn into prepared pan. Bake for 50 mins or until toothpick inserted in center comes out clean.
5. Cool 5 mins in pan. Remove from pan and complete cooling on a wire rack before slicing.

Nutrition:
Calories 99, Total Fat 3 g, Carbs 18.1 g, Protein 3.5 g

Easy Cornbread

Prep Time: 10 mins |Servings: 10 | Cooking: 25 mins
Ingredients:
- 1 cup cornmeal
- 1 cup flour
- 1/4 cup sugar
- 1 tsp baking powder
- 1 cup low-fat (1%) buttermilk
- 1 egg, whole
- 1/4 cup margarine, regular, tub
- 1 tsp vegetable oil (to grease baking pan)

Directions:
1. Preheat oven to 350 degrees F.
2. Mix together cornmeal, flour, sugar, and baking powder. In another bowl, combine buttermilk and egg. Beat lightly.
3. Slowly add buttermilk and egg mixture to dry Ingredients:.
4. Add margarine and mix by hand or with mixer for 1 minute.
5. Bake for 20–25 mins in an 8 x 8-inch, greased baking dish. Cool. Cut into 10 squares.

Nutrition:
Calories 178, Fat 6 g, Protein 4 g, Carbs 27 g

Classical Homemade Biscuits

Prep Time: 5 mins | Cooking: 12 mins
Ingredients:
- 2 cups all-purpose flour
- 2 tsps baking powder
- 1/4 tsp baking soda
- 2 tbsps sugar
- 2/3 cup low-fat (1%) buttermilk
- 3 tbsps + 1 tsp vegetable oil

Directions:
1. Preheat oven to 450 degrees F.
2. In medium bowl, combine flour, baking powder, baking soda, salt, and sugar.
3. In small bowl, stir together buttermilk and oil. Pour over flour mixture and stir until well mixed.
4. On lightly floured surface, knead dough gently for 10–12 strokes. Roll or pat dough to 3/4-inch thickness. Cut with a 2-inch round biscuit or cookie cutter, dipping cookie cutter in flour between cuts. Transfer biscuits to an ungreased baking sheet.
5. Bake for 12 mins or until golden brown. Serve warm.

Nutrition:
Calories 99, Fat 3 g, Protein 2 g, Carbs 15

Soft Bread

Prep Time: 5 mins | Cooking: 1 hour
Ingredients:
- 3 large eggs, beaten
- 1-3/4 cups sugar
- 1/2 cup vegetable oil
- 1/2 cup cinnamon applesauce
- 1 tbsp vanilla extract
- 2 cups zucchini, shredded or grated
- 3 cups self-rising flour
- 1/2 cup walnuts or pecans, chopped

Directions:
1. Preheat the oven to 350° F.
2. Spray a non-stick 9- by 5-inch loaf pan with cooking spray.
3. In a large bowl, whisk together the beaten eggs, sugar, oil, applesauce, and vanilla.
4. Add the zucchini. Stir with a large spoon. Sprinkle in flour. Stir well.
5. Pour batter in the loaf pan. Sprinkle nuts over the batter. Bake for 1 hour, or until a toothpick comes out clean. Cool for 15 mins on a cooling rack.
6. Loosen bread from the sides and remove the bread to cool completely on the rack. Once cool, slice and serve. (Hint: The bread slices even better when partially frozen.) Store individually wrapped leftovers in the freezer.

Nutrition:

Calories 320, Carbs 48 g, Protein 5 g, Fat 12 g

Savory Muffins

Prep Time: 5 mins | Servings: 12 | Cooking: 25 mins
Ingredients:
- nonstick cooking spray
- 2 eggs
- 1/2 cup applesauce
- 1/4 cup granulated sugar
- 1 tsp vanilla extract
- 1-1/4 cups whole wheat flour
- 1 tsp baking soda
- 1-1/2 tsps ground cinnamon
- 1/2 tsp ground ginger
- 1/4 tsp ground cloves
- 2 cups grated zucchinis (about 2 small zucchinis)
- 1/2 cup raisins
- 2/3 cup toasted and chopped pecans or walnuts

Directions:
1. Place an oven rack in the middle of the oven. Preheat oven to 350F.
2. Spray muffin pan (12 muffin cups total) with nonstick cooking spray and set aside.
3. In a large bowl, stir together eggs, applesauce, granulated sugar, and vanilla extract.
4. In a separate bowl, stir together flour, salt, baking soda, cinnamon, ginger, and cloves.
5. Stir flour mixture into egg mixture until just barely blended (there may be a few small lumps).
6. Gently stir in zucchinis, raisins, and nuts.
7. Divide batter evenly among muffin cups.
8. Bake 20 mins or until a wooden toothpick inserted in the center of a muffin comes out clean.
9. Remove muffin pans from oven and let muffins stand for 5 mins and serve warm.

Nutrition:
Calories 142, Carbs 21 g, Fiber 3 g, Protein 4 g, Fat 5 g

Cherry Tomatoes Muffins

Prep Time: 5 mins | Servings: 12 | Cooking: 25 mins
Ingredients:
- nonstick cooking spray
- 2 eggs
- 12 cherry tomatoes
- 1-1/4 cups whole wheat flour
- 1/4 tsp salt
- 1 tsp baking soda
- 1/2 tsp ground ginger
- 2 cups grated parmeasn
- 2 cups grated zucchinis (about 2 small zucchinis)
- 2/3 cup toasted and chopped walnuts

Directions:
1. Place an oven rack in the middle of the oven. Preheat oven to 350 degrees F.
2. Spray muffin pan (12 muffin cups total) with nonstick cooking spray and set aside.
3. In a large bowl, stir together all the Ingredients:
4. Divide batter evenly among muffin cups.
5. Bake 20 mins or until a wooden toothpick inserted in the center of a muffin comes out clean.
6. Remove muffin pans from oven and let muffins stand for 5 mins and serve warm.

Nutrition:
Calories 142, Carbs 21 g, Fiber 3 g, Protein 4 g, Fat 5 g

Chapter 14: 4 Weeks MEAL PLAN

DAYS	BREAKFAST	LUNCH	DINNER
1	Swiss Chard Omelet	Spinach Parmesan Dip	Black-Bean and Vegetable Burrito
2	Hearty Pineapple Oatmeal	Italian Cheese Sticks	Baked Eggs In Avocado
3	Zingy Onion and Thyme Crackers	Delicious Bacon Delight	Black-Bean Soup
4	Crunchy Flax and Almond Crackers	Squeaky Beef Stroganoff	Loaded Baked Sweet Potatoes
5	Basil and Tomato Baked Eggs	Sloppiest Sloppy Joe	Chicken and Broccoli Stir-Fry
6	Cool Mushroom Munchies	Cane Wrapped Around In Prosciutto	Quick Chicken Fajitas
7	Banana and Buckwheat Porridge	Majestic Veal Stew	Honey-Mustard Chicken
8	Delightful Berry Quinoa Bowl	The Surprising No "Noodle" Lasagna	Grilled Chicken, Avocado, and Apple Salad
9	Fantastic Bowl of Steel Oats	Worthwhile Balsamic Beef	Turkey Cutlets with Herbs
10	Quinoa and Cinnamon Bowl	Friendly Chipotle Copycat	Easy Roast Salmon with Roasted Asparagus
11	Awesome Breakfast Parfait	Ground Beef And Green Beans And Tomatoes	Shrimp Pasta Primavera
12	Amazing and Healthy Granola Bowl	Lamb Spare Ribs	Cilantro-Lime Tilapia Tacos

13	Cinnamon and Pumpkin Porridge Medley	Curry Lamb Shanks	Lemon-Parsley Baked Flounder and Brussels Sprouts
14	Quinoa and Date Bowl	Moroccan Lamb Tajine	Pan-Seared Scallops
15	Crispy Tofu	Crispy Chicken Egg Rolls	Baked Cod Packets with Broccoli and Squash
16	Wholesome Pumpkin Pie Oatmeal	Italian Meatballs	Garlic Salmon and Snap Peas In Foil
17	Power-Packed Oatmeal	Garlic Parmesan Wings	Southwestern Chicken and Pasta
18	Chia Porridge	Quick Jalapeno Crisps	Buffalo Chicken Salad Wrap
19	Mouthwatering Chicken Porridge	Crispy Egg Chips	Chicken Sliders
20	Simple Blueberry Oatmeal	Broccoli Sticks	Black-Eyed Peas and Greens Power Salad
21	The Decisive Apple "Porridge"	Halloumi Cheese Crunchy Fries	Butternut-Squash Macaroni and Cheese
22	The Unique Smoothie Bowl	Marinated beef Kebabs	Pasta with Tomatoes and Peas
23	Cinnamon and Coconut Porridge	Low-Carb Zucchini Lasagna Rolls	Healthy Vegetable Fried Rice
24	Morning Porridge	Pesto And Goat Cheese Terrine	Portobello-Mushroom Cheeseburgers
25	Vanilla Sweet Potato Porridge	Green Crackers	Pork Salad with Walnuts and Peaches
26	A Nice German Oatmeal	Special Cucumber Cups	Baked Chickpea-and-Rosemary Omelet

| 27 | Morning porridge | Crispy Egg Chips | Steak tacos |
| 28 | Chia porridge | Greek beef | Asian pork tenderloin |

Conclusion

So you're resigned to being a "fatty" for the rest of your life. You've come to accept it. You've come to love your "curves." You've made peace with the extra inches on your frame. You've found coping mechanisms for your thunder thighs forever touching each other with every step you take. You're fine with yourself as you are. Not because you haven't tried. Oh boy, what haven't you tried?

You've purchased every weight loss pill out there. You've gone to the gym religiously. You've tried cardio then weight training.

You've tried every fad diet known to man. You've starved yourself deprived yourself of good Nutrition:, purchased a lot of sugar-laden "fat-free" products which food companies have continued to push as the better option. Yet where has all this effort taken you? Nowhere. What's all the pain, the suffering, the self-loathing gotten you? Nothing. So, of course, it makes so much sense to just give up and focus on learning to love yourself as you are!

But what if I told you there's a way to the lean body you've only ever dreamed of? What if I told you could finally know what it's like to fit into those size 8 skinny jeans you bought many summers ago to spur you to lose that weight? What if you could finally wear whatever you really want and feel confident no matter what?

Well, there is a way. You ready? And It's called the DASH diet.s

Made in the USA
Coppell, TX
13 January 2021

48044786R00092